Hull
26/9/12

Hertfordshire
COUNTY COUNCIL
Community Information

2 9 MAY 2002

1 8 NOV 2002
2 5 JUN 2003
1 0 MAY 2005

2 6 AUG 2005

H50 130 852 8

Please renew/return this item by the last date shown.

So that your telephone call is charged at local rate, please call the numbers as set out below:

	From Area codes 01923 or 020:	From the rest of Herts:
Renewals:	01923 471373	01438 737373
Enquiries:	01923 471333	01438 737333
Minicom:	01923 471599	01438 737599

L32

THE HUNGARIAN REVOLUTION OF 1956

The Hungarian Revolution of 1956

Reform, Revolt and Repression
1953–1963

Edited by
György Litván

English version edited and translated by
János M Bak
Lyman H Legters

Longman
London and New York

Longman Group Ltd
Longman House, Burnt Mill
Harlow, Essex CM20 2JE, England
and Associated Companies throughout the world.

Published in the United States of America
by Longman Publishing, New York

© Longman Group Limited , Győrgy Litván, János M Rainer, 1991

© Reform–Revolt © János M Bak, Győrgy Kozák, Győrgy Litván, János M Rainer, 1996

English language adaptation and updating © János M Bak, Lyman H Legters, 1966

Chapter 1 © George Schöpflin, 1996

The original Hungarian edition of this book, *Az 1956-os magyar forradalom: Reform–felkelés–szabadságharc–megtorlas. Olvasókönyv*, was published by Tankönyvkiadó, Budapest, 1991

This English-language edition, translated and updated, first published by Longman, 1996

ISBN 0 582 21505 6 CSD
ISBN 0 582 21504 8 PPR

British Library Cataloguing-in-Publication Data

A catalogue record for this book is available from the British Library

Library of Congress Cataloging-in-Publication Data

1956–os magyar forradalom.   English
    The Hungarian Revolution of 1956 : reform, revolt and repression, 1953–1963 / edited by György Litván ; English version edited and translated by János M Bak, Lyman H Legters.
        p.   cm.
    Includes bibliographical references and index.
    ISBN 0–582–21505–6 (csd). — ISBN 0–582–21504–8 (pbk.)
    1. Hungary—History—Revolution, 1956.   I. Litván, György.
II. Bak, János M.   III. Legters, Lyman Howard, 1928–   .
DB957.A1713   1996
943.905'2—dc20

95–45648
CPI

Set by 20 in 10/12 Bembo
Produced by Longman Singapore Publishers (Pte) Ltd
Printed in Singapore

The original Hungarian text of this book was written by the members of the Institute for the History of the 1956 Hungarian Revolution (Budapest):

> János M Bak
> Csaba Békés
> Gyula Kozák
> György Litván
> János M Rainer

Consultant   András B Hegedűs

Assistants   László Eörsi
Zsuzsa Kőrösi
Adrienne Molnár
János Tischler

This Longman version has been edited and translated by
János M Bak
Lyman H Legters

With a specially contributed historical introduction by
George Schöpflin

And an Afterword by
Peter Kende

The editorial and translation work for this book was partially supported by a grant of the Soros Foundation, Budapest

Contents

Contents

Preface

The Parliament of the Hungarian Republic, the first freely elected one in more than four decades, began its legislative work on 2 May 1990 by enacting the following declaration:

> This freely elected Parliament regards as its urgent task to codify the historical significance of the October Revolution of 1956 and its struggle for freedom. This illustrious chapter of modern Hungarian history can only be compared to the 1848–49 Revolution and war of independence. The Revolution of 1956 lay foundation for the hope that it is possible to achieve a democratic social order, and that no sacrifice for our country's independence is made in vain. Although the ensuing suppression reinstated the old power structure, it could not eradicate the spirit of 1956 from people's minds.
>
> The new Parliament assumes the responsibility to preserve the memory of the Revolution and the ensuing struggle for freedom.
>
> The Parliament underscores its determination to do everything in its power to secure multiparty democracy, human rights, and national independence by proclaiming in its first session the following law:
>
> (1) The memory of the 1956 Revolution and its struggle for freedom is herewith codified.
>
> (2) October 23, the day of the outbreak of the Revolution of 1956 and the beginning of the fight for freedom, and also the day of the proclamation of the Hungarian Republic in 1989, shall henceforth be a national holiday.

The path leading to this legislative proclamation and thus to the establishment of a moral foundation for the new Hungarian Republic was a long one, starting with a revival of the memory of the Revolution.

Virtually all of the oppositional tendencies that emerged in the mid-1980s eventually found their intellectual roots in the tradition of the Revolution.

In 1986, on the thirtieth anniversary of the Revolution, a group of veterans of 1956 including some writers and historians, together with oppositionals of the younger generations, gathered for a scholarly conference. The meeting was not just a pious remembrance of 1956 but rather a revival of the Revolution's ideas and programme in critical juxtaposition to the political, economic and social situation that was steadily worsening in those years. The international situation also called forth a reassessment of 1956. Gorbachev's reforms and the withdrawal from Afghanistan brought the issues of earlier Soviet policies back to the current agenda, including the 1956 intervention.

In the spring of 1988 a group, the Committee for Historical Justice (TIB), was formed in Budapest with a membership including relatives of the 1956 martyrs, victims of the repression, leaders of the revolutionary workers' councils, writers, artists, and social scientists. The Committee's proclamation demanded the rehabilitation of the victims of the communist dictatorship before and after 1956 as a precondition for the renewal of Hungary's political life, referring first of all to the victims of the post-1956 repression. The proclamation read in part as follows:

> For three decades, overgrown with weeds in the remote Section 301 of the municipal cemetery in Rákoskeresztúr, hundreds of the victims of the vengeful neo-Stalinist restoration that began on 4 November 1956 have rested. Relatives are not even allowed to know in which corner of the desolate area their loved ones are buried.

The founders of the Committee also demanded that it be possible to undertake research freely on the period of the Revolution, including publications about 1956 and access to the documents bearing on the repression, and to circulate in Hungary the foreign publications on the subject. They ended their proclamation with these words:

> We call on everyone to remember on 16 June 1988 all those who fell in the fighting, those driven to their deaths, and those who were executed. Whoever can do so should place flowers on the anonymous graves of Section 301 of the cemetery where our martyrs rest.

On that day, thirty years after the execution of Prime Minister Imre Nagy and his fellow martyrs, a symbolic gravestone was unveiled in Paris at the Père Lachaise cemetery. This initiative of the Paris Section of the Human Rights League was supported by numerous writers, politicians and Nobel laureates from around the world. Hungarian émigrés, oppositional politicians, French socialists and a leader of the Italian Communist Party spoke on behalf of the honour of the executed Nagy and his comrades and in the memory of the 1956 Revolution, demanding an honourable interment of the martyrs of the Revolution.

In Budapest on the same day several hundred demonstrators gathered at the anonymous graves of the executed in Rákoskeresztúr. This silent demonstration was followed later in the day by a similar one at the 'Batthyány Memorial Light', a monument to Hungary's first parliamentary prime minister, who was executed by the Habsburgs in 1849, thus dedicating the memorial to an 'Eternal Light' also for Imre Nagy. The police attacked the peaceable demonstrators, arresting and brutalizing many of them. The streets and squares of the city echoed on this day with the names of Nagy and his comrades.

In January 1989, Imre Pozsgay, a communist politician who wished to gain support in the power struggle within the party leadership, declared that 1956 was not – as maintained by his party for more than three decades – a 'counter-revolution', but a 'popular uprising'. Of course, in Hungary most people had always refused to accept the Kádárist denigration of the Revolution and tried to avoid calling 1956 by its official appellation. But at this juncture the declaration was tantamount to an open challenge of János Kádár's entire regime. Under dictatorship, words can acquire extraordinary weight. (That is why the choice of words in the 1990 Law on the Memory of the Revolution was of great significance: the events of the Fall of 1956 were for the first time proudly declared a 'revolution' and a 'struggle for freedom', using the same words that have been applied to the worldwide acclaimed revolutionary resistance of Hungary against the Habsburgs and their Tsarist allies in 1848–49.)

In the spring of 1989 there were a number of events that brought the memory of 1956 to the attention of the general public. A meeting was held in commemoration of the Petőfi Circle, the intellectual harbinger of the Revolution, and publications on the Revolution were prepared for circulation as samizdat literature. Although officially prohibited, this material was in practice distributed freely. Then, the ceremonial interment of Imre Nagy, Miklós Gimes, Géza Losonczy, Pál Maléter and József Szilágyi on 16 June 1989, organized by the Committee for Historical Justice, became a turning point in the decline of the Kádár regime and a symbol of its fall.

Imre Mécs, who as a student of the Technical University had once been sentenced to death, spoke to the hundreds of thousands gathered at the largest square in Budapest:

> Today is a day of mourning as the nation looks back on thirty-three lost years. Things would be quite different if the erstwhile Soviet leaders had not drowned our Revolution in blood! They committed not just a crime but also a historical mistake as they prevented the Hungarian people with great brutality from finding its own path. They also brought harm therewith to their own peoples, great harm! The maelstrom of history has now brought our buried truths back into the light.

And Viktor Orbán, leader of the newly founded Alliance of Young Democrats, speaking for the generation born after 1956, fastened his gaze on the sixth coffin, arrayed next to those of the victims of the Nagy trial as a memorial to the 'unknown freedom-fighter', said:

> We know that the victims of the Revolution and the repression were in their majority youths of our age and condition. But that is not the only reason to regard the sixth coffin as ours. Our nation had its last chance in 1956, down to the present day, to take the course of western development and build its economic well-being. It is a direct consequence of the bloody repression of the Revolution that we have had to assume the burden of insolvency and search for a way out of the Asiatic dead end into which we were pushed. Truly, the Hungarian Socialist Workers' Party robbed today's youth of its future in 1956. Thus, the sixth coffin contains not just a murdered youth but also the next twenty – or who can say how many? – years of our lives.

As is well known, the ceremonial funeral on 16 June 1989 was followed by the rapid demise of the Soviet client-state system: the change of the Hungarian party leadership, the free travel of East German refugees out of Hungary, then the fall of the Berlin Wall, the 'velvet revolution' in Czechoslovakia, the final victory of the Polish opposition, the collapse of communist dictatorship in Bulgaria and Albania, and in December, the overthrow of the Ceauşescu regime in Romania.

The transformation in Hungary was perhaps the most tranquil of all. It was a meaningful symbol of the peaceable change of regime that the opposition agreed that the less compromised government ministers of the Communist Party lay a wreath on the grave of the martyrs. Parenthetically, political developments of the intervening five years have shown that this 'frictionless transition' had both a positive and a negative aspect. On the one hand, the country avoided major disruptions, including the indulgence in witch-hunts and recriminations of the sort that usually accompany such transformations. On the other hand, the shift in power was not complete enough to remove the influence of old centralizing tendencies and étatist attitudes in the economy and public administration, thereby occasioning some disillusionment among those who had suffered under the fallen regime. However, all that was foreseen but by a few of the contemporaries, and the agenda of 1989 was a different one.

As the Parliament, immediately after passing the Act on the commemoration of the 1956 Revolution, elected as President of the Republic of Hungary the writer Árpád Göncz, who had spent years in prison because of his activities during the Revolution and the subsequent resistance, it seemed that, in the spirit of national unity of that time, 1956 would really provide the basis for the moral and political legitimation of the new order. Since then it has become clear that tendencies only dimly perceived in the days of Revolution and resistance raise doubts about an unproblematic tradition of the 1956 experience. As the 'revisionists', i.e. the former inner-party opposition, expected something different as an outcome of the successful uprising than did the representatives of the democratic parties defeated in 1947–49, different too from the expectations of the Christian conservative camp or the radical anti-communists, just so variously do the descendants of these tendencies now interpret the message of 1956. The year 1956 serves still as a banner of legitimation, but no longer as legitimation of a common democratic programme of the entire nation. Inevitably, former comrades-in-arms against the Kádárist regime endorse different programmes for today and relate to 1956 in very divergent ways.

In the summer of 1991, as the discussions grew sharper, the Institute for the History of the 1956 Hungarian Revolution, founded two years before, was asked to provide a synthesis of the history of the reform era, the Revolution and the repression that could be used in schools. President Árpád Göncz expressed his feelings about that book in his Introduction: 'It is my heartfelt wish that it may help to convey the significance of 1956, especially to the generation that has no personal association with the events of those two weeks'.

The present volume is not just a translation of the original. Amplifications and changes were made at many points, taking account of the relevant results of discussions carried on since the original appeared and of numerous new studies of details. It also utilizes the insights gained from newly discovered documents, many from archives in Budapest, Moscow, Washington and elsewhere that were opened up in the past few years, above all on international politics and, in particular, on the methods, plans and conduct of Soviet decision-making.

The lapse of time means that not only in Hungary but throughout the world, fewer and fewer people recall the events of the 1950s from personal experience. Earlier monographs on 1956 (listed in the Bibliography at the end of this volume) could build only on secondary evidence and the reminiscences of eyewitnesses and participants, without access to the archival sources, especially the trial records and diplomatic correspondence, as these became available only recently. Indeed, the older treatments of the Revolution are out of print. Therefore, we wished to make available to English-speaking readers the results of our research and analysis. Since most recent research has been published only in Hungarian, we have not included formal references to sources and particular literature: interested specialists can find their way to the articles and monographs or to the archival material through the publications of our Institute.

For the benefit of readers unfamiliar with modern Hungarian history, we include a chapter on the wider historical background of the 1956 Revolution. We are grateful to our London colleague George Schöpflin for supplying a summary of Hungary's situation and development after the Second World War with which our volume begins. We also felt that almost forty years after the events, a retrospective epilogue is needed which would place 1956 in the context of our times. Peter Kende, who has written extensively on the Revolution in the past decades in Parisian exile, volunteered to add a few thoughts to this book. We are grateful to him, just as we are to the members and staff of our Institute as well as to our publisher for having helped us to produce this book. It is with this cooperative effort that we – a team of former participants and young researchers of 1956 – place our perception of the Revolution on the 'table' of the international public.

Spring 1995

Gy. L.

We are indebted to Mrs. Eva Hay on behalf of the estate of Gyula Hay and Random House UK on behalf of the translator, for permission to reproduce extracts from *Geboren 1900* by Gyula Hay, translated by J. A. Underwood, pubd. Hutchinson, London, 1974. pp 302ff.

Hungary after the Second World War

G. Schöpflin

In the final year of the Second World War, Hungary found itself the last satellite of the Third Reich, occupied by the German army since March 1944, and exposed to the main thrust of the Soviet forces advancing on central Europe. Attempts by the regent, Admiral Horthy, in October 1944 to leave the Axis and negotiate a separate peace – poorly prepared and betrayed by pro-Nazi army officers – led only to the imposition of an openly terrorist-fascist Arrow Cross government under Ferenc Szálasi. However, parts of the military did make contact with the Allies and they, together with individuals representing anti-fascist resistance, were able to convene a Provisional National Assembly, once the eastern parts of the country were freed of Nazi rule by the advancing Red Army.

THE DEMOCRATIC EXPERIMENT 1944–48

The Provisional Assembly convened at Debrecen on 21 December 1944 constituted a radical and fundamental departure from the canons of the political order which had ruled in Hungary for centuries. It represented a symbolic declaration that from then on the narrow, neo-feudal elite, which had sought to exclude pressure from society and popular partici-pation from political power, would have to yield its hegemony of power to new, more widely based forces. It held the promise of the creation of a democratic political system and the modernization of Hungary through the resolution of the plethora of social and economic problems which the old elite could not or would not tackle. Hungary had tried twice in the preceding century to enter the road toward civil transformation and modernization: in 1848–49, when the joint forces of Habsburg and Romanow stopped it, and then in 1918, when the short-term policies of the Entente caused its defeat first to the communists, then to the counter-revolution of Horthy and associates. The democratic experiment after the Second World War started out over the ruins of the authoritarian interwar system and promised a new departure to wide strata of the society. Its eventual failure and suppression by Stalinist totalitarianism has lent the years 1944–48 – characterized by true enthusiasm and pluralist attempts at change – a certain allure. This should not, at the same time, blind one to the weaknesses of this system and to the very real difficulties to which Hungarian politicians had to address themselves.

The beginnings of the experiment were decidedly inauspicious. The country was still at war. The capital Budapest and Transdanubia (Western Hungary) remained in German hands and in these districts the Szálasi government's Arrow Cross detachments were carrying out a reign of terror against Jews, the left, and other putative enemies. The Red Army, which had entered the territory of Hungary several weeks earlier, had earned itself the dislike of those affected by its depredations. War-damage was extensive and the task of material reconstruction was enormous. Political reconstruction looked no easier. The newly emerging political forces were suspicious of the communists who had returned to the Hungarian political stage after the débâcle of the transient Hungarian Soviet Republic of 1919, and were regarded as the agents of the liberating or, as some preferred, 'liberating' power, the Soviet Union. Many experienced politicians had perished or had compromised themselves with the previous regime or were going into exile.

Nor was there any broadly based consensus as to the way in which the system was to be rebuilt. Many questions, like what future role the old elites should play, the form of the constitution (Hungary was still technically a monarchy), the national issue and the frontiers, the relationship between the state and private sectors, and the nature of control over the state by society required answers. From the outset, therefore, the democratic experiment had the appearance of a somewhat haphazard affair, in which a variety of political forces and groupings, with relatively few aims in common, found themselves obliged to cooperate.

Revival of political life

The 230 delegates who assembled in the Calvinist Church in Debrecen – a symbolic venue, for this was where Louis Kossuth had proclaimed

Hungarian independence from the Habsburgs in 1849 – were a decidedly mixed collection who had come together either from the areas already liberated or who had hazardously made their way through lines eastwards or had been brought there by the courtesy of the Red Army.

The Provisional Assembly sat for two days and elected a provisional government which was to rule Hungary for over eleven months. The government which emerged from the Debrecen assembly was headed by General Béla Miklós, commander of the First Honvéd Army who had changed over to the Soviets. Among its members were two army generals, representatives of the former liberal, socialist and peasant opposition and two communists, the agrarian specialist Imre Nagy, who was joined later by Ernő Gerő. It functioned under close Soviet supervision exercised through the Allied Control Commission (ACC), as well as by decisions of Red Army commanders locally, and was strongly influenced by initiatives made at the outset of Hungary's newly revived political life, that is, even before the convening of the Provisional Assembly.

The most crucial of these were the proclamation of the National Independence Front on 2 December 1944 in Szeged and the beginnings of organized political activity in the newly liberated areas. In both these, the communists played an active and visible role. There is, indeed, evidence that the communists were even instrumental in launching the activities of other political parties. The Front proclaimed itself in being with the participation of the Communists, the Smallholders' Party (FKGP), the Social Democratic Party (SZDP), the National Peasant Party (NPP), the Civic Democratic Party (PDP) and the Free Trade Unions, as the leading forces of new Hungary.

The establishment of this organization not only was an innovation in terms of Hungarian political practice but also had its elements of continuity. It was new in that it was constituted by hitherto largely unrepresented political and social forces, but inasmuch as it sought to build up a hegemony over political life and the excluded political organizations of which it disapproved – the old elite – it had a haunting similarity to the government party of the *ancien régime*. At this point there was no attempt at political pluralism outside the Front and political opposition was not regarded a necessary element of democracy.

The programme of the Front was heavily influenced by the programme of the communists, which had been published just a few days earlier. As a basic precondition of success, Hungary had to participate in its own liberation, break with Hitler and support the Red Army. It declared pro-German elements and the Arrow Cross the enemies of the new order (but not the defunct Horthy regime) whose supporters had to be purged from Hungarian public life and who, therefore, could not

3

hold office. The programme called for land reform, the nationalization of mines, the oil industry, electricity generation, insurance and state supervision of banks and large industry. Private enterprise, as against this, was to have a positive role in the reconstruction. The programme called for the introduction of an eight-hour working day; for the legal recognition of the right to strike; for protection of the working conditions of women and minors; paid holidays and unemployment benefit for those out of work. In foreign affairs, Hungary should adopt a democratic foreign policy, meaning close cooperation with all neighbouring countries, as well as the United Kingdom and the United States, and it should pursue a policy of 'close friendship with the mighty Soviet Union'.

The communists, backed as they were by their Soviet controllers, attempted to be the most dynamic force, but did not seek monopoly of power straight-away. While this policy may have been motivated by a certain self-restraint – based on their historic experience of 1919 and the popular-front ideology of the war years – their caution stemmed above all from Stalin's ukase (edict) who at that point still observed the joint agreement of the Allies on a democratic, coalition strategy.

Soon after its election, the provisional government declared war on Germany and received the Allies' armistice terms, nullified the Vienna awards of 1938 and 1940 thereby returning Hungary to its Trianon (1920) frontiers and accepted obligations to make war reparations in the amount of $300 million to the Soviet Union, Czechoslovakia and Yugoslavia.

Political life in Hungary revived fairly slowly at the national level, a process which was in any case obstructed until the liberation of Budapest. However, locally where issues impinged on leaders more immediately, decisions had to be taken and the political vacuum created by the collapse of the old regime filled by whoever was at hand. 'National committees' were formed in towns and villages, frequently, but not always, following communist initiative.

Although the siege of Budapest lasted until 13 February, much of the capital had been effectively liberated earlier. Pest (the eastern and larger part of the capital) had seen the end of fighting by mid-January and political organization had slowly begun even before this. Although the capital lay in ruins and all the bridges over the Danube were blown up by the retreating Germans, people were keen to leave the air-raid shelters and start reconstruction. Life returned quickly to the capital, even as the war shifted westwards until the entire territory of the country was emptied of German troops around 4 April.

State of the parties

As already suggested, the communists were the first to launch their political activity, starting their operations in the wake of the Red Army, sometimes arriving within hours of the end of fighting. District branches were set up rapidly, the recruitment of members was given a high priority and the membership rose correspondingly rapidly from the 3,000 members at the end of 1944 to 150,000 by May 1945 and to about half a million by October of the same year, to reach the one and a half million mark by 1949. There were certainly a few thousand convinced communists (some of them keeping their faith ever since 1919) and they had their sympathizers. Many intellectuals, opposed to the conservative course of the interwar years joined, too, and so did young people looking for alternatives. Poor peasants and workers with ideas about radical social change also found their way to the party, but probably the great majority – above all, after 1947–48 – were those who joined for career or existential reasons. Finally there were many Arrow Cross small-fry, for whom the opening of the door into the Communist Party was a heaven-sent opportunity to escape responsibility for their past misdeeds lightly. These differences in the origins of the membership resulted in a heterogeneity in their quality and some members were far less experienced than others.

There were also significant differences between the attitudes of the Muscovites, who returned from Soviet exile, and the Home communists, those who had spent the war years and before in the underground. Muscovites enjoyed the prestige of the Soviet connection in the eyes of the Home communists and they used this to establish a pre-eminence over all party matters and to put the stamp of Sovietization on the Hungarian party. They tended to adopt a cautious, almost reformist approach to the future, in concert with the Soviet policy of the times. The Home communists, on the other hand, were more impatient. Some of them wanted to continue where they had left off in 1919; others had been radicalized by their experience in the wartime underground and demanded the introduction of communism straight-away. The subordination of the underground party to the new leadership from the Soviet Union was, however, soon completed after the arrival of Mátyás Rákosi in Budapest in late February. Bolshevik discipline and obedience prevailed.

Rákosi had been picked as the party's new leader in the Soviet Union and had been its head from 1940 onwards. He had played a minor role in the 1919 Soviet Republic, but had advanced to the status of a communist hero thanks to the life sentence imposed on him under

Horthy and the publicity he received then and later. Nor can the elimination of many leading Hungarian communists during the Soviet purges of the 1930s, including their leader Béla Kun, have been much of an obstacle to his advancement either. Rákosi was a consummate tactician, a man capable of charm as well as of sadistic brutality, of loyalty to the Soviet Union and of utter dogmatism. He was flanked in the leadership by his fellow Muscovites, Ernő Gerő, Mihály Farkas and József Révai. Gerő could hardly have presented a greater contrast to Rákosi's bonhomie. He was a cold, humourless, inflexible technocrat, who, however, shared with Rákosi the traits of dogmatism and loyalty to the Soviet Union. He was in charge of economic strategy and to some extent of party organization. Farkas was generally regarded as a semi-literate sadist, whose role in the leadership was assured by his Soviet connections, notably in the military. Révai's dogmatism and dedication were also paramount, but in his case these were coupled with an undoubted intelligence and sophistication. They made him a fearsome opponent for his intellectual antagonists and the heavyweight in ideological debates.

All four of the top Muscovites were of Jewish background, a factor which seriously complicated popular attitudes towards communism. There had been a connection between the left and Jews from the early years of the century and the popular identification of communism with Jews – well exploited by the interwar regime – had created the stereotype figure of the Judaeo-Bolshevik in the eyes of many people. From this it was an easy step to regard communism as a Jewish device, especially in the aftermath of the holocaust for which the responsibility of non-Jewish Hungarians had not been clarified then or later. This confusion of attitudes was exacerbated by the communists' more or less deliberate reliance on cadres of Jewish background to undertake the anti-fascist purification of Hungarian life. From the communists' point of view, Jews were absolutely reliable in this role because by no stretch of the imagination could they have been tainted with Nazism. From the non-Jewish and non-communist majority's standpoint, the prosecution of war criminals by Jews could and did assume the appearance of a Jewish revenge, because their other qualifications for this role seemed less salient. The entire question of reciprocal attitudes, Jewish and non-Jewish, communist and non-communist, remained as a kind of semi-visible undercurrent throughout the post-war period of Hungarian history and surfaced only occasionally.

Of the other parties, the Social Democrats (SZDP) found themselves in competition with the communists for membership, influence and power from the outset. The party, though having a strong tradition of organization, activity and even parliamentary representation until 1944, was in some disarray with the end of hostilities. Several of the party's senior leaders were either abroad or had failed to survive the war, so that leadership was in the hands of the so-called left wing under Árpád Szakasits, a weak, easily influenced and rather ineffectual man. In terms of membership, the SZDP was not unsuccessful. It attracted the bulk of the heavy industrial workers (except for those who joined the communists) and from most other industrial centres as well. The lower middle class tended to see in the SZDP a force that could protect them from the communists. By December 1945, the SZDP had around 2,000 organizations in the country as a whole. The most serious political ballast which the SZDP was obliged to bear was its unresolved relationship with the communists. The fear of 'reaction' was crucial in the post-1944 period in determining SZDP attitudes, for the party could neither afford to be outflanked on the left by the communists nor could it appear to be supporting measures which might genuinely aid the middle classes. On the other hand, there was, equally, anxiety that the communists were only waiting for the moment when they might swallow the SZDP and eliminate its political independence. All these fears were enhanced by the so-called 'unity document' which the underground leadership had signed in October 1944 and which to a large extent committed the Social Democrats to close cooperation with the communists virtually as the first priority. This unresolved relationship prevented the SZDP from undertaking more effective cooperation with the Smallholders, even where the interests of the two parties coincided.

The Smallholders (FKGP) were, like the Social Democrats, an established party which had operated legally before and during the war. In the aftermath of the liberation, however, they found themselves in a radically new situation for which the Smallholder leadership was in no way prepared. Not only did the party become the pre-eminent representative of the peasantry, but in addition the bulk of the political base of the old elite gave it its support, having no other political home to go to. In this way, the FKGP had a difficult double role to play: it was simultaneously the political home of the rural population, including sections of the poorest agricultural workers, and of the urban, professional classes. These different segments of the party tended to pull in different directions. This somewhat ad hoc quality of the party, together with the speed with which it had come together, made it that much easier for the communists to attempt to break it down into its component parts again. Furthermore, the leadership of the party remained in the hands of its old pre-war and wartime leading figures, like Zoltán Tildy, Ferenc Nagy and Béla Kovács. They were certainly courageous and determined politicians, but they were handicapped by their relative lack of experience on a broad front, by their unwillingness to engage in the devious tactical manoeuvres which circumstances required and to some extent by the impatience of many of their supporters with the 'political game', which they associated with the manipulations of the old regime. The killing of the best known politician of the Smallholders in the anti-fascist resistance, Endre Bajcsy-Zsilinszky, by the Arrow Cross was a grievous loss, for he would undoubtedly have stiffened the party's leadership in this respect. In the main, the party stood for western-style pluralism and for a pro-western orientation, while respecting the interests of the Soviet Union. But the different parts of the de facto coalition which constituted the party looked to different options on a variety of policies and issues.

Similarly, the heterogeneity and a certain anachronism dug the grave of the short-lived small Liberal party, the Civic Democrats (PDP), which tried to unify the relatively liberal former supporters of the interwar system with its truly liberal oppositionals. And in any case, the spirit of the age could not have been further from classical liberalism, which never had a serious following in Hungary.

Finally, the National Peasant Party (NPP) began virtually as little more than the rural branch organization of the communists, but thanks to some of its leading figures – intellectuals with various reforming ideas who had been associated with the anti-fascist March Front movement of the 1930s and the strong tradition of agrarian radicalism in eastern Hungary – the party captured something of a mass base and exercised a political influence out of all proportion to its size. The party's main merit was perhaps to have offered a forum for István Bibó, a seminal figure in post-war Hungarian thinking, who was crucial in formulating the ideology of the 'Third Road' for Hungary, a social and political system neither Soviet nor western.

While much of the political focus in these early months concentrated on the re-emergence of political parties and their activities, below the visible level of events a not altogether silent struggle was taking place. Communist strategy was aimed from the outset at establishing power at two levels – in party politics and in the institutions of state and society. To ensure their influence and to extend it as far as possible, they sought to 'colonize' institutions by filling important posts with trustworthy appointees. Central to this strategy was control of the security services: the secret police and its military counterpart. These were never brought under effective political control, but for all practical purposes remained the private army of the communists. Government ministries were similarly, though perhaps not so extensively, colonized as well and to a large extent the practice grew up of regarding different ministries as doing the bidding of the political party which controlled them. An analogous process was taking place in the trade unions, in the radio (an important medium of communication), in the economic sphere, in the administration of justice, and in local government. The 'national committees' of the early months were successfully marginalized by a joint effort of communists and Smallholders, both interested in strengthening central administration.

As the initial shock of the liberation and of the end of hostilities wore off, and as it emerged that the communists were not bent on the immediate introduction of a Soviet republic, the other parties began to flex their muscles. The country, it was felt, was in a sufficient state of readiness by the autumn for elections to be held. These marked a major turning point.

Land reform

The issue of land reform was one on which all the four parties agreed, but agreement stopped at the principle; the extent, the means and the instruments of redistribution were a matter for marked disagreement. While the dismantling of semi-feudal latifundia – that had been accomplished in the neighbouring countries by the 1930s at the latest – was certainly long overdue, the maximum and the ideal size of holdings and the procedure of reform was open to debate. As early as January 1945, agitation for immediate, radical land reform was launched by the communists, in which they were backed by the National Peasants. The communist-NPP proposal rejected immediate collectivization, which would have frightened and antagonized the peasantry, and opted instead for the outright expropriation of large estates. The communists then encouraged the formation of 'land-claimant committees' to oversee the reform. The other parties, however, disliked the radical nature of this approach and queried all aspects of it. In the end, after weeks of argument, the matter was resolved by Soviet intervention. The Soviet representative on the ACC, over which western influence was marginal, Marshal Voroshilov, instructed the provisional government to accept a Soviet plan, which was duly done.

The actual redistribution was carried out by some 3,000 land-claimant committees, aided by the Soviet military and the communists. The peasants themselves proved to be cautious in exercising their option, for fear that the former owners might return. Some 35 per cent of Hungary's arable land was redistributed among more than 600,000 landless peasants and dwarf holders, albeit this still left some 300,000 for whom there was no land left, to say nothing of the thousands who returned from Soviet POW camps 'too late' to announce their claims. With this step, the predominance of latifundia in Hungarian agriculture was terminated and one of the bases of the landed gentry was destroyed. Whether the hundreds of thousands of small plots without capital and expertise would have in the long run survived, cannot be decided as they were not left much time to consolidate. At any rate, the country was able to feed its population in the first post-war years, and wide strata of the rural population became supporters of the new system.

Elections

The autumn of 1945 saw the first public test of the distribution of political power. There were local elections in Budapest (7 October) and a month later (4 November) general elections were held. These proved to be a major débâcle for the communists, who had entered both with unrealistically high expectations. In Budapest, the communists persuaded the Social Democrats to fight the elections on a joint list. Rákosi confidently expected that the two workers' parties together would sweep the board in the most industrialized part of the country. Reality was different. The Smallholders emerged with a small absolute majority of the votes, the two workers' parties scoring little more than one-third. This result was a bitter pill for the communists, not only because it inherently falsified their basic assumptions about the extent of their support, but also because it appeared to suggest that their tactics were wrong as well.

The general elections confirmed the trend. The three left-wing parties polled respectably at well over two-fifths of the popular vote (SZDP 17.5 per cent, MKP 17 per cent, NPP 7 per cent), but the Smallholders emerged with a solid overall majority of 57 per cent. There were two important lessons in these results. An overwhelming (approximately two-thirds) majority – at least 60 per cent of the FKGP and half of the SZDP voters – took a stand against the communists. On the other hand, something like half of the electorate – all voters of the MKP and NPP, about half of those of the SZDP and perhaps one-third of the FKGP – expressed its will for radical changes in politics, economy and culture, beyond the programme of a western-style 'bourgeois' parliamentary democracy.

The first requirement was to settle the character of the government. The ACC left no doubt that it would only countenance the continuation of the coalition. This dispensation created an almost unique form of governance, one in which the coalition comprised both the government and the opposition. The FKGP provided the prime minister, but had only seven portfolios, while seven went to the MKP, SZDP and NPP. In addition, Rákosi, István Dobi of the Smallholders and Szakasits were made ministers of state, having the de facto status of deputy prime minister. The strategy that the FKGP adopted, therefore, was to keep the coalition going until the eventual peace treaty would, it was hoped, result in the departure of Soviet forces from Hungary, after which the country would be free to deal with its own internal affairs. The peace treaty, signed in February 1947 in Paris, did not bring the hoped-for independence. The dismantling of the ACC meant only that western Allied military presence – however powerless it might have been from the beginning – ceased, but the Soviet troops remained 'in order to secure transit and supply routes for the Red Army in occupied Austria.'

From democracy to dictatorship

In fact, the FKGP proved unable to win the first of many challenges they had to face. The communist objective was to regroup and to try and fragment the other parties, above all their main obstacle to power, the Smallholders. They recovered relatively quickly from the shock of the elections and, in any case, found themselves obliged to defend their positions against a strong wave of anti-communism encouraged by the election result. The communist counter-offensive was palpable in the labour movement; in agriculture; in the emasculation of the armed forces; in pressure for stepping up the purge of the civil service; and in overt politics. In February 1946, the MKP passed a resolution to attack 'reaction' in the Smallholders: the so-called Left Bloc was formed, consisting of the MKP, the Social Democrats, the NPP and the Trade Union Council. This effectively institutionalized the system of 'opposition-within-the government' and helped to isolate the FKGP. To back up the pressure, the Smallholder prime minister, Ferenc Nagy (who had succeeded Tildy on the latter's elevation to the Presidency of the Republic, which was proclaimed by the consensus of all parties in 1946), received a series of demands from the ACC which Hungary was in no position to meet. Each time the Smallholders launched an initiative to halt the Left Bloc offensive, they would come up against a Soviet counter-thrust with which they were powerless to deal.

It is still not clear whether Stalin had decided as early as 1944–45 to incorporate the whole of eastern Europe into the Soviet bloc (while

Allied consensus merely assured him of this region's belonging to the USSR's sphere of influence) or developed this strategy only in the course of the ever cooling atmosphere between the wartime Allies. It is probable that there was to be a difference between two zones. In the strategically most important bordering countries (Poland, Romania, Bulgaria), Stalin insisted on immediate communist take-over. The countries further west, such as Finland, Czechoslovakia, Hungary and Austria, were to follow a course of long-term transition, and only in 1947 did the communist parties obtain the order to take power. However, in Finland the democratic powers were able to stop the undecided communist bid, while in Austria the four-power occupation frustrated such steps. In Czechoslovakia the putsch of 1948 established communist domination for four decades in a situation where the Communist Party was already well entrenched.

In Hungary, the communists liquidated their political rivals and opponents in several steps and by so-called salami tactics: slicing up their opponents with the help of allies or agents on the 'left wing' of the coalition parties. The first victim was, of course, the FKGP with its threatening size. Its slicing-up began with the expulsion of the most vehemently resisting 'right wing' (Dezső, Sulyok and his friends), with the assistance of the centre and the 'left', only to be followed by the centrists themselves, led by the secretary-general of the party, Béla Kovács – abducted to Siberia by the Soviets – and Prime Minister Ferenc Nagy, who was forced into exile, being accused of participating in 'a conspiracy against the state'.

After the destruction of their main opponents, the MKP risked a new election, hoping to change parliamentary balance to their favour. In the 1947 elections, strongly manipulated, the communists became the strongest party with some 100 deputies. The restructured National Independence Front managed to win 60 per cent of the votes, but the opposition – mainly the (essentially Christian-Democratic) Popular Democratic Party and the National Independence Party – were strong enough to be eliminated only by extra-parliamentary methods. The 1947 elections, in effect, marked the end of the democratic interlude in Hungary. There were to be a few more steps until this slow process of winding up the experiment was concluded, but the point of no return had been passed.

The following twelve months have become known as the 'year of the turning point'. It was during this period that the drive to transform Hungary into a fully fledged Soviet-type state reached its climax. This drive had various aspects: the sacking of non-compliant civil servants, the nationalization of large, then medium and finally of all enterprises, the liquidation of all associations not controlled by the communists, the ending of the freedom of the press and the breaking of the power of the churches.

The decision to finalize nationalization was in many cases preceded by the take-over of enterprises by workers with communist encouragement. This was paralleled by the abolition of the right to strike and the subordination of the trade unions to communist rule. Thus, once the NPP was virtually absorbed by the communists, only the Social Democrats remained as serious rivals. At the turn of 1947–48 the 'left wing', led by the crypto-communist György Marosán, attacked and finally expelled the old, respected leaders of the party and declared its readiness for the union with the communists. At the 'unification congress' of June 1948 the Hungarian Workers' Party (MDP) was founded, defined as a Marxist-Leninist avant-garde. (Even its name, just as that of all east European state parties, such as the Polish PZRP, the German SED or the Romanian Workers' Party, was personally approved by Stalin.). This move also had an important symbolic significance, in that it notionally made the MDP the sole repository of proletarian legitimacy.

The process can be regarded as having been completed with the promulgation of the new Soviet-type constitution in August 1949, codifying, among others, the 'leading role' of the sole surviving party, the MDP, in state and society. It is clear in retrospect that the communists were accelerating their push for complete power and that the final stages were rushed through. The impulse appears to have been the Cominform meeting at Szklarska Poreba in Poland in September 1947, where the decision to complete the imposition of the Soviet model on the whole of eastern Europe was taken. The notion of 'people's democracy' meant from then on its exact opposite: the liquidation of all aspects of democracy by dictatorship. Those who believed that some kind of 'revolutionary democracy' might mean a long-term transition from 'bourgeois democracy' to the 'dictatorship of the proletariat' (such as Georg Lukács) were forced to denounce their earlier ideas.

Social and economic change

The 1945–49 period had been one of major upheaval for Hungary. The country witnessed a massive transformation, some of it real, some of it superficial. The old elite was shattered by its wartime defeat and only partly recovered itself sufficiently to articulate its political wishes. In any event, it accepted that some change, including wider access to political participation, was inevitable. How far this was to go was another matter and the professional classes expected that their technical skills would be needed by whatever government was in power. In this they were mistaken, for the communists regarded political loyalty as the supreme qualification and expertise as something of a distraction under the new dispensation. Additionally, the galloping inflation in 1945–46 destroyed the economic bases, the lifetime savings and insurance of the entire middle class, professionals and entrepreneurs alike.

In the autumn of 1946 the Third Congress of the MKP issued the slogan: 'We rebuild the country not for capitalists but for the people' and demanded the introduction and fulfilment of a three-years' plan of reconstruction. This plan, which followed a successful stabilization of the new currency, the Forint, in August 1946 was aimed at eliminating the war damage and found wide support among the population. However, the MKP soon used it for pushing through its own agenda. Soon after the plan's inception, the communists argued that it could not be accomplished without the nationalization of the major banks, and by the end of 1947 this was done. When in 1948, all enterprises employing more than 100 workers were 'nationalized', the entire economic system was changed and the state's role as administrative, proprietor, entrepreneur and organizer began to merge. Planning embraced ever wider sectors of the economy.

The peasantry, particularly those whose aspirations for land had been satisfied, proved to be relatively supportive of the new status quo and were fearful of losing their gains through collectivisation. The workers, some more radical than others, found that their hopes for a more equitable system were frustrated, notably with the elimination of their political and trade union representation. At the same time, the communists were successful in attracting to themselves a generation of previously low-status activists – peasants and workers – whom they promoted into positions of power. There were serious, though rather rough-and-ready attempts at refreshing the elite by children of the earlier disadvantaged. It was for this reason that the old professional elite, with its standards of solid professional rather than political criteria, had to be removed – to make room for what was later to be called the New Class. True, many of the enthusiastic young men and women, who planned 'to turn the world upside down', were also eliminated in due course, when servile obedience to the central party-line became the sole criterion for acceptability.

What was particularly striking about this period was the very wide range of social, political, economic and religious activity that was characteristic of Hungary at this time. While there was no question of Hungary having reached at best a partially developed level of social complexity, with grave areas of underdevelopment in terms of equal access to resources, society was not homogeneous but extremely varied in its aspirations, expectations and choice. Much of this was released in the new-found opportunity of the 1944–48 period, as was indicated by the very high number of institutions which the communists decided to liquidate.

In a word, in the aftermath of the war Hungary showed itself to be a complex, modernizing society, with clear aspirations for autonomy for individual and group action. The level of this went far beyond what the new political order could tolerate and the Stalinist period saw these processes reversed and stifled. In this context, Hungary embarked on an enforced rehomogenization, with far-reaching consequences for later years.

STALINISM

The basic principles of the Stalinist political order were remarkably straightforward. A political organization calling itself 'communist party' – a misnomer, for it was not a 'part' of society but sought to encompass the entire polity – declared itself to be in possession of the sole key to the future, to have found the only road to the perfect society, that is, communism. Not only was the party, therefore, engaged in the construction of perfection, but also it alone had the right to determine the criteria by which that perfection was to be defined. This was the essence of Marxism-Leninism. It offered a number of very clear political advantages to the new rulers. By definition, it is impossible to question or doubt perfection, hence anyone who disagreed with what the party was doing was a hostile conspirator flouting supreme rationality. This device effectively saved the party from having to justify what it was doing by any criteria other than its own. There was one further important consequence of this dispensation. Marxism-Leninism was a quintessentially political doctrine, claiming that all questions could be resolved by political means. Hence the political sphere ruled supreme, transcending all others and subordinating all other activities – social, economic, religious, family – to the rationality and power of the polity.

In its ideal form, the state entirely encompassed society and eliminated all social autonomy. All decisions, initiatives and action were in the hands of the state and the role of society was reduced to that of the passive extra in the Grand March into the Future. This dispensation ran counter to the values and traditions of Hungary, which were much closer to those of the European mainstream, in which society is creative and the state is reactive, albeit Hungary, in common with the rest of central and eastern Europe, had had a strongly étatist tradition. But the legacy of patterns of autonomy were such that the newly imposed system was operating against rather than with the grain of social aspirations.

At the centre was Stalin himself controlling the Soviet party and the Soviet Union. Through his east European allies, the east European parties and Soviet advisers in eastern Europe, he controlled seven countries, Hungary among them. The Hungarian communists had probably greater difficulties in imposing their project on society than any other satellite party. As mentioned before, the supreme leadership – the so-called quadriga – was of Jewish origin and spent the previous decades in jail or exile. Moreover, none of the other communist leaders came to be as opposed to society as they did, for there was nothing that the Moscovites could 'bring home as present' to their nation. (The Soviet occupation zone of Germany, later the GDR, was a special case for itself.) For the Poles the Soviets guaranteed the new borders in the west (even if they took away the east), the same was true for Romania, where the border with Hungary (Transylvania) was also guaranteed by the USSR. In Czechoslovakia a Slavic nation-state was established by the disenfranchisement of the German and Hungarian population – with Soviet and communist approval. The Bulgarian tradition of Russian friendship was also helpful to the communists. Furthermore, with the exception of Romania (and, again, the GDR), these were all Slavic countries, while Hungary's cultural and – because of its role in the war as an ally of Germany – political position was the exact opposite. The returning Muscovite leaders were aware of these handicaps; it is known that they still contemplated in Moscow what 'dowry' they could bring home. But Soviet politics did not leave space for any such thing. Rákosi's clique had, therefore, absolutely no national basis, which made them even more keen to win Stalin's favours, outdoing all the other satellites in 'revolutionary vigilance' against the slightest deviation from the Soviet model.

The party controlled the state, the state controlled society and these two, together with the now transformed social institutions, controlled the individual. But because traditions of social autonomy had had the chance to develop and, possibly, because they had acquired particular strength in the years immediately after the war, these were seen by the communists as requiring urgent extirpation. To this end, coercion on a mass basis was used.

Terror was the instrument to make perfection stick. Finally, the actual targets of Stalinism, as applied to Hungary (and the rest of eastern Europe) constituted a major anomaly. Whereas Stalin insisted that the goals to be pursued by each communist country – 'the sole road to communism' – were the ones developed under him in the Soviet Union in the 1930s and declared by him to be the immanent objectives of socialism, in reality these were nothing more than the temporary, contingent requirements of Soviet development, determined by Soviet conditions, like the abundance of raw materials, cheap labour and enormous distances.

In concrete terms, therefore, the Stalinist model consisted of the accelerated construction of a heavy industrial base. In the main, military or military-related objectives tended to receive priority. Thus the actual industries favoured were heavy metallurgy, especially steel, extractive industries, energy and transport. The approach was to emphasize the largest scale feasible, to build and to operate these by obliging the population to make the maximum effort in the process. The costs of the investment were borne by the population which underwent a squeeze on its consumption.

The problem from the Hungarian standpoint was that the model was wholly inappropriate to local conditions. Even if the country was in need of serious modernization and the development of different branches of industry, Hungary did not have plentiful natural resources; being a small country, it did not function according to the spatial relationships that obtained in the Soviet Union; and even the Hungarian labour force possessed a higher level of skills than its Soviet counterpart had done in the 1930s. The result was that Hungarian politics, society, economics were forced into a Procrustean bed that actually represented a large step backwards, a process of development.

Rákosi's Hungary

The years 1949–53 were all the apogee of Rákosi's power; and, as he described himself, he was Stalin's most apt pupil. The system that he created followed the Soviet model as closely as possible and at all levels, as far as is known, Hungarian initiatives were supervised by Soviet advisers with far-reaching competence. The party itself was run by Rákosi, flanked by Gerő, who oversaw the economy; Farkas, who held the security brief; and Révai, who supervised culture. The other institutions of the party acted under strict central control.

The last important non-communist opponent in the party's way was the Roman Catholic church and the personality of the Primate Josef, Cardinal Mindszenty. Mindszenty chose to oppose the state on the issue of the secularization of education, the dismantling of the network of

religious schools, an issue on which he did not command the unconditional support of Hungarian opinion. Throughout 1948 the conflict
continued, until at the very end of the year, an 'anti-state conspiracy'
was discovered and Mindszenty was arrested. He was forced to confess
to implausible crimes (espionage, currency speculation) under duress
and sentenced to life imprisonment. But even after this, it took over a
year to repress the last vestiges of popular demands for religious education. The remnants of the Roman Catholic church – the Protestant
churches had been repressed earlier – finally accepted state supervision
in 1950.

The political institutions associated with the new order served its
purposes, however remote these objectives may have been from those
of Hungarian society. Thus the use of coercion, which had already
destroyed non-communist institutions, was then extended to real or
potential opponents within the party itself. With the outbreak of the
anti-Tito campaign in 1948, a ready-made pretext for dealing with
communist opponents of the Stalinist leadership was to hand. Essentially,
the charge of Titoism was a declaration that even within the party,
autonomous thought, before as well as after the take-over, was prima
facie grounds for persecution.

The principal communist victims of the purges had this in common:
they were not Muscovites, that is they had not spent time in exile in
the Soviet Union, but had been members of the party in illegality or
abroad. From Rákosi's standpoint, this made them suspect as potential
opponents. In the summer of 1949, László Rajk, who was an utterly
dedicated and loyal communist and had served it well as a ruthless
Minister of Interior, was arrested, together with a number of others.
His trial later that year was organized along the lines pioneered in
Moscow in the 1930s. 'Evidence' was discovered that Rajk had been
involved in a range of fantastical crimes, from Trotskyism to espionage
for Yugoslavia and the west. He was duly executed.

The deeper purpose of this and other show trials was to demonstrate
to the party and to society that there was only one truth and this was
known only to Rákosi and Stalin. The show trials were a symbolic
enactment of the party's claim to ominiscience and to the proposition
that all shades of disagreement with the party were tantamount to hostile
conspiracy, including different interpretations of communist doctrine.
The legal form used in these trials centred on public confession, indicat-
ing acceptance of the party's transcendental role in determining the
'truth'. They served, furthermore, to lay down in a particularly striking
way that the boundaries of what was acceptable and what was unaccept-

able were determined exclusively by the party and that all must now accept these. Resistance was pointless, the party controlled perfection.

A second political institution developed under the new order was the cult of personality. Stalin was the centrepiece of this and the ritual adoration of Stalin was enacted and re-enacted again and again, whether in the numerous places and factories named after him or the massive statue erected to him in Budapest. The cult of Rákosi followed closely behind. Rákosi was declared the *fons et origo* of the communist revolution in Hungary, the wise father and teacher, infallible, ever watchful and the keystone of the new order. Other rituals included the mass parades at which attendance was obligatory, the compulsory Marxism-Leninism classes and so on. All these had a similar purpose: to demonstrate that the party and only the party, as embodied in Stalin and Rákosi, constituted politics, that all else was illegitimate and antagonistic to the Wave of the Future, the historical inevitability of the class struggle.

A third institution of Stalinism was the continuous purge. It began within the party, but the message was meant for the entire society: if the powerful officials of the communist dictatorship can vanish from one day to another, how much more defenceless a simple citizen must be! The category of 'enemy' grew day by day. After the 'class enemy', the 'kulaks' and 'clerical reactionaries' came those who 'infiltrated the party', 'Trotskyist' and 'Titoist'. All those who spent some years in the west, even as fighters in the Spanish Civil War, were seen as 'cosmopolitans' and unreliable; finally Jews came to be accused as 'Zionist agents'. No one could feel secure from police terror, daily arrests, deportations and internments. The atmosphere of suspicion demoralized families, old friendships and close collegial circles alike.

In October-November 1951, almost half of the middle and lower level party officials were dropped; the total number of those purged between 1948 and 1956 was around 350,000. The purge, of course, was not restricted to the party. The severity of the regime and its readiness to use coercion was shown by the fact that around one-tenth of the population of Hungary was affected by police terror and, further, that those hit by coercion were in the main workers and peasants. The middle classes were naturally not left out. Between 1950 and 1951, a significant proportion of the urban middle class, primarily in Budapest, was compulsory resettled in the countryside – deported and/or interned – often in the most appalling conditions; over 100,000 people were affected.

Industrialization, collectivization and Russification

A fourth aspect of the period was forced industrialization. There were several underlying motivations in this. There was the general bias towards heavy industry in the Soviet model, as already noted. Additionally, the Stalinist period was one of war hysteria. The Kremlin was convinced, or at least acted as if it was, that a third world war was imminent; indeed, preparations for hostilities against Yugoslavia were well advanced by 1949–50. This required a rapid increase in the military capability of the entire Soviet bloc, which again emphasized heavy industry. To these might be added the personal ambitions of the planners, above all of Gerő, who masterminded the economy. These factors lay behind Hungary's development plan. They accounted for its unique features, which had the stated aim of transforming Hungary into a 'land of iron and steel'.

To achieve this, the First Five Year Plan (1950–54) adopted the most far-reaching targets and planned to raise industrial output by 204 per cent; at the Second Congress of the MDP in 1951, this figure was raised to an unbelievable 380 per cent. This, of course, was attainable only notionally, through the neglect of quality, through the distortion of production patterns and through a squeeze on consumption as the source of investment. Real wages fell by 18 per cent between 1949 and 1952 and this was accompanied by a levelling down of incomes, an equalization which brought the incomes of the managerial elite close to that of the bulk of the labour force. Nor was the Stalinist model helped by a shortage of managerial and industrial skills. The old technocratic elite had been ousted to make way for the politically reliable but otherwise inexperienced New Class and much of the old skilled working class was promoted upwards. The raw materials, notably of iron ore and coking coal, were imported from the Soviet Union. So was the technology used for this industrial construction, and it tended to be obsolete or obsolescent.

In effect, the Stalinist model of industrialization saddled Hungary with an autarkic industry, which functioned at high cost, which resulted in the destruction or weakening of the existing industrial structure, which significantly lowered the standard of living and which was generally inappropriate to Hungarian conditions.

Much the same could be said for Stalinist agricultural policy. It was decided that agriculture should be collectivized, despite earlier promises that the party had no intention of doing so. The political motivation behind this move was to extend the power of the state in the countryside by subjecting it to industrial-type control. The economic argument was that only by exacting the maximum from agriculture could industrialization be achieved. In sociological terms, the party imposed the concept of class on the village and arbitrarily decided that the well-to-do-rich and middle peasantry constituted an exploiting class, the kulaks. At the height of the collectivization drive, there were some 70,000 people on the kulak list. In this way and through the imposition of compulsory deliveries, punitive taxation on private farmers, constant intervention by agriculturally ignorant officials and the pursuit of occasionally wholly irrational crop policies, it was expected that the countryside would accept the party's strategy. In the event, the results of this strategy were close to disastrous. The persecution of the kulaks eliminated the most efficient farmers, who were prosperous precisely because they were the most skilled producers. The passive resistance on the land brought with it a fall in output and food shortages.

The intelligentsia – hit by the economic decline and disintegration together with the rest of society – suffered additionally from the intellectual effects of Stalinism. Stalinism, claiming to be a perfect system, offered answers to all problems, those requiring specialized knowledge included. If all areas of knowledge are subject to class considerations, then it follows that there can be no autonomous or objective knowledge, even in fields like medicine or engineering. Hence these fields were subjected to the leading role of the party and to politicization regardless. Thereby the role of the intelligentsia, the bearer of specialized knowledge, was made superfluous. But because this social group had possessed (and still possessed) a claim to autonomous knowledge, it was regarded by the party as politically suspect and it was constrained to undergo the most far-reaching resocialization. The party's first task, as it saw the situation, was to socialize the socializers, those whose function in society was to transmit information. In this way the entire intelligentsia, including the humane, cultural and artistic intelligentsia, were caught up in the party's drive for total control.

In the purported absence of autonomous judgement, the function of the creative intelligentsia – particularly of those who were in the forefront of creating new values – was to be transformed into apologetics. Writers, poets, artists, actors and musicians alike were required to promote the political role of the party and not to exercise their independent judgement, which could not exist under Marxism-Leninism. All this was furthered by a determined Russification of cultural life, the compulsory learning of Russian and the adoption of Russian styles, paralleled by a witch-hunt against western ideas. The sycophantic odes to Stalin, the overblown, fulsome language, the synthetic optimism were the surface symptoms of this. The outcome was a stultification and, indeed, simplification of cultural patterns, whereby simple answers were forced on to situations of complexity, with attendant distortions. While a simplistic rhetoric of '500 years of struggle for national independence' was applied in order to win the nation, all aspects of national tradition and Hungarian pride were prosecuted as 'chauvinist deviation'.

On the brink of crisis

The overall result of Stalinization, with its massive mobilization and coercion, was that by 1953, Hungarian society was close to breaking point. Tensions were accumulating and the political system had no means of releasing them. In the spring of 1951 the ration card for groceries was reintroduced, setting off strikes in some plants. Industrial workers, beset by obligatory political assemblies and the daily half-hour liturgy of reading the party's daily in addition to the general hardships, were strained to breaking point. The peasants' situation was no better, thanks to mandatory deliveries and taxes and the insistence that they join the agricultural cooperatives (kolkhozes) or give up their land to the state farms.

Discontent was increasing and the level of economic output was stagnating, as an overburdened workforce retreated into passivity. The peasantry was apathetic and sullen. The intelligentsia was cowed by the threat and practice of terror. Within the party, however, doubts did not exist or where they did, they were stifled. The Stalinist policies managed to make the communists' assumption about everyone being an 'enemy of the regime' a self-fulfilling prophecy. At Stalin's death on 5 March 1953 Hungary looked calm on the surface, but underneath pressure was mounting and needed very little to turn it into something highly explosive.

CHAPTER TWO

The Path to Revolution

Just as Stalinism had been imposed on Hungary by the Soviet Union according to purely Soviet precepts and needs, so it eventuated with de-Stalinization. The new Soviet leadership that emerged from the succession struggles after Stalin's death was faced with an entirely unprecedented situation and sought to resolve the legacy of Stalinism by whatever methods could be made acceptable to a wide enough circle within the power elite. This then became the new strategy of socialism and it was imposed on the Soviet Union's satellites in eastern Europe without further thought as to whether conditions there might not require alternative strategies of decompression.

However, the policy of the 'New Course', initiated by the Soviet leadership, stimulated in Hungary more than just a correction of the very worst effects of totalitarian rule. Budapest did not, to be sure, experience an uprising of the sort that occurred in the German Democratic Republic, and the local strikes did not match the scale of worker protest in Poland and Czechoslovakia. Yet the changes that ensued in Hungary went deeper than those in the other satellite states. One may attribute this to the fact that Hungary's communist leaders were the spearhead of Stalin's anti-Tito campaign, which the Soviet leaders preferred to forget after the dictator's death. Or to the fact that party leader Mátyás Rákosi, who was 'more Catholic than the Pope' in following Moscow's directives, had alienated the people more completely than had any other satellite leader. Or perhaps to the circumstances that the Hungarian Stalinists were the first to lose their influence in the wake of changes in the Kremlin. At any rate, the harshly self-critical tone of the Hungarian party leadership and the ideas of the intellectual opposition that crystallized within the party went well beyond the cosmetic alterations envisaged by Moscow. And it was under the leadership of Imre

Nagy that a serious attempt was made at fundamental reform of the system.

The pervasive terror of the state security apparatus and the steady deterioration of living conditions had, as already indicated, made virtually the entire population into opponents of the system. Rákosi and his associates had been warned in the Kremlin, and not without reason, of a popular uprising. The decisive negotiations that took place in Moscow from 13 to 16 June 1953, completely closed to the public of course, were a perfect example of the fact that even positive changes could occur in the Soviet bloc only at Soviet initiative.

The Soviet party Presidium sharply criticized the Hungarian comrades for their economic and social policies emphasizing Rákosi's personal responsibility. Malenkov, Beria and Khrushchev cited exact numbers of those arrested, on the catastrophic situation in the countryside, and on the inordinate expenses on the military. The Hungarian leadership was instructed immediately to correct the entire political line. Rákosi was forced to resign as prime minister and hand over that post to Imre Nagy, the son of a western Hungarian rural family and an old communist who had spent decades in the USSR, but not in the émigré leadership. As Minister of Agriculture in 1945, he had acquired popularity for the land reform and had criticized Stalinist agrarian policies as early as 1949. The Soviet leaders also 'proposed' that Minister of Defence Farkas and Minister of Culture Révai resign, and the Central Committee discuss the leaders' self-criticism.

FIRST ATTEMPT AT REFORM IN THE SOVIET BLOC

In the ensuing Central Committee meeting of the MDP on 27–28 June 1953, the policies of the 'quadriga' (Rákosi, Gerő, Farkas and Révai) were subjected to unusually open and critical comment, complying to the directives of Moscow. The leadership was charged with being autocratic and thus causing anxiety, hardship and hatred. Rákosi's personal responsibility and the activities of state security (ÁVH) were openly discussed. The outcome was an exceptionally detailed and unambiguous resolution condemning the hitherto prevailing policies of state and party. (Characteristically, this extremely important document was not published then or in the thirty years of the Kádár regime. Only in 1986 did it appear in a party journal intended for internal use.)

It is worthwhile to quote some passages from this resolution, for they reveal how extreme the situation was for the country and its people when leaders of the ruling party were moved – even if only for internal use – to such sharp formulations.

> The Plenum of the Central Committee of the MDP declares that the party leadership, with Comrade Rákosi at the helm, has made serious mistakes in its political programme and practical work of the past years. These mistakes have had negative consequences for the living standard of the population in general and especially of the working class; they have weakened the relationship between party and working class and have in general negatively influenced the relationship between party, state, and working masses; they have caused grave problems in the economy. . . .
>
> It was a sectarian policy that regarded industrialization as an end in itself without considering the interests of the working class and working people. This false economic policy revealed certain boastfulness as well as an element of risk-taking, in so far as the forced development of heavy industry presupposed resources and raw materials that were in part just not available. . . .
>
> The party leadership neglected agricultural production and pushed collectivization at a much too rapid tempo. . . .
>
> The overly rapid collectivization of agriculture discloses a serious error, the more so as Imre Nagy urged against this policy within the party leadership; but that leadership not only failed to accept his position but falsified it as 'opportunistic' and penalized him for it. . . .
>
> The satisfaction of the needs of the people was ignored and thrust into the background, with the result that the workers' living standard was reduced. . . .
>
> The mistakes in the party's general line and in economic policy contributed greatly to the application of administrative measures against workers, such that people were victimized by the police and the courts while enduring rough and arbitrary treatment by officials. . . .
>
> From the beginning of 1951 until 1 May 1953, the police imposed penalties in approximately 850,000 cases. . . .
>
> Between 1950 and the second quarter of 1953, 650,000 cases came before the courts with penalties imposed in 350,000 of them. . . .
>
> We still have a system of internment that is subject to great arbitrariness and is not defensible eight years after the end of the war. . . .
>
> Excessive reliance on administrative measures – fines and such – has aroused ill feeling among workers affected and has been especially damaging to the relationship of state and party to farmers. The wholesale application of such measures, along with the affronts to legality and the resulting uncertainty about justice, has also led the old intelligentsia into an attitude of resignation. . . .
>
> The Office of State Security (ÁVH) has been inappropriately led by the party and personally by Comrade Rákosi. It was improper For Comrade Rákosi to give direct orders to the security forces as to how they should conduct investigations, whom they should arrest, and how they should mistreat prisoners (which is legally forbidden). Moreover, Comrade Rákosi has in many instances given false orders, which have interfered with the search for truth. . . .
>
> Boastfulness and the cult of personality are also the rule in the military; in the army leadership these are coupled with the tendency to force the

expansion of the military without regard for the economy, for which Comrade Mihály Farkas is chiefly responsible. . . .

Instead of a collective leadership, we have direction by one individual, and Comrade Rákosi is largely responsible for the associated cult of personality. . . . Because of direction left in the hands of one individual, the development of a genuine collective leadership at the pinnacle of state and party was hindered. The number of cadre positions held by leaders of Hungarian lineage is small, and the few who have attained high position often have only formal authority. Leadership is concentrated in fact in the hands of a foursome: Comrades Rákosi, Gerő, Farkas, and Révai. . . .

The absence of collective leadership has led to mistakes in the party's general line, its economic policy, and its personnel policies, all of which has contributed to ideological backwardness and the incorrect development of the relationship between party and state and the masses.

Parliament accepted the resignation of Rákosi and ratified the new government on 4 July 1953. Prime Minister Imre Nagy announced the government's adoption of the policy of the New Course. His speech did not emphasize the criticism of Rákosi's policies but rather, of necessity and understandably, the new goals, means and methods; it had a powerful effect throughout the country and even internationally. The venerable scholar Oscar Jászi, a leading radical thinker of the turn of the century and a minister in the Hungarian Republic in 1918, wrote in a letter from the United States, where he had been in exile for more than thirty years: 'As I read Imre Nagy's speech, my heart leaped with joy. See, I said to myself, the Soviets have adopted our revolutionary programme of 1918 in all its relevant features; the mistakes, crimes, and stupidities of the Soviet system have now been unmasked.'

Beyond the substance of the speech, it was its tone, its elevated style and its authentic-sounding Magyar that separated it from the usual boring lectures of the functionaries and resonated in every corner of the country and with simple citizens, arousing hope in a time of general disillusionment and lethargy. The new prime minister's speech was carried directly over the radio and tens of thousands felt that this communist politician was their man, that he was different from others.

The new government's initial measures appeared to justify people's trust. It was decided that the kulak list was to be abolished, withdrawal from the cooperatives – even the dissolution of kolkhoses – permitted, and the internment camps, including the infamous forced labour camp in Recsk, closed. Internment was eliminated from the inventory of available sentences altogether, extra-legal police sentencing was to be terminated, and a revision of the so-called 'show trials' was begun. It seemed that the pressure exerted by the holders of power for some four or five years was going to be relieved.

REFORM OR RESTORATION: A TUG-OF-WAR

There were of course many who were discomfited by this relaxation, notably the party apparatus and state security forces in fear of losing their unrestricted power. Rákosi himself, as soon as he had overcome his initial insecurity, began agitating and then openly attacking the New Course and its consequences.

Just one week after Nagy's programmatic speech, at a gathering of the Budapest party activists on 11 July, Rákosi proclaimed bombastically that there will be no real change. 'A kulak remains a kulak, with or without the list', he said to enthusiastic applause from the party functionaries in the audience. As one expert on this period remarked, this meeting represented 'basically a campaign of mobilization signalling counter-attack'. It was the beginning of the effort to undermine the relaxation and all reform aspirations of Nagy and his allies. Rákosi's message to the party apparatus was clearly understood: they now knew where 'mobilization' or 'increased activity' was expected, where to 'put on the brakes', and where to engage in open sabotage.

A tug-of-war developed between Rákosi and Imre Nagy and the latter's associates that would last for three years. Kádárist propaganda later preferred to characterize this struggle as an unprincipled contest for power, but it turned in fact on very important differences of principle – in political outlook and also in character – between the two camps. Rákosi's entire past, especially his excessively enthusiastic conduct of a Stalinist policy since 1948, his arbitrary and dictatorial style of rule, and his leading role in the purges and show trials stamped him ineradicably. He was clever enough to know that a genuine renewal would lead ineluctably to his political demise, and he was familiar enough with the Soviet system to realize that the personal consequences could prove still worse.

As a convinced communist, Imre Nagy believed, on the other hand, that the objectives of socialism could be realized in unity with the people, without resort to terror or intimidation. He was the only leading communist politician to whom the idea was not strange that there were people of different political persuasion in the country and that they had the right to their views. At this stage he had not yet entertained the notion of restoring the multiparty system, but his effort to make the Patriotic People's Front into an operative organization in 1954 signified his concern to fashion for non-communists a kind of representation and public forum. His gradually evolving programme of social and political reforms may rightly be seen as a prefiguring of those ideas that appeared years later in certain west European countries under the label Eurocommunism. This was not just a matter of inner-party personnel questions. This first attempt at communist reform hinged, as it would fifteen years later in the Prague Spring, on the possibility of creating, without Stalinist measures, socialist conditions in consonance with humane values and national distinctiveness. Such notions were of course not yet framed in abstract theory but rather appeared as goals derived from everyday practice and in discussion as to how to solve the challenges of the economy and public policy.

Nagy had to fight vigorously for every step in the implementation of the government's programme. Many were of the opinion, then and also later, that this straightforward and honourable politician lacked the necessary energy and practical sense, skill and determination. There was, to be sure, something 'professorial' about him, a quality that some found sympathetic, and yet he had in 1953–54, in his first term as prime minister, achieved unquestioned successes: the rise in living standards, advancement of agriculture and light industry, improvement of legality, and a certain autonomy of state institutions vis-à-vis the party.

Rákosi, supported by the party apparatus, made every effort to isolate and weaken Nagy, who was however not without support himself. Besides the general endorsement of his policy especially among farmers, he had the support of the intellectuals, the artists and the writers.

REVOLT OF THE WRITERS

The writers, and especially the communists among them, who took their creed seriously and were irritated by the contradiction between word and deed, between dishonest party propaganda which they had supported wholeheartedly and actuality, welcomed the new government programme and its public defence as a true liberation. That was of great importance for the future. At least since 1848, in Hungary as elsewhere in east-central Europe, writers understood it as their duty to lead their people out of servility, like the pillar of fire that directed the Israelites out of the desert into 'the promised land' (as Sándor Petőfi, poet of the Revolution of 1848, deployed the metaphor). In the role of people's conscience, the writer of the post-war period was not just posturing. The Writers' Union weekly, *Irodalmi Újság* (Literary Gazette), became the publication of choice for Nagy sympathisers as of 1953–54 and therewith, the country's favourite newspaper. Each edition, limited to 30,000–40,000 copies, was sold out on the first morning after delivery.

The young poet Sándor Csoóri published two poems in *Irodalmi Újság* on 1 August 1953 in direct response to Imre Nagy's speech. The one entitled 'Pamphlet' sounds like the collective avowal of a whole generation of writers:

> Up until now I had lived on the topmost heights,
> and from there everything I saw seemed good and bright
> and my favouring fortune drew a curtain
> across my eyes, hiding harsher reality.
> I lived on there among miraculous numbers,
> amid overfulfillings, seeing nothing of how
> my people strained, how they staggered under
> heavily burdening, exhausting destiny.
>
> (Translated by Kenneth McRobbie)

On 7 November 1953, *Irodalmi Újság* published under the title 'While Writing' a speech given by István Örkény at the Writers' Union that expresses the same self-critical posture along with just a hint of accusation:

> It was not our intention to write books that offer only a distorted picture of the world, books as hollow as an empty nut . . . yet we have written such books. We have done this – certainly not all of us and not only such books were written. . . . I praised loyalty and discipline . . . and it was a pleasure to be obedient. . . . I was free, free like a cork bobbing on the waves. Now I have become a writer and participate in the work that changes the river's course. . . . And what should the mission of the writer mean now? – now after the government's announcement? It means that the writer writes without false colouring. It means that the writer, and no one else, has responsibility for what he writes. That he may experiment and stop being a mere illlustrator.

A change in the perception of things, the gradual emancipation from ideological blinders, had begun. That was doubtless one of the most important results of Imre Nagy's New Course and, as would become evident, one of lasting effect. It was not a matter of change in the viewpoint of the general population, for the workers and peasants and sectors of the intelligentsia for whom the communist standpoint was alien did not have ideological blinders to lose. They had seen things as they were anyway. But that could help little in changing the system for it had been impossible to initiate change from below, for all decision-making, even at the local level, was monopolised by institutions and officials subject to party control. Changes in the thinking of 'those within' was, therefore, of central importance.

The ever-increasing oppositional stance of this inner-party intelligentsia was motivated largely by the fact that they were deeply ashamed and embarrassed for having uncritically supported Rákosi's murderous politics over several years. Now, awakened, they perceived the bitterness and anger of the people, and regarded it as their duty to express them. Their public actions were in fact the tip of that mighty iceberg on which eventually the ship of Stalinist dictatorship broke apart.

At first there were only a few in the ranks of the communist intellectuals who had the courage or the ability to stand up to their newly won convictions. It was a minority, consisting mainly of writers and journalists, who began to see more clearly, and only *Irodalmi Újság* was brave enough to represent their point of view. But it was decisive for developments in the future that the process of disillusionment spread beyond the narrow group of writers and poets and became general in scope. The discussion of literature and literary politics gained in liveliness as more and more voices were raised on behalf of honest language. The 'Imre Nagy Line' offered an alternative to the Stalinist ideology and political practice, the option of a humane, rationally achievable socialism that would accommodate national distinctiveness more fully. If one was dissatisfied, as a communist, with existing conditions, that did not imply a leap into some void or that one was to embrace 'western' or 'capitalist' ideas. Of course, it was not irrelevant either that the expression of dissatisfaction was no longer coupled with fear for one's life or freedom.

An important political and ethical stimulus to widening disenchantment came from the political and juridical rehabilitation. The innocent victims, those who had survived, of the show trials were released from prison starting in 1954, at first individually and without publicity, the communists first and gradually the social democrats as well. The poet László Benjámin dedicated a poem to the universally venerated old communist and anti-fascist fighter Sándor Haraszti in which he described the confusion and conflicts of conscience that arose when old friends and comrades, appearing suddenly from the shadow-world, were encountered once again.

> This is the way with us, Sándor: lying accusation
> stabbing you so quickly down into whichever hell.
> From where my voice is rising calling out to you:
> 'Believing in your guilt, I was the guilty one.'
> (Translated by Kenneth McRobbie)

It is a sign of the time not only that this poem could be written, but also that it had to be circulated in individual copies and could be printed only in the summer of 1956. The subject of the show trials and the rehabilitations was strictly forbidden, in large part because of Mátyás Rákosi's personal involvement in the persecutions. If the poet declares himself guilty, how great must be the guilt of those who concocted the charges and then consigned the victims to torture and solitary confinement for years?

TRIUMPH OF THE OPPONENTS OF REFORM

In the autumn of 1954 it appeared that Imre Nagy had won out over the Rákosi-Gerő clique. On 24 October at the congress of the revitalised Patriotic People's Front, which the prime minister wanted to become an 'open forum for the sovereign people and the conscience of the entire nation', Nagy spoke about the end of the tug-of-war and his confidence that the reform politics could now be implemented rapidly and energetically.

At the same time, the party members at the offices of *Szabad Nép* held a meeting that lasted three days and issued in heated debate. The majority of the editors and the staff attacked the policies associated with the Stalinist party leadership and the direction of the newspaper itself. Copies of the minutes of the meeting were distributed to the party school, the Hungarian Press Agency, the Hungarian Radio, and other institutions. That had all the earmarks of a rebellion and struck at the system's 'central nervous system'. The response was prompt. The spokesmen were expelled from the editorial staff of the newspaper, their positions filled by loyal party members, 'workers who could wield the pen powerfully'. The signal for an undisguised counter-offensive against Nagy's reform policies and in general against the freer and more critical atmosphere was an article in the purged *Szabad Nép* against the 'exaggerated' and therefore 'unhealthy' criticism coming from writers and journalists.

Party chief Rákosi, who had returned from a lengthy sick leave in the Soviet Union, already knew that the winds in Moscow were blowing in a different direction. Soviet party leaders were alarmed by rearmament and NATO membership for the Federal Republic of Germany and, to some extent, uneasy about the ferment unleashed by Nagy's policies. It was desired that 'order' should again prevail in Hungary. On 1 December Rákosi informed the Hungarian Politburo of the Soviet posture, and opinion quickly shifted in Rákosi's favour. Imre Nagy had not defended his position energetically enough, thus the outcome was a Politburo resolution on 'the dangers of rightist opportunism'. As in 1953, the crucial decision was made in Moscow. With Rákosi and Nagy in attendance, the Soviet Presidium on 8 January 1955 considered the situation in Hungary. This time the strong critique was aimed not at Rákosi's usurpations but at Nagy's 'rightist deviation'.

In response, Nagy was not prepared to show remorse, as was usual in Bolshevik practice, but remained true to his convictions. The ensuing events took place as if according to a script. (The only thing unforeseen by the director was the mild heart attack that overtook Imre Nagy because of the tensions of February; for that reason the final reckoning had to be deferred a bit.) Rákosi's conclusive blow to Nagy's reform policy, the first socialist reform attempted in eastern Europe, unfolded in three stages.

From the Central Committee meeting of 2–4 March 1955, a resolution emerged that, while not explicitly abrogating the resolution of June 1953, did define as 'principal danger' the 'party-damaging, anti-Marxist, opportunistic and right-leaning' tendency represented by Imre Nagy. The resolution returned the development of heavy industry to the centre of concern, condemned the agrarian policy pursued since June 1953, and labelled the democratic and national accents within the Patriotic People's Front as nationalistic and contrary to the dictatorship of the proletariat. It was typical of the servile conduct of the upper echelon of the party that it was just this leadership group that had, five months before, given its enthusiastic endorsement to Nagy's suggestions for hastening the reform process.

At this point, according to the unwritten but well-established rules of the Communist movement, Imre Nagy should have offered humble self-criticism and promised to subordinate his convictions to the new political line. But Nagy, absent because of his illness, emphatically declined to do this, explaining that he was open to the discussion of all questions but only if that were done publicly. He had offered to resign but Rákosi refused the offer, for Nagy's refusal to humble himself had only increased his public acclaim and it was not enough to terminate Nagy as prime minister. He had to be destroyed politically.

It was not difficult for Rákosi to bring the party apparatus into line. The Central Committee decided on 14 April to dismiss Nagy from all his offices: he was not only removed as prime minister but also expelled from the Central Committee and the Politburo. He was soon denied his professorship and membership in the Hungarian Academy of Sciences as well. And at the end of 1955 came the final blow as the faithful old communist was dismissed from the party.

Rákosi may have believed that the Imre Nagy case was now settled for good. But if so, he deluded himself, for the inner-party struggle – that would lead to the emergence of a significant nucleus of opposition within the party – began now in earnest.

Nagy's successor was the 33–year old András Hegedüs. In the spring and summer of 1955 it appeared that Rákosi had succeeded in regaining the full power that he had enjoyed before June 1953. It had again become apparent that he could depend on both the sectarian fanaticism and the cowardice and servility of the party cadres. The well-known theoreticians of communist ideology and many professionals, especially economists, all of whom had for the preceding years been celebrating the New Course and arguing for the necessity and advantages of the new economic policy, did an abrupt about-face and outdid each other in repudiating their 'incorrect' views.

Those who did not choose to play this game could reckon with party disciplinary procedures and even the loss of positions and privileges. Miklós Vásárhelyi, former deputy head of the cabinet press office established by Nagy, described his own experience: 'No one who stood in Rákosi's way could feel secure. His vengeance knew no bounds. One might be dismissed, replaced, transferred, retired, or exiled to the provinces. Penalties were assigned without mercy to Central Committee members, state and party officials, newspaper editors, writers, journalists, and well-known reputable intellectuals.'

But Rákosi did not grasp that times had changed, that the era of 'classical' Stalinist politics was over. On the one hand, the means of exercising real terror and repression were no longer available. On the other hand, in the two years since Stalin's death, since Imre Nagy's governmental declaration and the discovery of the actual circumstances of the show trials, Stalinist ideology had revealed obvious fissures. Blind obedience and fanaticism, even faithful party thinking, were slowly disappearing. It was possible to exclude Imre Nagy from public life, but it was no longer possible to break his spirit or to isolate him completely.

IMRE NAGY AND THE FORMATION OF THE ANTI-STALINIST OPPOSITION

In the spring and summer of 1955, despite (or perhaps because of) the constant attempts at repression and Nagy's refusal to yield, a circle of sympathizers began to develop around Imre Nagy, consisting of communist intellectuals who were now consciously oppositional. Most of them were old communists released from Rákosi's jails, who would sit with Imre Nagy on the defendants' bench once the Revolution had been put down. Sándor Haraszti, a veteran of interwar Hungarian communist underground and an anti-fascist fighter, who had spent four years in prison under Rákosi, was highly esteemed by the younger generation of communist intellectuals and by Imre Nagy as well. Szilárd Újhelyi came from the anti-fascist March Front of the late 1930s, held important posts in cultural policies after 1945, and was jailed in 1951 for concocted accusations. József Szilágyi was an upright man who, on the strength of his underground work for the Communist Party between the wars, became for a short time chief of police and party official after 1945, but whose straightforwardness brought him increasingly into conflict with the leadership. Others included Géza Losonczy, also from the anti-fascist resistance, who became briefly a commissar of culture under Rákosi only to end up in jail on trumped-up charges, and was keen to atone for his earlier dogmatism by fighting for reform; Ferenc Jánosi, Nagy's son-in-law, who had been active as a Protestant chaplain in the resistance and became a colonel in the People's Army after 1945; the journalists György Fazekas and Tibor Méray; and the writer Tibor Déry. Two dynamic young men and well-regarded journalists, Miklós Gimes and Miklós Vásárhelyi, formed the nucleus of the loose grouping, to which some other young journalists belonged, most of whom participated in the above-mentioned 'rebellion' in the editorial offices of *Szabad Nép*.

In the months that followed, the circle steadily grew until, by the middle of 1956, it included practically the whole party group in the Writers' Union, many journalists, artists, teachers and members of the technical intelligentsia. The majority consisted of party members, including those expelled from the party, and persons who were ideologically close to the party. Many were graduates of the People's Colleges (NÉKOSZ), which had been established in 1945 for the benefit of students from worker and peasant families but were dissolved already in 1949 in connection with the Rajk trial.

In assessing the potential of the developing opposition, one must bear in mind that, as mentioned before, only movements from within the prevailing structures had any chance to succeed. In the years of repression there had of course been resistance by individuals and groups having nothing in common with the communists. There had also been youths who sought to organize and distribute leaflets, but activity of that sort against the regime was quickly discovered and dealt with by the police. Thousands were jailed and hundreds executed on charges of resistance and sabotage, and not all of these were mere concoctions: people did try to oppose the Soviet-imposed, Communist dictatorship. But their courage changed only their own fate. It was characteristic, incidentally, that one of these illegal groups found its most promising venue of activity in the regional branch of the communist youth organization (DISZ). The young oppositionals in the small town of Békéssámson used the DISZ as camouflage for their illegal activity. But most of those who dared to engage in such heroic actions ended in prison or on the gallows, and after 1953 the regime had no reason to fear any challenge from outside party ranks. This was not peculiar to Hungary, by the way, but was typical of the political system throughout eastern Europe. (Poland was perhaps a partial exception because the Catholic Church could provide the non-communist opposition a modicum of protection while affording legal channels for the circulation of non-communist thinking. But even that was possible only because the Church did not openly challenge the regime on any basic issue.)

Thus, the oppositional group around Imre Nagy became the first significant anti-Stalinist reform movement of the post-war period in east-central Europe. Although unorganized and not very numerous, this group played a decisive role in Hungary's public life from summer 1955 to autumn 1956. By unmasking the party dictatorship, it hastened the decline of the regime and paved the way, albeit unintentionally, for the Revolution.

Much of their importance is explained by the special relationship obtaining between Imre Nagy as leader and the group surrounding him. Rákosi and his cohorts would have had an easy time with a small group of unknown personalities. But Nagy had long enjoyed general respect in the public consciousness. He was the only popular communist politician who had, by reason of his governmental programme in 1953 and the steadfastness of his defence of the New Course, conquered the hearts of his countrymen. And he was far from being unknown outside Hungary. Still, by himself he could have been swiftly isolated and, despite the respect he enjoyed, reduced to a forgotten relic. But the force of Nagy's great popularity was intensified by the intellectuals among his followers: they supported him after his fall, encouraged his activism, and secured his continuous contact with the public.

Contact with the public was a vital function, for despite his acuity and strength of character Imre Nagy retained party discipline as a primary value, and that imposed narrow limits on his ability to act. After his removal he composed one protest memorandum after the other, all addressed either to the Soviet or the Hungarian party leadership. Although he showed them to his close political friends, he insisted that they not reach a larger circle. (Only in 1957 did these writings appear abroad as his *On Communism: In the Defence of the New Course.*) Nagy did not want to become the leader of an underground group or even the perpetrator of so-called factionalism; but his followers knew that party discipline was a recipe for defeat in any struggle with the Rákosi clique, for they – as experience showed – managed at all points to determine the correct party line and to apply it as they saw fit.

The Writers' Memorandum

The case of the so-called Writers' Memorandum was a telling example of the party leadership's habit of setting the proper course. In the autumn of 1955 some oppositional journalists thought the time ripe for an open protest. One item of the protest, for example, was the elimination of Imre Madách's play, *The Tragedy of Man*, from the repertoire of the National Theatre on the grounds that the nineteenth-century classic of Hungarian drama had depicted the utopian-socialist commune in an ironic manner. Another item was the official obstacles to playing the works of Béla Bartók in Hungary. Sixty well-known writers and artists, all party members, signed the memorandum, among them the old communist Tibor Déry and the Stalin Prize laureate Tamás Aczél. The writers' act was categorized as factional, that is as a deviation from the party line and thus damaging to the party. The reaction against the protesters produced a massive pressure that led to the withdrawal of the signatures – except for a 'hard core' of some ten of the signatories. At the end of November the Central Committee addressed the 'rightist tendencies appearing in literature' and in its resolution named Aczél, Déry, Julius Háy, Tibor Méray and Zoltán Zelk as representatives of the harmful tendencies.

An assembly of the Budapest regional party activists was called against the unrepentent writers. One of the targets, the old communist playwright Julius Háy, described the event decades later in the following words:

> One date I remember well – 6 December 1955. We, writers – that is to say a selected dozen or so of us – were instructed individually by telephone to report to the Metalworkers' Union building for a literary debate . . .
>
> A man came up to me. The face was familiar: it belonged to one of Rákosi's bodyguards. He had some printed sheets in his hand. I was against being handed printed sheets by Rákosi's bodyguard. My name sprang out at me in bold print: 'J.H. . . . peddling the idea of freedom of literature'. . . . A further five or six names were mentioned in the text in connection with other similar charges . . .
>
> A tall, fair-haired, fat-faced man . . . delivered a defamatory speech against writers in general and against ones in bold type in particular. Beside him sat Rákosi, surrounded by his numerous bodyguards. . . . A number of Party and union officials and one or two writers loyal to Rákosi made speeches reiterating the general and personal accusations – 'peddling freedom' and so on – prescribed on the printed sheet.
>
> I waited with growing impatience to see who among us accused would rise to answer. No one. Suddenly a crazy idea flashed through my mind and I immediately translated it into action: I wrote my name on a piece of paper and passed it up to the presidium.
>
> It was my blameless and naive intention to explain in simple terms what

it was that we writers actually wanted. . . . My very first sentence was interrupted: Rákosi himself echoed my vocative 'Comrades' in a tone of mockery. This was a signal for the others. Rákosi conducted the catcalls with his eyebrows. Thereafter I was interrupted every second. Yells and cries of derision came at me from all sides. . . .

Sitting opposite me in the front row and standing at all the exits were numbers of thugs like the one who had thrust the printed sheet into my hand. I could see the muscles rippling and the guns gleaming beneath their jackets. They were poised to spring – a twitch of Rákosi's cheek and I should be torn in pieces. All at once I knew what it felt like to be delivered up to lynch justice.

(J Hay *Born 1900*, translated by J A Underwood, London: Hutchinson, 1974, pp. 302ff.)

Then at the end of December, as the final act of Rákosi's campaign, came the aforementioned decision of the Central Control Commission on the expulsion of Imre Nagy from the MDP.

AFTER THE TWENTIETH CONGRESS OF THE CPSU

At the turn of the year from 1955 to 1956, the political climate became as frigid as in the years before Stalin's death. Early in 1956, as a kind of warning, there were even politically motivated arrests and sentences. After Nagy's expulsion and the party resolution on 'literary life', the reform movement and inner-party opposition lost their elan. The immediate future held little prospect of change. The only hope was the Soviet party congress due to occur in February 1956.

The dreary opening reports and speeches provided little nourishment for that hope at first. But already in March one heard rumours of that closed session in which Krushchev gave a secret speech lasting several hours and disclosing the horrific crimes of Stalin (more precisely, a part of them), followed by the demand for a decisive break with Stalinist ideology, the harmful thesis of a steadily intensifying class struggle, the doctrine of the inevitability of war, and the inhuman conduct of the erstwhile 'wise leader'.

That raised the curtain on the last act of Rákosi's political career. He tried at first to deflect the fatal consequences of the Twentieth Congress and its 'spirit' for his own position. He argued that the Soviet party congress would only justify him, because the activity of his Hungarian party had conformed to this new spirit since 1953, thus making political or personnel changes unnecessary in Hungary. But the Twentieth Congress, universally overrated as an epochal and irreversible event at this time, gave renewed impulse and perspective to the party's internal opposition. Now Rákosi's removal could be anticipated. There was no doubt that he was the major obstacle to any renewal. Because of his personal responsibility for the Rajk trial and other show trials, it was in his most basic interest that nothing change. That made him hated and vulnerable at the same time. People had not forgotten how 'Stalin's best Hungarian pupil' had boasted in 1949 of the many 'sleepless nights' he had spent for the sake of unmasking hostile agents and enemies such as Rajk and accomplices.

His boundless ambition would now cost him dearly. He tried in vain to escape destiny, first with hypocritical remorse, then by shifting all blame to the Generals Mihály Farkas and Gábor Péter, former heads of the security services. The number of those demanding his removal grew steadily through the spring and summer of 1956. Soon the whole country was awaiting his resignation. Even the performance of Shakespeare's *Richard the Third* in the National Theatre led to demonstrations, for in 1956 the public had no trouble recognizing Rákosi in the bald tyrant of the play.

There are many who believe that, if Rákosi had been removed from his position promptly, the revolutionary eruption and its bloody accompaniment would not have occurred. That can be neither proved nor excluded in retrospect. From the perspective of that time, such a step was exactly what a responsible leadership would have done. But there were two elements in the situation, the Soviet leadership and the Hungarian party's Central Committee, that stood in the way of that move.

The Kremlin was conscious of the danger, to be sure, but was primarily concerned to protect the Hungarian party. The Soviet leaders, and especially Mikhail Suslov who was 'visiting' Budapest in the summer of 1956, feared that Rákosi's removal would weaken the party, so they attempted to strengthen his hand. The same considerations governed the outlook of the Hungarian party leaders. There were many old communists among them who realized that Rákosi was driving the party and the country toward catastrophe. That was no secret within the narrow circle of leaders, which included János Kádár, who had once suffered imprisonment at Rákosi's instigation and had since been rehabilitated and made district party secretary of County Pest. Kádár and his associates later tried to portray their role as that of a 'centre' opposed equally in the first half of 1956 to Rákosi's 'dogmatic-sectarian' leadership and to the 'splintering-revisionist' forces around Imre Nagy. That may have been true of some of them in a purely emotional sense, but in political actuality there was no sign of any such formation. In the intensifying power struggle, Kádár and his group distanced themselves from the persecution of Imre Nagy but did not oppose Rákosi.

'BUDAPEST SPRING' OF THE PETŐFI CIRCLE

With the Stalinist restoration of 1955, the hated ruling party deprived itself of its last remaining social underpinning, for the greater part of the communist intelligentsia had by now been decisively alienated. The thousands of young intellectuals who had become active after 1945 in the Communist or the National Peasant Party, who could identify out of conviction with the slogan (the words of the marching song of the People's Colleges), 'We'll turn the world upside down tomorrow', now, after all the years of bitter disappointment and countless 'corrections' of the political line sought as adults for a new orientation and routes to political renewal. The Petőfi Circle – originally planned as a discussion group for young intellectuals under the supervision of DISZ – afforded this generation a forum in which they could recapture the enthusiasm of their youth. The erstwhile comrades who had often travelled different roads in the early 1950s (some remained more or less within the 'establishment', some spent years as labourers) now met again in the Petőfi Circle and, what is even more important, practised an independence of thought that contrasted sharply with almost a decade of ideological strait-jacketing. Gábor Tánczos, a 'veteran' of the youth movement after 1945, was chosen as secretary of the Petőfi Circle. The authorities certainly did not foresee that they had in fact created the opening wedge of future intellectual revolt.

The first gatherings of the Circle in March 1956 were not much more than reunions of activists from the former League of Hungarian University Students (MEFESZ) and the National Association of People's Colleges (NÉKOSZ). But the evening on Yugoslav literature already drew a numerous audience, and shifted into a declaration of sympathy for Hungarian-Yugoslav friendship. It was clear to all in attendance, including the state security personnel in civilian dress, that the lively interest in the subject was actually an expression of protest against Rákosi, who had spearheaded the anti-Tito campaign.

In May and June the Petőfi Circle staged its famous public discussions, six evening sessions devoted to topical issues of economics, history and ideology, with the audience always exceeding the capacity of the auditorium. Some two thousand people sought to attend the evening discussion devoted to philosophy; a different location had to be found for such a crowd and finally the audience, with Georg Lukács leading the way, found its way into the largest lecture hall of the university. But a still larger auditorium had to be found when the meeting on anti-fascist resistance took place in the Officers' House of the People's Army; likewise the evening devoted to press and public information, at which some seven thousand people appeared.

The extraordinary nature of these events was a function not only of the subject matter, but also of the quality of the presentations and the hitherto unimaginable open and unrestrained character of the discussions. In contrast to the conduct of the 'socialist' pseudo-Parliament, these discussions brought to the surface many of the pressing concerns and problems of public life, from economy to culture. Two important issues were, however, excluded by an unspoken consensus: the subordinate relationship to the Soviet Union and the single-party system. Any explicit reference to these pillars of the system would have immediately caused dissolution or worse. But by surveying the distortions and lies of the preceding years, be it in scholarship or the media, it was perfectly clear to all, what was really meant. At the meeting of Second World War resistance veterans Szilárd Újhelyi formulated the statement: 'We are not trying here to rehabilitate particular groups; rather, a whole country, a whole people must be rehabilitated!' That elicited such thunderous applause that it constituted a sign of readiness for decisive protest.

With anger and growing uneasiness, the Rákosi group pursued the now plainly evident oppositional activity of the Petőfi Circle and the parallel case of the increasingly radicalized Writers' Union as they registered growing resonance among the people. But in the prevailing atmosphere of relaxation, it was not possible to terminate this unruly behaviour until occasion presented itself at the end of June. On the evening of 27 June, the Petőfi Circle sponsored its so-called 'press debate' that lasted into the early hours of morning. On the 28th, the workers of Poznań, Poland, took to the streets in protest against miserable living conditions, rising production norms and falling wages. And there was no authority prepared to negotiate with them about their demands. Instead, the Polish state threatened the workers, and the ensuing confrontation between security forces and regular troops on the one hand and the demonstrators on the other ended in bloodshed. According to official reports, a hundred people died on this day in Poznań and those injured were estimated at more than a thousand. These developments in Poznań, where workers rose against the 'worker-and-peasant state', gave a powerful impulse to the ferment inside the Polish Communist Party.

This bloody encounter sent a signal to the Hungarian party leadership that harsh measures were in order if they wished to avoid open confrontation. A Central Committee resolution of 30 June attacked Imre Nagy and his intellectual sympathizers in sharp terms and ordered that the activities of the Petőfi Circle be suspended. Its ruthless tone and thundering clauses threatened to end the little freedom of speech that had been achieved in the preceding months. We now know that the Circle loomed large in the reports of the Soviet embassy, and the Budapest residents of the Soviet secret service, as a dangerous core of resistance that had to be extinguished. On 12 July at a session of the Politburo, Rákosi promised the 'complete liquidation of the Nagy conspiracy'.

Two serious charges were brought against the Petőfi Circle, both later kept alive by the Kádár regime and the courts of justice. One was that the Circle had been directed by the so-called Nagy Group; the other that it had moved an inner-party debate to the streets. In retrospect, one must acknowledge that both charges were well founded. Gábor Tánczos, who had become a harsh critic of the Rákosi-line, directed the activities of his associates masterfully and coordinated his plans with Losonczy and Vásárhelyi, who in turn kept Nagy informed. As for involving the public, the Petőfi Circle had moved consciously beyond the group of disappointed communist intellectuals to the widest extent that was then possible. By questioning the moral and intellectual basis of the regime, the Petőfi Circle and the engaged writers became spokesmen for the painful experiences of the populace. The more politically receptive citizens of a repressed and lethargic society were aroused to consciousness by such activity; the silence was broken, there was more breathing space, and public criticism had become possible. It was the accomplishment of the Petőfi Circle precisely that it moved the concerns of the nation, regarded by the ruling party as its own internal affair, out into the 'street', that is into the awareness of a widening public.

That the Circle's influence was not confined to its own original founders is shown by the fact that in autumn 1956, as the Budapest branch of the Circle had begun its debates on education, agriculture and health care, similar intellectual discussion groups were forming in several cities, mainly by university and college students and faculty. The great interest in public discussion of political topics is shown also by the plans for a series of lectures in the metal works in Csepel with speakers invited from the Petőfi Circle. The youthful organizers of the Petőfi Circle deliberately sought contact with the older generation and with certain non-communist personages such as the former president of the republic Zoltán Tildy – until then under house arrest since 1949 – who spoke at the debate on agriculture.

INTERNATIONAL CONTEXT

All these developments in Hungary were, of course, closely connected to the changes in the international situation after the death of Stalin. During the years from 1953 to 1956, and indeed right up until the collapse of communism, east-central Europe's fate was determined by the European political status quo which had come about in 1945. The two superpowers which dominated the post-Second World War bipolar world order, the United States and the Soviet Union, considered it to be the cornerstone of east-west relations. Yet, there were some new elements in the policies of both.

After Stalin's death, the new Soviet leadership attempted to make significant changes in both the domestic life and foreign policy of the empire. In the late 1940s the Soviet Union – whose economy had still not recovered from the trauma of the Second World War – began spending heavily in order to keep pace with the United States in the arms build-up which had begun with the Cold War. Following the formula which had proved effective in the 1930s, the capital necessary for weapons production was to be generated through an extensive diversion of resources from the agricultural and consumer goods sectors of the economy. It is for this reason that the new Soviet leadership, especially during Malenkov's premiership (1953–55), attempted to mitigate domestic unrest by establishing a more balanced economic structure marked by reduced emphasis on heavy industry, particularly arms production. However, the Soviet plan to reduce expenditures on arms could be implemented only within the context of a general improvement of east-west relations, which had until then been based upon mutual fear of direct confrontation.

Accordingly, beginning in 1953 Soviet foreign policy became much more flexible and for the first time since the closing stages of the Second World War the Soviet Union displayed a willingness to negotiate and compromise with the western powers. This change in Soviet comportment ultimately opened the way for an end to the Korean War and led to such a significant reduction in east-west tension that the mid-1950s are justifiably referred to as the first period of détente.

Soviet foreign policy in the years preceding 1956 was marked by attempts at a rapprochement with Britain, France, and the rest of western Europe as well as the United States without seriously considering any change in the status quo. With the onset of détente, the Soviet Union's relations with the west, based on a growing parity in the balance of power as well as a mutual respect for the post-Second World War status quo in Europe, was to receive a new definition. Although Moscow did in fact respect the sanctity of the European spheres of influence through-out even the chilliest years of the Cold War, western Europeans were none the less constantly worried about the possibility of a Soviet attack. The new course in Soviet foreign policy gave rise to a greater sense of security in western Europe. The increased Soviet inclination towards negotiation was also largely due to the fact that even though they had, with the development of the hydrogen bomb, largely caught up to the United States in the arms race, the differing geopolitical location of the two countries still left the Soviet Union in a vulnerable position since it was not capable of direct attack on the American continent until the intercontinental ballistic missile was developed at the end of the 1950s. The Soviet shift to a more conciliatory foreign policy also had another, more concrete motivation: they hoped to prevent the rearma-ment of West Germany by sowing discord within the western alliance.

The Soviets none the less clearly defined the limits of the compro-mises they were willing to make throughout the entire course of nego-tiations with the west, and it soon became obvious that they were only disposed to discuss issues such as that of the status of Germany and Austria which the great western powers had been unable to agree upon among themselves. The irreconcilability of Soviet and western positions regarding the reunification of Germany ultimately prevented the sides from reaching any kind of agreement, and when West Germany had joined NATO, the question was taken off the agenda for quite some time. The resolution of the Austrian question nevertheless demonstrated the willingness of the Soviet leadership to bargain with the west: in exchange for a pledge to withdraw their troops from the country, the Soviets were able to get the western powers to agree to permanently uphold Austria's strict neutrality and to allow those eastern European countries which were not already members of the United Nations to join the world organization. However, the Soviets never considered the issue of the satellite countries to be negotiable; in fact, since the Soviet Union's ratification of the Austrian State Treaty would remove the legal basis for continued presence of its troops in Hungary and Romania, the Soviet Union used this as an opportunity to strengthen the cohesiveness of its empire by establishing the communist bloc's military alliance, the Warsaw Pact, one day before the signing of the treaty on Austria.

Even though the Soviet leadership officially considered the question of the post-war European status quo to be non-negotiable, this did not mean that they had given up on the idea of expanding the Soviet Union's sphere of influence. Soviet expansionist ambitions centred now on the new countries born in the wake of the rapid disintegration of the colonial empires after the Second World War – the Third World.

Contrary to the strong-arm methods it had used to subjugate eastern Europe after the Second World War, the Soviet Union was able peaceably to bring these primarily Arab and Asian countries into its political orbit. People in these underdeveloped countries were often allured by the Soviet social and economic model emphasizing equality and centralized planning. Beginning in the mid-1950s Soviet foreign policy was aimed at exploiting opportunities for ideological expansion into the Third World through intensive propaganda and, where necessary, economic aid. By this time the Soviets had also begun discreetly to provide some of these countries with arms and military advisers. Soviet prudence in this area was proved later at the time of the Suez crisis: not only did the Soviets completely exclude the option of providing direct military support to Egypt, but also Soviet military specialists and advisers immediately left the country so as not to become embroiled even indirectly in conflict with the western powers. A few days later, when it became clear that the United States itself would compel Britain and France to cease their armed attacks on Egypt, the Soviets resumed their propaganda strategy of portraying themselves as the champion of the independence of the Arab countries and the small peoples of the world in general.

A primary objective of the new Soviet leadership was to repair the cracks and fissures which had appeared in the socialist bloc through the break with Yugoslavia in 1948. In May of 1955 Khrushchev and Bulganin went to Belgrade in an attempt to make amends with Tito, blaming Stalinist policies for the deterioration in relations between the two countries and communist parties. Throughout 1955 and 1956 the Soviets made several conciliatory gestures toward Yugoslavia, such as giving public sanction to the tenet that there could be more than one valid way to build socialism. The Soviet leadership, which was still capable of thinking only in 'might makes right' terms, did not really believe in what they were saying: their policy of conciliation toward Tito was, in fact, designed to bring Yugoslavia slowly and peacefully back into the socialist camp and, more specifically, to draw it into the Warsaw Pact. These steps, however, did not imply that Moscow was prepared to accept the Yugoslav model for its east European satellites. Soviet foreign policy in east-central Europe was to maintain stability at any cost. The Soviets were so keenly aware of the mounting social unrest in East Germany that in early June of 1953 they instructed East German party leaders to introduce a more liberal political direction to their country. This, what was to be a short-lived period of reform in East Germany not only was marked by a reduction in heavy industrial production and a corresponding increase in the production of consumer goods, but also meant reduced restrictions on travel abroad, the suspension of the collectivization of agriculture, an end to curbs on religious practices and even, for a short time, the removal of the word 'socialism' itself from the regime's propaganda vocabulary. The Berlin uprising in June 1953 erupted despite all these precautions, and partly because the GDR leadership was reluctant to follow the instructions from Moscow. Soviet political intervention to suppress the turmoil was vigorous and concise, though Moscow continued to try to moderate East Germany's radical policies.

It was the same concern which made the Soviets intervene politically in Hungary and replace Rákosi with Imre Nagy in June 1953. And though the permissible pace and scope of post-Stalin political reform in eastern Europe depended greatly upon which faction happened to have the upper hand in the incessant power struggles within the Soviet leadership, there was never any question in Moscow that the satellite states would remain inside the Soviet empire. But they were prepared to consider a moderate revision of the principles underlying relations between the Soviet Union and its east European allies. This revision found expression in the Soviet leadership's pronouncement of 30 October 1956, which, contrary to earlier assumptions, was formulated before the upheaval in Poland and Hungary, in mid-October at the very latest, and was merely updated in accordance with the new political developments. Beyond outlining considerably more equitable foundations for relations between the Soviet Union and its satellite states, this pronouncement asserted unambiguously that each country had the right to find its own way toward internal political reform as long as it did not stray beyond the confines of the Soviet bloc.

The Soviets were, however, extremely wary of Yugoslavia's growing influence in eastern Europe, suspecting reasonably that what people knew of the Yugoslav socialist model – with an active popular front and extensive workers' self-management as well as consideration for local and national concerns – might prove to be more attractive in this region than the Soviet pattern. Therefore, at the end of the summer of 1956 the presidium of the CPSU sent a secret communiqué to the leaders of the satellite countries cautioning them that the Soviet Union took a dim view of exaggerated promotion of the Yugoslav model.

The policy of the Eisenhower administration (1953–56) toward those countries of east-central Europe that had landed in the Soviet sphere of influence after the Second World War was characterized by a peculiar duality. Eisenhower had made the so-called peaceful liberation of captive nations an integral part of his campaign platform; he firmly believed that the Truman administration's policy of containment of communism was not befitting the United States as leader of the free world and that ultimately only a more offensive posture would compel the Soviet Union to surrender its east European domains. Accordingly, the US government devoted considerable sums toward funding of subversive radio stations and other such organizations as well as eastern European emigré organizations. Reference to liberation of the captive nations – though exactly how it was to be accomplished was never made clear – was, all the way up until October of 1956, a mandatory component of all high-level US political pronouncements, which were subsequently transmitted to eastern Europe by various propaganda organizations, particularly Radio Free Europe. All this served to create the illusion, not only in eastern Europe and the United States, but throughout the entire world, that the United States, which had in fact never shown any real interest in the region, had made the liberation of these nations the cornerstone of its foreign policy and of east-west relations in general.

In reality, however, US foreign policy of this era was based on a thorough pragmatism characterized by recognition of the post-Second World War European status quo and the prevailing balance of power with the Soviet Union as well as the avoidance at all costs of superpower conflict. The United States, together with the other western powers, tried to exploit the new disposition of the post-Stalin Soviet leadership in order to open the negotiations regarding issues which they found to be vital to their interests such as ending the Korean War, disarmament, reunification of Germany, and the status of Austria.

Thus, particularly after the US government discovered that the Soviets had made unexpectedly rapid progress toward developing an intercontinental ballistic missile, the United States sought to mitigate east-west political tension by finding an acceptable modus vivendi with the Soviet Union – one which was to become known to the world as peaceful coexistence.

The communist countries of eastern Europe did not receive a prominent role in this process since the United States, in its typical great power way of thinking, considered the Soviet Union to be its only legitimate negotiating partner. During this period of east-west reconciliation and rapprochement the western powers sought to put the issue of the so-called satellite states on the negotiating table with the Soviets; but it became quickly apparent – especially at the time of the Geneva summit in July of 1955 and in the interval prior to Khrushchev and Bulganin's official visit to Britain in April of 1956 – that the Soviet Union, which in certain respects had already surpassed the United States in the arms race, was willing to negotiate only from a position of strength. In this way the Soviets were prepared to discuss only issues which had not yet been settled from their perspective and any mention of previous foreign conquests continued to activate a Stalinist rejection reflex.

Thereafter the United States and the other western powers considered the question of eastern Europe to be of secondary importance to that of overall east-west détente, a position which is quite understandable when viewed from an international political perspective. Though they had not abandoned hope that the peoples of eastern Europe would eventually regain their independence, by the autumn of 1956 western political officials had come to the conclusion that, for the time being, the Yugoslav political model – 'national communism' – offered these countries the greatest opportunity for gaining a certain degree of both internal and external autonomy.

Thus the western powers – contrary to what was to become one of the principal elements contained in communist propaganda for decades thereafter – not only did not help to ignite the Hungarian revolution or the resistance of Poland to Moscow, but also did not even remotely expect that an open conflict, let alone an armed uprising, would erupt in one of the Soviet satellite states. The western powers had no pre-existing strategy – except that military intervention was absolutely ruled out of the question under any circumstances – designed to deal with such an unexpected event.

RÁKOSI'S FALL, GERŐ'S ENDGAME

There is much to suggest that Rákosi was determined to use the events in Poznań as an excuse to proceed harshly to end the political crisis he had inflicted on Hungary. Reportedly, he had ordered the development of a 'hit list' containing some 400 names, including the most stubborn 'oppositional elements'. But there was no time to execute such actions. On the strong urging of President Tito, who demanded that the most active promotor of the 'anti-Titoist campaigns' be removed, the Soviet leadership decided to get rid of Rákosi. The drama then unfolded in the usual manner: Politburo member Anastas Mikoyan arrived unannounced in Budapest on 13 July, a few days before a scheduled Central Committee meeting, and informed Rákosi of his dismissal. It was announced publicly on 19 July, officially explained as the result of health problems. To avoid any further difficulty, the unseated tyrant was loaded in an airplane and sent off to Moscow.

The former number two man in the leadership, Ernő Gerő, an old Moscow favourite, now graduated to Rákosi's post as first secretary, and János Kádár was elevated to Central Committee secretary. The rearranged leadership now also included, for example, the former social democratic politician, György Marosán, whose eager assistance in the liquidation of the Social Democratic Party in 1948 had been 'rewarded' by Rákosi with five years in prison.

Perhaps at this stage it would still have been possible to deflect the threat of an uprising. But that would have required both the Soviet and the Hungarian leaders to make more basic and convincing changes, that is, to reinstate Nagy as prime minister and to name Kádár as first secretary. In that way it might have been possible to generate enough trust to sustain a new beginning. First Secretary Gerő did announce a policy of a 'clean slate', but the half-hearted personnel changes were not enough to restore the credibility of the state and party leadership. Further, the people had gradually overcome their fear. Gerő was scarcely more beloved than Rákosi, but he inspired less fear. And his uncertainty was evident within a few weeks of his taking office.

By September 1956 it had become abundantly clear that the rehabilitation of the communists among the regime's victims must be initiated without delay, also that a solution to the 'Imre Nagy problem' was urgently needed. Gerő and Kádár would have preferred to settle these matters quietly and without publicity. Nagy had indicated in negotiation that he would accept reinstatement in the party as a solution. But the issue of rehabilitation took on complications. Júlia Rajk, widow of the most prominent victim of the Rákosi era, who had herself spent years in prison after the execution of her husband in 1949, demanded a ceremonial reinterment of László Rajk's remains and his unqualified rehabilitation. In her efforts she could count on the support of the entire inner-party opposition and other major social forces. There was nothing left for the party leaders but to meet her requirements even as to the details of the ceremony. In order to avoid having to participate themselves, the party leaders with Gerő and Kádár at their head set the date for the reinterment of their own victims to coincide with their visit abroad. Whether by chance or intentionally, the reburial ceremony was set for 6 October, a day that had been celebrated in remembrance of the thirteen generals of the Honvéd army executed in 1849 in Arad by the Habsburgs.

The appearance of hundreds of thousands at the cemetery was a conspicuous demonstration not only of the guilty involvement of the regime but also of its weakness. After the dreary official speeches with their conventional phrases, a brief address really caught the attention of the subdued and weary crowd as the writer Béla Szász spoke in the name of those charged in the Rajk trial:

Executed as a result of trumped up charges, László Rajk's remains rested for seven years in an unmarked grave. Yet his death has become a warning signal for the Hungarian people and for the whole world. For the hundreds of thousands who pass by this coffin desire not only to honour the dead man; it is their passionate hope and their firm resolve to bury an entire epoch. The lawlessness, arbitrariness, and moral decay of those shameless years must be buried forever; and the danger posed by Hungarian practitioners of rule by force and of the personality cult must be banned forever.

Truly, the gathering had sensed the uncertainty of the leadership, the extent to which the wounded apparatus of power had left a vacuum, and the realization that the decision as to who commands the streets was no longer the prerogative of the authorities. On the afternoon following the ceremony, a small group of students delivered the proof of that as they arranged a demonstration at the memorial to the martyred prime minister, Count Batthyány, thus widening the protest beyond the confines of the communist movement into a national one. The day was like a dress rehearsal for the events of 23 October, except that new forces would then take the stage and assume the leading roles.

CHAPTER THREE

From Mass Protest to Armed Uprising

Thus, in the autumn of 1956, an ever more insecure and nervous power structure was faced with an ever more popular opposition – in its own ranks and beyond. The resonance of the intellectual rebels widened and their call for profound change, as it was to become clear, could count on the support of the entire population. Although uprisings can always be traced back to a particular event, the causes of this outburst are extremely complex, the results of prolonged developments. The Hungarian uprising represented the eruption of a long-smouldering crisis of 'socialism' of Stalinist type. In retrospect, one might say that the uprising was also the first general crisis of the system in its entire history.

Of course the loss of power did not begin on the morning of 23 October. Already after the burial of László Rajk the armed forces were put on alert, but these measures were soon rescinded. The situation was more than tense but the leadership did not want to acknowledge it. As Nikita Khrushchev would later remark contemptuously, they preferred to take an extended swimming holiday on the Adriatic Sea. The true state of affairs was correctly assessed by none of the political actors involved. The Soviet leaders had, to be sure, deposed party chief Mátyás Rákosi, but his replacement by Gerő was in effect a signal that no fundamental changes were intended. On the other hand, the inner-party opposition expected the realization of its gradually evolved plans for reform to occur by virtue of a power shift within the existing system.

THE WARSAW EXAMPLE

The Polish example was what suggested that such a political strategy could succeed, for Władysław Gomułka had been elected party chief there despite the quite different intentions of the Soviet leadership. The Polish reform movement, encouraged by the Twentieth Party Congress of the CPSU and fortified significantly by the workers' rising in Poznań in July 1956, reached its peak at the Eighth Plenum of the Polish United Workers' Party (PZRP) which met during 19–21 October. There had been rumours already that fed the hopes for major changes in personnel. Gomułka laid claim to the position of first secretary: although he had been driven from the party leadership in 1949 and spent three years in prison, his popularity was in no way diminished.

On the first day of the Plenum, the Soviet delegation arrived, bent on preventing the change in Polish party leadership. Khrushchev, accompanied by Mikojan, Molotov and Kaganovich, threatened military intervention, and some of the Soviet troops stationed in Poland were actually set in motion toward Warsaw. Some Polish army units were also on the way to the capital by command of Defence Minister Rokossovsky (who was at the same time a marshal of the Soviet Union). The dramatic negotiation between the Soviet leaders and the Polish Central Committee (now including Gomułka) came to a close early on 20 October: the Soviet delegation acceded reluctantly and approved the personnel changes. The Chinese Communist Party had figured significantly in the outcome when it voiced disapproval of a military intervention, as had Gomułka's assurance that nothing would alter Poland's close ties to the Soviet Union.

When the Polish Politburo membership was chosen on 21 October, the most compromised politicians of the Stalinist period were excluded, and Gomułka was formally elected as first secretary of the party. In his ensuing speech, he promised fundamental changes, revised the assessment of the events in Poznań (hitherto officially attributed to the 'agitation of spies and agents of the imperialist intelligence services'), and announced a 'Polish way to socialism'. His speech was printed in full in the next day's *Szabad Nép*. The inner-party opposition in Hungary felt confirmed in its efforts. The average citizen got another message from Polish developments, however: it is now time for actions that are not only possible but even mandatory, for if one shows enough firmness even the Soviet leaders will back down.

PRELUDE: THE STUDENT MOVEMENT

Several days passed before the Hungarian press reported the events of 15–16 October 1956 in the southern university city of Szeged. In a student assembly there it was proposed that the former independent

League of Hungarian University Students (MEFESZ) be re-established. Within a few days all of Szeged's institutions of higher education had endorsed the proposal and the student demands had been formulated. In addition to educational matters and the social needs of students, the inventory of demands included unmistakably political objectives.

In part the student protest stemmed from the intellectual opposition within the party during the summer and autumn of 1956. As mentioned before, just about all university cities saw the formation of intellectual discussion groups resembling the Petőfi Circle. The local press and especially the provincial literary journals suddenly became freer and livelier in tone. Sensing the dwindling influence of their own organization, the leaders of the communist youth began, albeit timidly, to consider reforms.

At the same time, the entry of the students into the political life of Hungary signified a decisive turn, one that can properly be called a 'prelude' of the revolution, not just because they opposed the Stalinist leadership under First Secretary Gerő – the inner-party opposition did that too – but because they left the reform initiators far behind in three crucial respects.

The students' first step, forming their own independent association, already made it evident that their resistance was much more radical than that of the inner-party opposition. By organizing something new, independent of the centre and democratic in its principles, the students broke fundamentally with the centralized Stalinist institutional structure. The assembled members elected their provisional officers and participated fully and directly in the formulation of the student demands.

The second crucial point was that the students did not rest content anymore with criticism of existing circumstances and the formulation of vague reform ideas. They pressed demands: after the example of the revolutionaries of 1848 with their demands for civil rights, parliamentarianism and national independence, the students at universities throughout the land prepared manifestos. If these differed in detail and formulation, they displayed basic attitudes that were astonishingly similar.

The third decisive feature was that the students did not stop with lists of demands. On the contrary, their elected spokespersons delivered the resolutions to other universities, to the factories, and to both local and central officials and offices. They wanted to see their demands converted into action and they made clear, at the same time, that they were themselves committed to action in the form of demonstrations and strikes.

In the week leading up to 23 October there were assemblies in universities all over the country, all with nearly identical results. The great student gathering on 22 October at the Technical University of Budapest then became truly a 'dress rehearsal' of the revolutionary uprising.

The original intent of the gathering, as organized by the official youth association, was to counteract the independent actions of the student body. But after a report from Szeged delegates and under the influence of news of successful reform in Poland, the direction of the assembly was simply taken out of the hands of the communist youth functionaries, as the great majority voted to join forces with the Szeged students in the new independent MEFESZ. Late in the evening, as demands were being formulated for the gathering of several thousand, strictly educational matters soon faded in favour of political positions.

The most influential speakers were József Szilágyi, a supporter of Imre Nagy, who attended a correspondence course at the Technical University, and Lieutenant-Colonel István Marián, head of the reserve officer training at the same institution. As the closing proclamation put it, the evening had indeed developed into 'the sunrise of modern Hungarian history'. As the evening wore on, the growing self-confidence and lust for freedom produced increasingly sharp formulations and ever more radical demands. Thus, the characteristic short-term goals of the communist opposition (appointment of Imre Nagy as prime minister, calling a party congress, reassessment of norms and quotas in industry and agriculture, etc.) were expanded to include general democratic and national demands: multiparty system, free elections, civil rights, national economic independence, and reinstatement of Hungarian national holidays and symbols of state. And as the prerequisite for any reform programme came finally the unconditional demand for withdrawal of Soviet troops. Many variants of the already legendary Technical University programme were circulating, containing ten or fourteen or sixteen points depending on who had made notes and when they had been recorded, suggesting the impulsive and spontaneous nature of the evening's proceedings.

The participants naturally wanted to reach a larger audience than could be done through circulation of copies and by means of publication in the student paper *A Jövő Mérnöke* (Engineer of the Future). But the delegation that approached Hungarian Radio had no success. The officials there refused to put on the air such demands as those for free elections and the withdrawal of Soviet troops. That was the occasion for resorting to a demonstration called by students for the next day to show solidarity with the Polish reformers and, at the same time, to publicize their own demands. (The twin objectives were most clearly expressed on the signs carrying the slogan: Poland is our Example –

Follow the Hungarian Path!) The idea of a political demonstration was simply 'in the air' during this time. The students of the faculty of arts at the University of Budapest had the same intention, and on the morning of 23 October the plans of the initiators at both universities were coordinated. Students from the Technical University wanted to march in silence and without signs; those from the other universities meant to march with signs and flags. The meeting place was the monument to General Bem, the legendary Polish revolutionary who had led Hungarian forces to victory in several engagements with Habsburg and Tsarist military units in 1849.

23 OCTOBER

Aside from the demonstration of indignation that greeted the loss of the world soccer championship in summer 1954, for nearly a decade the streets of Budapest had not seen a spontaneous mass demonstration. It was hardly to be expected that the authorities, accustomed to officially organized marches, would react complacently to the announcement of a student demonstration. Yet their uneasiness over popular expressions of discontent did not seem particularly intense in this instance. The most important decision makers found themselves at the time on an extended state visit in Yugoslavia. The delegation, which included Prime Minister Hegedüs and János Kádár as well as Ernő Gerő, sought to secure the support of President Tito, returning to Budapest only on the morning of 23 October. In a Politburo meeting called directly after its arrival, the party leadership was united in the view that the demonstration should be forestalled. József Révai and György Marosán said openly, 'If necessary we'll have to shoot!'

Other elements of the power structure were less confident and did not replicate the Politburo's determination. Leaders of the youth organization, for example, called on members to join the march, saying that the leading functionaries would be at the head of the march column. At the same time, the responsible officers of state security and police informed the political leadership that they had no suitable means available for a peaceable dispersal of the demonstrators. Sándor Kopácsi, police chief of Budapest who sympathized with the opposition, said that a police action would be unwise, suggesting that the police would not proceed forcefully against the protesting students.

The Politburo, in session constantly, had fallen apart, sensing its loss of control over developments. At 10:00 a.m. on 23 October it was announced on the radio that the university students would, at 2:30 p.m., stage 'a silent march to the Polish Embassy to show their solidarity with events in Poland'. The headquarters of the Writers' Union was named as the gathering point. But at 12:53 the Interior Minister's announcement was read: 'For the sake of preserving public order and safety, public meetings and demonstrations are prohibited until further notice'. Students and reform groups (Writers' Union, Petőfi Circle and editors of *Szabad Nép*) protested; before the advocates of a hard line could intervene, the radio announced at 2:23 p.m. that the minister's prohibition had been lifted.

The students had paid little attention either to the prohibition or its withdrawal; if anything the ban served as stimulus. The marches began early in the afternoon, one from the Faculty of Arts and the Petőfi monument, the other from the Technical University to the Bem monument (see Map 1). Their numbers grew rapidly as many workers and other sympathizers from all segments of society joined the students. The crowd that met finally in the late afternoon at the Bem monument numbered tens of thousands. Neither the official youth functionaries nor the party activists had any hope of 'channelling' the outburst. Members of the inner-party opposition, who at least in principle had a greater chance to influence the events, also tried to direct the demonstration into peaceful channels, but the Petőfi Circle's vehicle with its loudspeaker was lost in the crowd. And when Péter Veres, president of the Writers' Union, attempted to present a resolution endorsing the change in leadership in Warsaw as a worthy model for reform in Hungary, his voice was drowned out by the noise of the crowd. The demonstration grew and advanced like a mighty wave overcoming the inhibitions of fear.

Recruits in the barracks on Bem Square, forbidden to open windows, climbed to the roof and raised Hungarian flags in a sign of solidarity. Flags also appeared in the crowd but with the Soviet-type insignia of the people's republic cut from their centres. The crowd's slogans kept getting more radical ('Rákosi into the Danube! – Imre Nagy into the government!'); the reformist slogans gave way to anti-Soviet accents ('If you're a Hungarian you're with us!' and 'Out with the Russians!'). But the students' demand that the Sixteen Points, adopted the preceding evening by the students of the Technical University, be broadcast continued to be refused.

Instead at 8:00 p.m. Radio Kossuth broadcast a provocative speech by Ernő Gerő in which the first secretary sharply condemned the 'nationalistic demonstration'. The party leaders had still not grasped that this was not just a display of indignation that could be managed with vague promises and half-hearted measures – such as reinforcing security at the radio station – that would show their firmness. The protest had

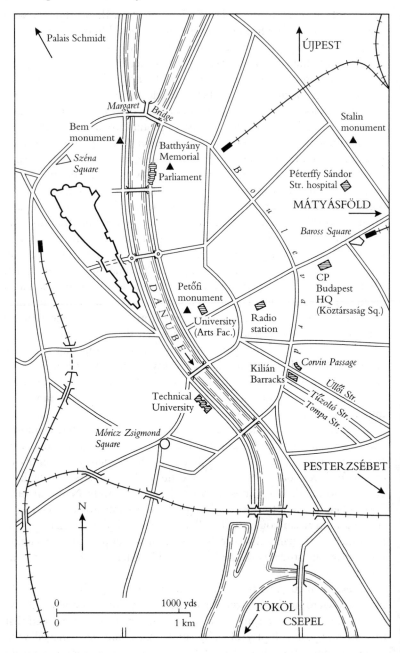

1   Central Budapest 1956

developed its own dynamic that was no longer susceptible to the old style of 'crisis management'. As the crowd surged from Bem Square over the Margaret Bridge in the direction of Parliament as darkness fell, this fact was certainly not yet clear to Imre Nagy and the oppositionists either, though they had not spent the day in the Politburo meeting.

Imre Nagy, who by chance had returned to the capital from Lake Balaton – where he was a guest at a wine harvest – on the morning of the 23rd, met that forenoon with some of his close political allies. Even these leaders of the inner-party opposition exhibited less than complete enthusiasm for the demonstration. They feared provocation – that Gerő might shift responsibility to them and eventually place them under arrest. For that reason they cautioned the young protestors, when the latter sought them out, to maintain discipline and order. Yet in another sense the members of this group were optimistic: after hearing of Gomułka's elevation to party chief they were certain that changes would take place in Hungary. For the eventuality that Imre Nagy might be returned to political leadership, they fashioned a list of individuals who should be dismissed from the leadership and of the replacements they wished to have at Nagy's side. After this meeting, Nagy remained at home where friends visited him and kept him posted about the events in the streets. He was there in the early evening when the call came from the Politburo that he should go to the Parliament building and calm the crowd waiting there for him.

Some two hundred thousand people had gathered in front of the Parliament building and in the neighbouring streets: students, workers, people from all walks of life, calling for Imre Nagy. Thousands demonstrated at other places, especially at the Stalin monument at the edge of City Park and in front of the radio station where the crowd insisted that the student demands be broadcast. The extremely tense atmosphere, stimulated by the commitment to change ('Now or never!' was one of the slogans heard), could be expected to erupt at any moment.

Imre Nagy showed himself about 9 o'clock in the evening, looking down at the crowd from a balcony above the square. His very choice of greeting, 'Comrades!' triggered disappointment, and still more so as in his speech he proposed 'internal party negotiation and clarification of the situation' as the practical way to implement the government programme of June 1953. He urged the crowd to go home, and his urging was heeded. The square emptied, but the people left frustrated, even angry. There was deep disappointment with Nagy's speech, which had ignored the demonstrators' demands. Soon thereafter the Stalin monument was toppled. It was not an easy task to remove the colossus. Ironworkers came with tools, several heavy trucks pulled it with ropes until it finally fell, leaving merely a pair of bronze boots on the pedestal. Hundreds took part in smashing the statue of the hated foreign dictator to pieces. About the same time, the situation changed at the radio station: the defending forces thought to resolve the crisis by force when the crowd appeared to storm the building. Shots rang out. The demonstrators were now armed, partly with weapons from the soldiers sent to strengthen the building's defence and partly with guns taken from barracks of the People's Army. When they really did storm the building, the armed uprising had begun.

THE POLITBURO'S SEARCH FOR A SOLUTION

While all this was going on in the streets of Budapest, the Politburo was meeting still at party headquarters. Ernő Gerő had already called Moscow that afternoon, as the student meeting turned into a mass demonstration, asking the Soviet leaders for help. As is clear from recently released materials from Communist Party archives, Gerő had requested military support from both Ambassador Andropov and somewhat later from Khrushchev himself. Having just reached a resolution in Warsaw, obviously through concessions to a united Polish party leadership, Khrushchev was not prepared at this point to order the intervention of Soviet troops in Hungary. But because Andropov assessed the situation as critical, Moscow agreed to military intervention on the condition that the Hungarian government make a formal request. At Andropov's instigation, Marshal Zhukov received the order to send tank units into action in Budapest several days before Prime Minister Hegedűs's letter of request for intervention reached Moscow. As Imre Nagy left the Parliament building about 10:00 p.m. and went over to party headquarters, Gerő already informed of the armed clash at the radio station, was again calling Moscow. It was probably during this telephone conversation that Khrushchev finally agreed to military intervention.

While the Stalinist single-party-state was collapsing spectacularly in the streets of Budapest, the leadership set about, in the accustomed style of communist statesmanship, 'to manage the crisis'. Even Imre Nagy, whom the Stalinist faction could no longer ignore, did not manage to change the usual decision-making process of the top leadership. He must have been shaken and surely surprised by the day's events. Invited by his enemies and opponents to take part in the leadership, he could have simply left Gerő and his comrades to their fate or he could have offered his help subject to the meeting of certain conditions, such as personnel changes and the discussion of the demonstrators' demands. While his commitment to the party did not allow him to choose the former, he tried the latter by asking for Gerő's resignation, without success. But then he accepted the post of prime minister because he saw the catastrophic consequences of Gerő's policies and realized that the Soviets did not support his return to leadership. He lent his name and popularity to the rescue of the party while continuing the fight within the leadership for a peaceful solution.

The Central Committee met late in the evening, though only with those members present who had been able to reach the inner city. It was decided to define the uprisings as 'the work of counter-revolutionary, fascist forces' and to terminate it by means of military and security forces and Soviet troops. The next task was the reorganization of state and party leadership, and in particular the choice of personnel for leading positions. Nagy, already earlier reinstated in his party membership, was nominated to the Politburo and for the position of prime minister. Nagy himself had proposed in this meeting that Gerő be replaced as first secretary, but when the proposal did not command a majority he responded according to lifelong habit by accepting party discipline and the majority decision. First Secretary Gerő, viewed by Soviet leaders as the best guarantor of their interests, retained his position.

The results of the meeting under 'renewed' direction were broadcast the next morning, 24 October. A state of emergency was declared, all gatherings were prohibited, and the armed insurrectionists threatened with court-martial. It was also announced that Soviet assistance had been sought for restoring order. Finally, personnel changes were noted: József Révai, Interior Minister László Piros, and a few others were dropped from the Politburo, replaced by Imre Nagy and two other representatives of the inner-party opposition, Ferenc Donáth and Géza Losonczy, who, however, were not present. They did not accept the election and protested against the Politburo's handling of the situation. Nagy, who took up his duties in the altered leadership on the morning of 24 October, had not taken part in framing the final version of some of the measures adopted that day, but since he was not able to forestall them they remained associated with his name. That gave rise in the days that followed to many of the political difficulties with which he had to contend.

Nagy, at that point virtually alone, separated from his political friends, probably hoped that the decisions on reform would not be made in the streets, but rather that the political leadership could take the necessary steps. But the masses in the streets, conscious now of their strength, reacted with their own weapons to the regime's show of force. A mass strike developed spontaneously: all public transportation in Budapest was closed down and the newspapers – except for some leaflets – did not appear. (By way of contrast, the telephone service continued to function throughout the fight; the radio came back on air from temporary studios.) The streets of the capital were still unsafe, but on 24 October; between skirmishes people gathered in groups to discuss the situation. The demands of the previous day receded into the background as the new circumstances unfolded: the intervention of Soviet troops had turned the uprising against a Stalinist dictatorship overnight into a national freedom fight.

A REVOLT FOR FREEDOM

Although virtually all lists of demand contained suggestions of reform within the existing system, they also referred to 'freedom and national independence'. When the uprising began, these two demands, linked closely together, shifted clearly into the foreground. On 25 October a reporter asked a 16–year-old freedom fighter why he took to the streets with weapon in hand; the answer was typical: 'Just as our freedom fighters of 1848 rebelled against foreign repression, so we cannot allow an alien oppressor to do as he pleases in our homeland'. The invocation of 1848 was virtually automatic in 1956 – and not only because the memory of that earlier time was still alive in Hungarian collective consciousness. For the Russian intervention contained the reminder that the Habsburgs could put down the Hungarian revolution in 1849 only with the help of the tsar's army. The demonstration of 23 October had begun at the monument to General Bem of 1849 fame. In framing the demands of 1956, remembrance of the revolution of 1848 was an important element both politically and emotionally.

The demand for freedom on 23 October meant above all: departure of the occupying army; termination of military, political and economic dependency; reconsideration of the treaties and agreements unfavourable for the country; and the reintroduction of traditional symbols in place of the emblems and uniforms of Soviet type. After the intervention of 24 October, the immediate withdrawal of Soviet troops fighting against the Revolution became the uppermost demand, first the withdrawal from Budapest and the larger provincial cities, but soon their removal from the whole country. The Soviet intervention had demonstrated that the stationing of troops in Hungary was chiefly to preserve the dependency relationships within the Socialist bloc and to serve the interests of the communist regime in Moscow, protecting them if need be with military force. Hence, the demand for withdrawal of Soviet troops was not only a question of national independence, but also a necessity for the success of any democratic transformation and any effective move against Stalinist dictatorship.

Dependency on the Soviet Union was opposed by those expressions of protest concerned with the review of international agreements, foreign trade treaties, and similar matters. Like the other satellite states, Hungary was, beyond the military occupation, both politically (thanks to Communist Party direction from Moscow) and economically entirely dependent on the USSR. Hungary's status as a client state was confirmed by the fact that government decisions, especially in the foreign policy realm had to be approved in Moscow.

The Soviet 'colonization' of Hungary proceeded in stages. Very little was known publicly about the status of the equipment and goods removed to the Soviet Union in 1945–46, or about the details of the legal reparation payments imposed on Hungary in the peace treaty. Hungary's contribution within the framework of the Council for Mutual Economic Assistance (Comecon, established in 1949) was guarded as if it were a state secret. Neither the public, nor the Parliament, nor the professional specialists were informed. But everyone knew, or, more precisely, thought they knew, that the Hungarian economy had been subordinated to Moscow's interests for at least a decade and that it had been forced to assist in the rebuilding of war-damaged areas of the Soviet Union and in offsetting the shortages of the poorly functioning Soviet economy. People were especially inclined to speculate about the destination of the two strategic materials, bauxite and uranium, and whether their extraction served Hungarian or alien interests. One could hear questions about who was processing Hungarian uranium or such slogans as 'Hungarian uranium belongs to the Hungarian people!' (Near Pécs in southern Hungary there was a small uranium mine and its ore went exclusively to the Soviets; Hungarian scientists were unable to obtain samples for their research.)

If during the Revolution the word 'freedom' meant first of all the liberation from Soviet occupation and colonial status, the positive sense of the concept of freedom was never absent and included freedom of expression, assembly, religion, conscience, education and organization. These civil and human rights, the basis of modern European political culture, were virtually all included in the 1949 constitution of the Hungarian People's Republic. But these rights existed only on paper.

Freedom of belief and of the press stood at the top of the lists of demands. Freedom to organize and assemble were already established de facto by the reappearance of the free student organization (MEFESZ) and by the workers' councils and revolutionary committees. The right to strike figured in every statement from the workers' councils. Equally frequent, though in diverse formulations, was the demand for free elections. Religious freedom, as much curtailed as freedom of opinion and expression by the party dictatorship, was mentioned explicitly in the programme of the workers' council in the Csepel industrial district.

Both the lists of demands and the revolutionary actions themselves gave expression to concern for the symbols of state and society. Among the changes insisted upon were the reintroduction of the so-called Kossuth coat of arms of 1848 (which had again become the official emblem of state in 1946), the celebration of 15 March as a national holiday commemorating the revolution of 1848, and the elimination of uniforms patterned after the Soviet style. After the uprising began, there was a demand to make 23 October a national holiday. These were of course not of the same significance as those directed against military, political and economic repression. Yet they were extremely important and they remained so in the decades that followed. When the new emblems were introduced, a newspaper remarked, 'How little this Hungarian Revolution demanded, and how reluctantly that little was granted!' We might add: and how much that little signified!

Symbols such as flag, state emblem and uniform have always functioned as a shorthand making understandable for ordinary people an otherwise opaque hierarchical, social or religious content. The red star, symbol of Soviet communism, appeared everywhere in both public and private places – on the flag and uniforms, on coins and stamps, on walls and roofs, as shop window decoration and free-standing monument. Another such symbol was the huge Stalin statue in Budapest's City Park and countless other pictures and busts throughout the country. The red star appeared immediately and everywhere following the communist take-over, signifying the regime's triumph; it was a corresponding symbolic act against repression when the star was cut from the centre of flags and hauled down from the roofs. Also symbolic was the demand for termination of mandatory teaching of Russian: the protest was aimed not at the language or the Russian classics but at the requirement that Russian be the only mandatory foreign language taught in the schools. The demands concerning the Kossuth-arms and the national holiday were not just negations of everything represented by the red star or the celebration of the Russian October Revolution, but were endorsements of the ideas of the 1848 revolution and war of independence, of the programme of the Hungarian Republic of 1946, and of the free, republican national tradition. The red-white-green flag with the Soviet-type state arms cut out became the symbol of the struggle against disrespect for the national traditions.

Decades later, people demonstrated against Ceauşescu's dictatorship in the streets of Timisoara under the the Romanian tricolor with the emblem of the people's republic cut out of its centre.

ARMED CONFLICT WITH SOVIET FORCES

The armed insurrectionists were the most decisive representatives of all these demands, the ones who gave an unmistakable answer to the exercise of official authority. And that was altogether clear to those in power.

In the night between 23 and 24 October, the party leadership formed a military council to coordinate measures to be taken against the uprising and, in keeping with the Warsaw Pact, to maintain direct contact with the commanders of Soviet troops in Hungary. The only reason that forces of the Hungarian People's Army did not launch massive interventions lay in the moral disarray and internal divisions within the leadership. Neither the political nor the military leaders could be sure that the soldiers would obey a command to shoot at civilians. Therefore, only units of the armed security forces fought alongside Soviet forces.

Soviet units arrived in Budapest early on the morning of 24 October. Judging by their actions and movements over the next three or four days, it is probable that, at least at the outset, they had no orders to attack. In any case, the strength of the two divisions stationed in the centre of the country did not seem to suffice for an attack. Therefore, the general staff commanded additional troops to Hungary as early as 24 October. It would also appear that the tactical threat of force, used successfully in 1953 during the East German rising, was expected to overcome the 'unrest'.

The fighters facing these forces were relatively small in number; at first only a couple of thousand of them pursued the struggle. And until 28 October they had not succeeded in occupying a single strategic objective (the building of the radio station, totally ruined and useless, was retaken by Soviet troops on 25 October). Yet they were everywhere in the capital, attacking the Soviet tanks in small groups and taking a toll on the Soviet soldiery. They were able to establish a few important bases for resistance: in Pest at the Corvin Passage and various points in nearby smaller streets (Tűzoltó Street, Tompa Street), in Buda at Széna Square and Móricz Zsigmond Square. In outer districts such as Csepel and Újpest there were larger armed groups (see Map 1 p. 56). The overall number of participants in the fighting in the course of the subsequent days can be estimated, on the basis of various sources, at ten to fifteen thousand.

Although virtually the entire population trod the stage of history, first during the Budapest demonstrations and then throughout the country, the armed fighters were mainly young people. Teenagers, young workers and apprentices, including young girls, were the principal ones who took up arms. They came mostly from the poorer districts of Budapest, and from the worker and apprentice barracks. Their fighting was less the result of conscious political decision than of bitterness over their hopeless situation and of rage at the appearance of the armed forces of state repression. Their experience of poverty and oppression was only intensified by generational tensions, miserable starting wages, and the regimentation of all forms of recreation specific to youth. Young people were especially irritated by the state-inspired boredom and ritually enforced modes of conduct. The marginalization of whole sectors of the population in the 1950s was especially hard on the young. Armed revolt seemed to offer a romantic or heroic route out of this situation. They found in the uprising all that was missing from their daily routine: the genuine solidarity that springs from the sharing of danger, the experience of human support and fraternity that came from the entire population, and the hope of breaking out of their despair.

The insurrectionists included only a few adults or people with a higher education. These few often became the leaders of armed groups, for they were the only ones with rudimentary military experience and the necessary qualities of political leadership. Others emerged as leaders simply because they were the bravest in the guerrilla-style attacks on the Soviet troops or Hungarian security forces. In Budapest the rebels included quite a few bullies and individuals who had come in conflict with the law – and not necessarily out of political conviction. But they too were swept along by the naïveté and unblemished bravery of the others. Rectitude was altogether characteristic in the days of the uprising: there was virtually no ordinary crime while the fighting was going on, the goods behind broken shop windows remained untouched, and leaders of the armed groups paid for supplies for their personnel. The resistance and endurance of the Budapest youth became a crucial political factor, for they were the ones who continued to fight against superior force during the critical time between 24 and 28 October. They confronted Soviet tanks with remarkable courage and the most primitive of weapons, Molotov cocktails and handguns. It was of course crucial that they could count on the moral and practical support of the whole population. After the first round of hostilities, on 31 October Leslie Fry, British minister to Budapest, cabled to the Foreign Office:

I have just been through some of those parts of the city in which the fighting was heaviest, and can only describe their condition as devastated. I was astonished also by the extent of many areas affected. It is nothing short of a miracle that Hungarian people should have withstood and turned back this diabolical onslaught. They will never forget nor forgive.

Although the freedom fighters were joined by many soldiers from the People's Army, including some officers, their groups could not be said to have much military training or any unified tactical approach. Those who had completed military service relied on their own experience in handling weapons; the younger ones applied the 'tricks' learned by watching films about war and partisan struggle. Leaders emerged from the ranks by displaying bravery and tactical talent during the fighting. Some groups elected their leaders: thus János Szabó (the legendary Uncle Szabó) at Széna Square, László Nickelsburg at Baross Square, László Iván-Kovács and later Gergely Pongrátz and his brothers in Corvin Passage, János Bárány in Tompa Street, István Angyal, Ottó Szirmai and Per Olaf Csongovay in Tűzoltó Street, and many others.

There was little or no consultation among the groups, but their style of fighting was remarkably similar. For most of the young fighters it was characteristic that they paid little attention to larger political issues, not at the outset of the fighting and not later. As Gergely Pongrátz recalled, 'Whoever had a weapon and fought for the students' 16 points was a comrade-in-arms.' Most decisive, as later became clear, was their determination to resist and to endure.

Imre Nagy, who had overcome the shock of 23 October, revised his position and announced on the radio at midday of the 24th that martial law would not apply to those who laid down their weapons. The deadline for laying down weapons was extended several times in the next few days. But the fighters – except when they landed in a hopeless position – would not give in. It proved impossible to smoke them out of their pockets of resistance, and groups that were broken up formed themselves again and continued.

The fighters were, in the most literal sense, committed to a struggle to the death. This was probably the main reason that the political leadership could not introduce a compromise and did not succeed, by partial reform or promise of reform, in restoring order. The other decisive reason was the revolutionary movement from below, the self-organization of the populace at the local level.

COUNTRYWIDE REVOLUTION

The news from Budapest mobilized people throughout the country. After 24 October there were demonstrations and expressions of protest in other cities and also in the smaller communities.

Revolutionary events played themselves out in similar fashion everywhere – as if the protagonists were all reading the same script. The first phase was usually a mass assembly of students, high school pupils and other youth. People took physical possession of those public spaces hitherto reserved to the hated official monopoly of force and available to the citizens only for the festive rituals organized and imposed on the community from above. The removal of the symbols of rule – the red star, Stalin statues and Soviet war memorials – was a symbolic cleansing of public places, a kind of iconoclasm expressive of spiritual liberation. Next came the framing of inventories of demands and the election of delegates charged with negotiating with official representatives. The nuclei of self-governing bodies also emerged until, finally, there developed, in many places, a direct confrontation with the forces of the old regime.

Armed engagement was largely absent from the revolutionary uprisings in the provincial cities, though in several places there was a single bloody encounter leading immediately to the collapse of the old regime. But continued military engagements, the violent aspect of the Revolution in Budapest, were not for the most part experienced personally by people outside the capital.

As the central apparatus of state power became paralysed, the commanders of the military and security units in the provinces displayed little inclination to resort to arms – with certain exceptions treated below. Heads of local party and government organizations had either fled or attempted to adjust to the new situation. Grassroots committees (revolutionary councils, national committees) formed everywhere, taking in hand the public business of the localities. On 23 October a workers' committee was formed to implement the demands of the employees in the locomotive factory DIMÁVAG in the heavy industry centre of Miskolc. On 24 October the first workers' council appeared in the electrical equipment factory Egyesült Izzó (Tungsram) in Újpest, taking over the direction of the factory in response to the countrywide general strike and the armed struggle. News of that development stimulated the formation of provisional workers' councils in factories all over the country.

In the larger communities, local revolutionary committees consisted of delegates from the workers' and students' councils, which were then enlarged, depending on local conditions, either with representatives of the 1945–48 coalition parties or respected people from the displaced governmental administration. In the smaller communities, the revolutionary councils were constituted according to the example of the workers' councils, their members directly elected from among trusted citizens. They assumed everywhere the tasks of governing. Gradually over a period of some days, a new leadership emerged, legitimized by the Revolution, consisting mostly of young people capable of serving the well-being of their communities under the difficult circumstances prevailing. In these variously named revolutionary entities, tens of thousands of individuals became active over the whole country; it quickly became clear that some of them possessed leadership qualities that could, given enough time, have led them to play important roles at the national level. Examples include Attila Szigethy, chairman of the revolutionary committee in Győr, the lawyer József Perbíró, chairman of the committee in Szeged, or the high school principal Árpád Brusznyai, chairman of the committee in Veszprém. District party secretary of County Borsod, Rudolf Földvári, took charge of the revolutionary transformation in his county.

The Revolution proceeded somewhat differently in the villages, where the change occurred quickly and peaceably as a rule, for the Stalinists simply resigned. The initiative of local revolutionary committees, where they existed, was confined to dissolving the agricultural producers' cooperatives (kolkhozes) and destroying the hated registry of mandatory deliveries. Beyond this, the village committees tried to preserve public order and, so far as they could do so, support the fight in Budapest through shipments of food. That item was of great value, not only for the survival of urban residents unprepared for the rigours of armed struggle but also as a way of raising morale in at time of great danger. Without any central organization, the trucks arrived from all corners of the country bringing potatoes, flour, geese, chickens, etc. The fighters and civilians alike saw in this a sign that their cause belonged to the entire country.

A feature of the revolutionary uprising in the provinces was the 'revolutionary of order', one who amidst revolutionary militancy and state of emergency sought to preserve order and safety, offering himself as organizer and broker. The smaller communities managed, despite all destructive forces, to keep their bearings and, up to a certain point, their inner cohesion. It was known which individuals to entrust with positions of leadership or assign organizational tasks, and which ones should be dismissed, driven out, or even arrested. In the self-governing institutions of the provincial cities, the participation of workers and army officers in the age group between 20 and 30 was noticeably high. In villages, many private farmers who had not yielded to the political pressure of the Rákosi era moved into public office. Those who had been active politicians in the coalition parties after 1945 enjoyed general regard and automatically assumed leadership posts.

The role played during the Revolution by the organs of self-government at the local level should not be underestimated. Budapest was the centre to be sure, but the rapid emergence of self-government in the provincial cities and towns exerted considerable influence on party and state leadership and on Imre Nagy personally. On this score the elements of self-government were on the same plane as the armed fighters. Without their political pressure, the Nagy government would probably have stopped halfway – somewhere between the platform of the party's internal opposition and the goals of the Revolution.

Basically, power in the country was divided. On one side were the revolutionary elements representing the demands of the people, above all the demand for withdrawal of Soviet troops, and along with them the workers' councils, the armed insurrectionists and the supporting populace. On the other side stood the official power structure in Budapest, still committed to the restoration of public order through military force. Nagy and the party leadership found themselves in a singular dilemma through the week after 23 October: confrontation with the whole population or acceptance of the demands of the Revolution.

CHAPTER FOUR

Victory and Defeat

The leadership of the ruling party, surrounded by Soviet tanks in its Budapest headquarters, was not prepared in the days after 23 October, even as its control over the situation was slipping away, to abandon its old methods. Of the members of the inner-party opposition, only Imre Nagy attended the Politburo meetings; Ferenc Donáth and Géza Losonczy did not attend, for they did not wish to be associated with the characterization of the current developments as 'counter-revolution' and sent their votes to the Politburo in writing. Their view was that basic reforms had to be instituted and only after that, if unrest remained, would a policy of the strong hand be defendable. Nagy was a 'prisoner' in two senses, though not as legend has it physically: he was a prisoner of an unchanging, insecure and irresponsible corps of party leadership and a prisoner of his own illusions, still believing that the problems could be handled according to the norms and habits of the Communist Party.

The rigid Stalinists, a majority in the Military Council of the Politburo, expected that military intervention would provide the solution. Units of the security forces were stationed on rooftops to guard the government quarters. That led, on the morning of 25 October, to the massacre of peaceful demonstrators in front of the Parliament building. There were thousands involved in the protest with their flags and placards, and some Hungarian and even Soviet tanks joined in, for the fighting seemed to be receding. Suddenly shots rang out from the roofs of government buildings. This was one of the bloodiest events of the Revolution, with more than a hundred dead and wounded. Similar occurrences took place in the next days in dozens of other cities, among them in Győr, Miskolc, Zalaegerszeg and Esztergom, where security forces, joined at times by military units, fired on demonstrators demanding weapons, or the participation of armed units on the side of the

Revolution, or the release of arrested insurrectionists. The order to fire issued at the barracks of the border police in Mosonmagyaróvár cost scores of dead and injured. Demonstrators in Kecskemét and Tiszakécske were fired on by airplanes of the Hungarian army.

Terror did not succeed: resistance was unbroken and the people continued to take to the streets. The only result of employing force was to increase hatred. Everywhere could be heard the demand that the state security apparatus be dismantled. The order to fire had the horrible consequence in Miskolc and Mosonmagyaróvár that several officers and men of the security forces and border police, held by the angry mob to be guilty, were seized and hanged.

When on 26 and 27 October the political leadership indicated a readiness to compromise, the Military Council, supported by the orthodox segment of the leadership, offered new proposals for the unleashing of Soviet artillery and air forces against the toughest resistance centre in the Corvin Passage and then the establishment of military dictatorship. It was mainly to Imre Nagy's credit that such plans were not implemented.

At the outset Nagy had not found a plausible alternative that he could offer convincingly, though he had been trying since 24 October to do so. The group around Nagy, most of the members of the Petőfi Circle, and most of the students had hoped, before 23 October and for a time thereafter, that the crisis could be resolved by means of radical changes within the ruling party in the spirit of the 1953 programme of the government. The Patriotic People's Front was to be expanded as a genuine mass organization, free and open discussion within the party was to be allowed, and the party's monopoly of power was to be given up. On the personal level, these ideas appeared as Imre Nagy's and János Kádár's alternative to Gerő's style of party leadership. Some of the fighters hoped for a purified Communist Party. István Angyal, a leader of the rebels in the Tűzoltó Street who was executed in 1958, wrote from prison:

> We felt that the party should put itself at the helm of the Revolution . . . so that all could see that the people were fighting for socialism. Socialism wanted to be fought for. . . . Had it occurred thus, we could have fought with united effort for the basic achievements of socialism, the nationalization of banks, businesses, and factories, and the land reform.

Clearly, the majority of the fighters, and of the civilians as well, did not share these ideas, as shown by the fact that Nagy's designation as prime minister did not have the desired effect: the fighting did not stop. Further changes in personnel seemed appropriate. The two Soviet presidium members, Mikoyan and Suslov, who arrived in Budapest on

24 October, agreed to the replacement of Gerő by János Kádár at the head of the party (as Imre Nagy had suggested). Since Gerő, Hegedüs and their allies remained in the leadership, the change at the top satisfied nobody, however. It remained for Imre Nagy to search for a genuine solution. Ever since 24 October he kept on arguing with both the Soviets and the Politburo that some compromise should be reached with the revolutionary movement in the country. That he on 28 October discovered the possibility of a solution was due in no small part to the mediating efforts of his friends in the party opposition.

IMRE NAGY ACKNOWLEDGES THE REVOLUTION

The inner-party reformers had sustained a shock because of the way events had unfolded, and the stance of Imre Nagy, who had yielded to his enemies and lent his name to repressive steps. But as they recovered from it, they tried to bridge the gap between Nagy and the revolutionary populace. Already on 26 October at the meeting of the Central Committee, Donáth and Losonczy proposed to recognize the uprising, stigmatized on 24 October as a 'counter-revolution', as a democratic national movement – without success. The many delegations that spoke with Nagy – Writers' Union, revolutionary committee of university students, individual oppositional writers and journalists – kept trying to instruct the head of government, who was or was believed to be insulated from the actualities of the situation, as to what was really happening in the country. The effect was that Nagy finally recognized that it would be impossible to accomplish significant change without fulfilling the demands of the population.

The steps that followed were motivated by that recognition. Courts martial were not invoked for arrested rebels; the deadline for laying down weapons was constantly extended; the Budapest police chief, Sándor Kopácsi, offered to negotiate with the fighters in the government's name; and the new revolutionary organizations were acknowledged as legitimate and self-governing institutions. The centre of political power was shifted from the indecisive party leadership to the new government that had been formed between 25 and 27 October, in which a few uncompromised old communists who had been persecuted under Rákosi, such as Georg Lukács, and also two well-known politicians of the FKGP, Zoltán Tildy and Béla Kovács, were included. This enlargement of the government brought Nagy into harmony with the initial reform demands, but the demands of the freedom fighters and the National Councils now went far beyond partial reform.

The decisive debate within the Politburo took place in the night of 27–28 October. Nagy proposed to declare a cease-fire, start negotiations with representatives of the insurrectionists and, as he put it, 'take the lead of the working masses on the move'. He also urged that the Soviet troops should return to their bases and that the security forces withdraw from the streets. János Kádár and the majority placed themselves on the side of Imre Nagy. The Soviet representatives Mikoyan and Suslov also accepted the change. They did not at that moment know what position the presidium in Moscow would adopt and, furthermore, they recognized that the Soviet forces stationed in Hungary had neither the numerical nor the tactical strength to overcome the uprising.

On 28 October the prime minister announced a cease-fire and truce with all participants of the uprising. In a radio address he called the events a 'wide democratic mass movement' instead of condemning it as counter-revolution. Nagy declared the government's intention to fulfil the major part of the revolutionary demands and its resolve to commerce negotiations for the withdrawal of Soviet troops from Budapest.

The leading institutions of the MDP were disbanded and leadership conferred on a presidium in which Nagy could count on majority support. Nagy announced the dissolution of the state security apparatus. The preservation of public order was shifted to police and army elements sympathetic to the uprising and to insurrectionist groups folded into the newly founded National Guard. The most compromised Stalinists of the party, with Ernő Gerő and András Hegedüs at their head, were flown to the Soviet Union. The prime minister nursed the hope that these measures would suffice by way of accommodation and that he, at the head of a cleansed party leadership positively disposed to policies of change, could begin to effectuate the reforms.

DEMOCRATIC BREAKTHROUGH

Within the next two days the fighting actually stopped. But Nagy's expectation that consolidation could proceed on the basis of the change of 28 October proved illusory. At this point, stabilization would have required the fulfilment of *all* the demands of 23 October, above all the introduction of a multiparty system and the recognition of the more radical national demands that had emerged during the fighting. In these circumstances it was not enough to close down the ÁVH and include a few non-communists in the government. Everyone was now demanding the immediate removal of Soviet troops, withdrawal from the Warsaw Pact and declaration of Hungary's neutrality: the armed fighters, political parties that mushroomed and were using the suddenly free press and radio to declare their positions, the workers' councils with their readiness for a general strike, and the provincial revolutionary committees.

Imre Nagy, freed of the fetters of the old MDP leadership and its tendency to hold back, finally announced the end of the single party system on 30 October and the formation of an inner cabinet including representatives of the parties of the 1945 coalition government. Besides Nagy, this cabinet included Géza Losonczy and János Kádár (MDP), Zoltán Tildy and Béla Kovács (FKGP) and Ferenc Erdei (NPP). The place reserved for the social democrats remained unfilled because of the hesitation of the SZDP leaders. It was announced that the government intended to involve the freedom fighters in the organization of new police entities, to remove the delivery quotas that burdened the farmers, and to negotiate the complete withdrawal of Soviet troops.

The Revolution had thus arrived at a stage where the way seemed to be open to the establishment of a multiparty system and parliamentary democracy. The Imre Nagy government accepted throughout the country by an overwhelming majority and with a programme – for a free, independent, democratic and neutral Hungary – that was wholly congruent with the demands of the Revolution, was oriented in the final analysis to the party political situation of the early post-war years. The non-communist party leaders, only a few of whom had found a modus vivendi with the communists in 1947–49, had spent years in prison during the Rákosi era and had been released only just before the Revolution (some also already in the years of Nagy's reform government in 1953–54). Although this 'broad coalition' seemed acceptable at the end of October, it must be noted that it included only the parties approved in 1945 by the Allied Control Commission under Soviet chairmanship. The conservative oppositional parties established in 1946–48, for example, the Popular Democratic Party and the Hungarian Independence Party, that had protested most vigorously against the communist take-over, were not included. These parties had been mercilessly destroyed by 1949 through police terror, their leaders imprisoned or exiled. Therefore, those elements standing to the right of centre could organize only slowly in October 1956, and the few days of freedom did not suffice for them to appear as significant actors in the political arena.

The demand for free elections with the participation of democratic parties was, as has been mentioned, a crucial point in the students' original demands and became widespread during the uprising. Some of the revolutionary organizations proposed that elections be held as early as February 1957; at the latest they should be held as soon as the Soviet troops had departed.

The idea of revolutionary democracy, as it was called at the time, was by no means exhausted by the formation of a multiparty government and by the appearance of political parties in public affairs. No less important among the ideal objectives of the Revolution was the establishment of grassroots democratic institutions on the level of factory and locality. The history of revolutions shows that such 'fighting units' emerge after the fall of an autocratic system of rule. They enter the power vacuum in order to take on public and governing tasks, but also, more importantly, to insure that smaller groups will be heard in political life. From the first days of the Revolution, the workers' councils were important politically and also as the instruments of social-political programmes. During the 'rearguard' fighting of November and December, the councils were almost the sole centres of resistance.

The revolutionary self-organization had no immediate precedents of significance; the councils were formed in factories and offices at the initiative of workers, technicians and white-collar staff. One should of course not forget that official history books about the CPSU hailed the soviets of 1905 and 1917. Communist teaching in the schools conveyed to people the lessons of successful insurrection. The workers' councils developed quickly as militant representatives of the political and economic interests of the workers. On them depended the decision on ending the general strike; the strike gave them the means to force the temporizers among the leaders to push on with the Revolution, lest they were prepared to assume responsibility for a completely crippled country. Since the workers' councils spoke for the best organized part of the population and could count on a million and a half people behind them, they were entitled to claim a role in decisions affecting the country's fate.

The emergence of these councils was, for example, what the political philosopher, Hannah Arendt, found most remarkable about the Hungarian 1956, when she wrote:

> In Hungary, we have seen the simultaneous setting-up of all kinds of councils, each of them corresponding to a previously existing group in which people habitually lived together or met regularly and knew each other. . . . The men elected were communists and non-communists; party lines seem to have played no role whatsoever, the criterion, in the words of a newspaper, being solely that there is 'none among them who would misuse his power or think of his personal position' . . . One of the most striking aspects of the Hungarian revolution is that this principle of the council system not only reemerged, but that in twelve short days a good deal of its range of potentials could emerge with it. . . . The rise of the council, not the restoration of

parties, was the clear sign of a true upsurge of democracy against dictatorship, of freedom against tyranny.

(H Arendt *The Origins of Totalitarianism*, 2nd edn, New York: Meridian, 1958, pp. 500–1)

One of the outstanding elements of political thinking and action in 1956 was the relationship of grassroots democracy and parliamentary system, the cooperation of local and factory councils and committees with party and governmental organs at the national level. Just as the governing parties did not desire a monopoly of political decision-making or the exclusion of the spontaneously emerging organs of revolutionary democracy, so did the councils not challenge the right to exist of the democratic parties or the role of the central government.

Although there were some who were uneasy about the onset of party competition and raised objections to the formation of parties, they did so only because they feared for the national unity that had been forged in the Revolution and was essential for a successful struggle. Thus, for example, the workers' council of County Borsod stated its concern about 'party wrangling'. On the other hand, the North Hungarian National Council stated plainly on 1 November that 'it was convinced of the propriety and necessity of the formation of democratic parties', and wanted only to suggest that the parties defer struggle among themselves until after the withdrawal of Soviet forces.

STEPS TOWARD CONSOLIDATION

Along with the basic decision for a broad coalition, the government undertook a series of practical initiatives designed to further consolidation. On 30 October at police headquarters in Budapest, a Revolutionary Defence Committee of the forces of public order was established to coordinate the National Guard composed of armed fighters, students and factory personnel. General Béla Király, who had been imprisoned on false charges until October 1956, was chosen as chairman. The Ministry of Defence was purged of the worst of the Stalinist generals and the revolutionary committee of the army declared its loyalty to the Revolution. Imre Nagy met on 30 October with the social democratic leadership with Anna Kéthly at its head and also established contact with the leaders of the armed rebels. He also received József Dudás, leader of a small armed group, who as spokesman for a 'National Revolutionary Commission' sought to bring pressure to bear on the government.

For the change to be successful, the communist party also had to renew itself. The party presidium dissolved the MDP on 30 October, and one day later the party re-formed under the name Hungarian Socialist Workers' Party (MSZMP). Imre Nagy, Zoltán Szántó, Georg Lukács, Ferenc Donáth, Géza Losonczy, Sándor Kopácsi and János Kádár were elected to its temporary executive committee. The erstwhile reformers organized themselves on a broad basis: on 28 October the Revolutionary Committee of the Hungarian Intelligentsia, in a meeting at Budapest University, accomplished the unification of the revolutionary organs of the university youth, the Writers' Union, the Petőfi Circle and the former NÉKOSZ. The resulting committee was regarded by many as the most influential 'lobby' for thoroughgoing reform, and it did play an important role in persuading the group around Imre Nagy that revolutionary moves were necessary.

Immediately after the declaration on restoring the multiparty system, the organization or reorganization of political parties began. As far as one can ascertain, some twenty parties were formed during the Revolution. In Budapest, leading personalities of the 1945–48 coalition period gathered in the old headquarters of their parties, confiscated in the preceding years, and provisional leaderships were formed. The major parties, FKGP, Social Democrats and NPP (now renamed Petőfi Party), were able to reassemble their staff in the last days of October, and appear on the political scene with their newspapers on the streets and well-attended meetings. Through their members coopted by Imre Nagy into the cabinet they were trying to influence the policies of the new government. Zoltán Tildy became effectively deputy prime minister in a very active way.

Party organization outside of Budapest went much slower. However, their representatives, well-respected intellectuals, teachers, farmers, priests and ministers were regularly elected into local revolutionary committees. Most characteristic was the slow revival of different Christian parties. They started from a most disadvantageous position: their leading personalities had just been freed from prison or had left the country fleeing Rákosi's terror many years before. A symbolic figure of the resistance and repression of the church in Hungary, Cardinal Josef Mindszenty, was set free from house arrest on 30 October and escorted by a local army unit to Budapest. Even if he did not take part in the organization of any party, his radio address on 3 November marked out a significant conservative platform.

Despite all the measures taken on behalf of consolidation, the population at large and many of the revolutionary groups remained mistrustful. More had been hoped for after the bloody sacrifices of recent days, essentially the complete and immediate fulfilment of all the national demands. Although Nagy recognized the revolutionary organizations on 30 October and asked them for their support, he did not get an immediate response. On the contrary, there was a continuing stream of delegations seeking to influence the government according to their respective ideas. The armed fighters did not want to lay down their weapons, not even for Hungarian troops; they were willing to join the police forces only as distinct units. This viewpoint had prevailed in the Kilián Barracks on 31 October as the National Guard was formed. Similarly, the workers' councils continued to watch and wait concerning the general strike: the slogan remained – 'until the Russians leave no one should return to work'.

There were also downright destabilizing forces at work. The hatred that had built up during decades was not overcome by the dissolution of the State Security service. It erupted on 30 October, for example, at the Communist Party's municipal headquarters on Köztársaság Square in Budapest. When armed insurrectionists sought to search the party building, they were arrested by the ÁVH units stationed there, which then opened fire on additional armed groups arriving at the square. The armed fighters then began a siege of the building, which was decided by the tanks of the army ordered to protect party headquarters, the personnel of which then – in all likelihood by mistake – fired on the building. At the end of the hours-long flight, in which Budapest party secretary Imre Mező, an ally of Imre Nagy, was fatally wounded, a number of ÁVH personnel who had surrendered were systematically slaughtered, some of them lynched and their bodies mutilated. These occurrences were sharply condemned in the days that followed by numerous revolutionary groups; the free press, the Writers' Union and leaders of armed fighters also spoke out against lynch-justice.

Political prisoners were freed from virtually all the prisons after 30 October. (Despite the rehabilitations, there had still been at least 4,000 people incarcerated for political reasons!) In many cases ordinary prisoners were also freed, people who had been sentenced, with or without grounds, as common criminals, in the Rákosi era. Quite a few of these joined the uprising, partly out of gratitude for their freedom, partly to demonstrate their honour and courage. If there were questionable characters among them, the revolutionary spirit swept them along too. Kádár's propaganda tried later to portray the rebels as criminals, but there is abundant evidence that the freedom fighters themselves penalized any lawlessness resolutely.

News circulated in Budapest on 31 October that the Soviet troop withdrawal, begun on the previous day, had been stopped. New units were arriving, concentrating their forces at the strategically important points, and encircling cities and airports. From this point on, the internal and external policies of the Nagy government were focused entirely on trying to avert the impending catastrophe. It was obvious that the country could not be defended, whatever the readiness for sacrifice. Under the desperate circumstances, the government decided that the best it could do would be quickly to establish internal stability in order to prevent the Soviets from engaging in further armed intervention under the pretext of restoring order.

In the first days of November, energetic measures were indeed undertaken to engender order – in people's minds and in the street. Governing bodies were formed around the cabinet. With the freedom fighters participating, the new organization of police forces was brought under unified direction, the rough-and-ready justice of the streets came to a halt, and command of the army fell to General Pál Maléter, who supported the uprising since 28 October. The relationship between local workers' councils and the revolutionary units had improved; the formation of parties proceeded at a dizzying pace; and other groups and sectors were establishing their own organizations. All of this was without effect on Soviet troop movements. Questions in this connection, sent through diplomatic channels, were answered by the Soviets with empty or deceptive phrases. Thus, the Nagy government again confronted a choice: either give up the revolutionary cause and assume leadership of a restoration, in the vague hope of some improvements, or mount a last heroic effort to rescue the Revolution. Imre Nagy chose the latter. Unilateral withdrawal from the Warsaw Pact (on grounds that the Soviet invasion had invalidated the treaty) and the declaration of neutrality were the final desperate steps in this direction.

WITHDRAWAL FROM THE WARSAW PACT AND DECLARATION OF NEUTRALITY

Imre Nagy's theoretical statements from 1955–56 show that he recognized the significance of independence long before the Revolution and that he was an advocate of neutrality for Hungary. At that time any practical implementation was unthinkable. But in his speech of 31 October he announced that negotiations concerning withdrawal from the Warsaw Pact have been initiated.

Imre Nagy had maintained no contacts in the west, and the western governments followed his activity during the Revolution with suspicion. In his efforts to advance independence and democratization, he saw as his natural allies the Soviet leaders regarded as anti-Stalinists as well as the new Polish leadership and Tito.

Gomułka's Poland had supported Nagy in the beginning and condemned the armed intervention of 23 October. Several Polish leaders visited Budapest from 28 to 30 October and met a number of times with Hungarian counterparts, especially with Nagy and János Kádár. The task of the Polish leaders was, apart from simply informing themselves about the Hungarian situation, to influence their Hungarian comrades against a radicalization that would preclude a solution of the kind reached in Poland. At the same time, on 29 October, a message from the Polish party to the people of Hungary was read on the radio and published in *Szabad Nép*. It was an appeal to end the bloodshed but one expressing support for the Hungarian national government and its programme.

President Tito also responded positively to the events in Hungary so long as he could regard them as a weakening of Stalinism. But he also warned, in his message of 29 October to the MDP Central Committee, against 'imperialist manoeuvres and counter-revolutionary elements' that might exploit the situation.

In the final analysis, Nagy was abandoned by both Tito and Gomułka. Hardliners were gaining the upper hand in Moscow, and Polish leaders viewed the Hungarian move to leave the Warsaw Pact as a danger for Europe's political map and, conceivably, for the Polish-German boundary. Tito, alarmed by the emerging multi-party system, chose to support Moscow.

The appeal by Imre Nagy to the United Nations on 1 November, in which he requested great power recognition of Hungarian neutrality (not, as is often written, requesting UN troops) reflected the fact that Hungary had no other choice but to go its own way. At 7:15 p.m. on 1 November, the prime minister released the following statement:

To the Hungarian people! The national government, profoundly responsible to the Hungarian people and their history, and in obedience to the united will of their millions, herewith declares the neutrality of the Hungarian People's Republic. The Hungarian people, on the basis of independence and equality and in keeping with the spirit of the UN Charter, wish to live in true friendship with their neighbours, with the Soviet Union, and with all peoples of the world. The Hungarian people hope for the consolidation and further development of the gains from the national Revolution without having to belong to any power bloc. The centuries-old dream of the Hungarian people has been fulfilled. The revolutionary struggle, fought by the people and their heroes, ended in the triumph of freedom and independence. This heroic fight made possible the upholding of our fundamental national interests in our international relations, namely, neutrality. We appeal to our neighbours, lands near and far, to respect the definitive decisions of our people. It is true that our people are united in this decision as they have never been before. Working Millions of Hungary! Support and strengthen our land with your revolutionary determination, by your unremitting labour, and through the preservation of order, the free, independent, democratic, and neutral Hungary.

THE LAST DAYS

The declaration of neutrality had a much greater echo at home than it got from its recipients (see Chapter 5). Consolidation now entered a new phase. The workers' councils of Budapest decided at their general conference on the evening of 1 November to terminate the general strike and call for the resumption of work on Monday 5 November. Work resumed at many plants already on Saturday 3 November. Many of the streetcars and buses were back in operation in Budapest; at some places a start was made in cleaning up the vestiges of battle. Delegates of the hitherto suspicious workers' councils met with Imre Nagy between 1 and 3 November and assured him of their support; the delegation from Győr, with Attila Szigethy at its head, did the same after a meeting with Nagy. Even the deceptive manoeuvres of the Soviet command increased hope: on the morning of 3 November, negotiations began in Parliament on the technical aspects of Soviet troop withdrawal. While support for the government was doubtlessly growing everywhere in the country, there already emerged political alternatives that opposed, along with the Stalinists, the reform-minded and patriotic communists, including Imre Nagy himself. These gradually crystallizing forces wrote the charismatic name of Cardinal Mindszenty as a prospective leader of the country on their flag.

On 3 November the cabinet was radically reconstituted. The new Communist Party, MSZMP, was represented by Imre Nagy as premier and acting foreign minister, and Géza Losonczy; the Social Democrats by Anna Kéthly, Gyula Kelemen and József Fischer; the Smallholders by Zoltán Tildy, Béla Kovács and István B. Szabó; and the Petőfi Party (formerly NPP) by Ferenc Farkas and István Bibó; all of them as ministers of state. General Pál Maléter was appointed Minister of Defence.

The press release on the new cabinet also listed the name János Kádár. It was he whose announcement was read on 1 November on the radio about the founding of the new communist party. In the cabinet meeting he had also supported the neutrality declaration and the withdrawal from the Warsaw Pact. Yet Kádár chose a direction exactly opposed to that of Imre Nagy. It is difficult to reconstruct his motives and plans during the hectic revolutionary days. In all likelihood he had supported the changes sincerely as long as they aimed at eliminating the Rákosist leadership and he could believe that they were approved by Moscow. But when he learned, probably from Ferenc Münnich, of the Soviet determination not to allow Hungary to leave 'the camp', he followed his 'communist duty' and changed sides. However, he informed neither the government nor the party leadership of his decision.

Kádár and Münnich went to the Soviet Embassy on the evening of 1 November, while Kádár's speech was played on the radio from an earlier recording. From the Embassy they left for the Soviet air force base in Tököl, and the next day were flown out to Moscow. On 2 and 3 November Kádár and Münnich took part at the meeting of the CPSU's presidium. It was at this time that the new Hungarian leader finally decided to accept the role that was foreseen for him. As a result, a declaration of forming a new government was accepted by the two Hungarian communists. The text had been prepared by the Soviets and was drafted in Russian before being translated into Hungarian. Kádár probably expected that Imre Nagy, faced with a fait accompli, could be persuaded to resign. On the other hand he made clear his unwillingness to cooperate with Rákosi and other old Stalinists staying in Moscow and waiting anxiously to be returned to power. Early on the morning of 4 November, just as Soviet troops were beginning their attack, Kádár and Münnich were flown back to Hungary, and announced the formation of a counter-government.

The Hungarian military delegation led by Ferenc Erdei and Pál Maléter, which was negotiating in Tököl at the Soviet headquarters concerning troop withdrawal, was arrested by Soviet security personnel on 3 November under the personal command of General Serov, head of the KGB.

During the night of 3–4 November sixteen Soviet divisions, including air force and armoured divisions, began their concentrated attack on Budapest (see Map 2). The Hungarian army was unable to offer serious resistance and was swiftly disarmed. Early on 4 November, Imre Nagy issued a brief statement about the Soviet aggression. Then, to avoid the arrest that threatened, he accepted President Tito's invitation and fled to the Yugoslav Embassy. Although there were still a few places in Budapest and elsewhere in the country where freedom fighters led a bitter struggle against the Soviet army, the days of freedom were past.

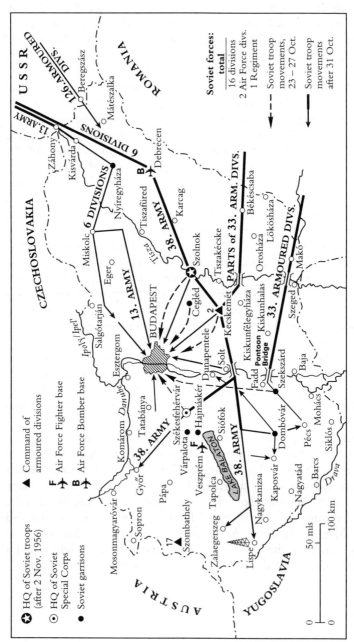

2 Soviet troop movements October–November 1956

CHAPTER FIVE

The Revolution and World Politics

From the narrative of events it is obvious that the Revolution's fate was decided by international politics, above all, by the decisions of the Soviet leadership, acting in the context of overall world politics. In order to understand these moves, it is necessary to survey the international implications of all that happened in Hungary after 23 October. If the events of the preceding years were connected to changes in world politics, after the outbreak of the armed uprising and the Soviet intervention, Hungary's fate came to be almost entirely dependent on the reactions of the great powers and other members of the world community.

HOPES AND ILLUSIONS IN HUNGARY

Although the claim has been interminably reiterated by communist propaganda, the west was not directly responsible for instigating the Hungarian Revolution. However, the previously mentioned hypocritical foreign policy of the United States toward eastern Europe undoubtedly contributed indirectly to the fact that social unrest in Hungary eventually manifested itself in the form of an armed uprising. Those young workers and students who risked their lives in taking up arms against the overwhelmingly superior forces of the Soviet military and the ÁVH were, for the most part, thoroughly convinced by all the misleading liberation propaganda that the west, particularly the United States, would make good on the promises to provide armed assistance to the Hungarian people if they rose up against Soviet domination, or at the very least that it would employ all the political weapons at its disposal in order to force the Soviet Union to acquiesce in the Hungarian desire for independence.

The principal foreign political demands of Hungarian society at the time of the Revolution were, for the most part, not founded upon an awareness of world political realities. This is due partly to the fact that the general public held illusions which hindered, and in some instances even precluded a clear assessment of Hungary's international circumstances, and partly to the general propensity of people to make unrealistic demands during the upheaval and agitation of revolution.

A significant portion of Hungarian society mistakenly believed (and still believes) that the spheres of influence established in Europe after the Second World War were just temporary arrangements and that the Revolution offered the western powers an exceptional opportunity to change them. The majority of Hungarians were only able to perceive those world political trends which were encouraging for their aspirations. Although the new orientation of east-west relations were leading to a rapprochement between the two world superpowers they continued believing in the unchanged US propaganda emphasizing that the United States would never write off the so-called captive nations. The armed freedom fighters in particular were counting on military intervention; it was precisely these people who harboured the greatest illusions regarding the world political environment, though they were generally aware of the fact that their struggle against the vastly superior Soviet forces would fail without outside support. Consequently the insurgents commonly appealed both personally to western journalists or diplomats and en masse before the Budapest legations of the western powers for political and military intervention as well as arms and ammunition.

It is important to note that the non-belligerent political entities which sprang up at the time of the uprising, such as the revolutionary and national committees and the workers' councils, did not make similar requests for western assistance. This was due partly to the general inclination toward self-restraint characteristic of the initial stages of the Revolution – for most people were quite aware that exaggerated repudiation of the Soviet Union would certainly provoke immediate Soviet intervention – and partly to the fact that most of these revolutionary organs were directed by intellectuals and workers who tended to advocate an essentially socialist 'Third Road' for Hungary which precluded the idea of western military intervention.

The widespread illusions regarding the will and ability of the United Nations to mediate a settlement of the Hungarian crisis are reflected clearly in the various revolutionary organizations and press. The Hungarian people viewed the UN (to which Hungary had gained membership in 1955) as being the pre-eminent forum for the resolution of international conflicts in general and not simply as an agent for conciliation between the great powers. Hungarian expectations regarding UN mediation were none the less of a most diverse nature: there was a universal hope among Hungarians that the Security Council or the General Assembly would be able to induce the Soviets to find a peaceful resolution to the Hungarian crisis; others went even further in their expectations, calling for UN observers or immediate intervention by UN military forces: there was even an 'eyewitness' who claimed to have seen an advance guard of UN forces at the border.

Practically from the very outset of the uprising the various revolutionary programmes gave special prominence to the demand that Soviet troops withdraw from Hungary, a contingency which was commonly regarded as an essential precondition for the general restoration of independence to the country. Hungarian public opinion at the time of the Revolution was unanimous concerning the question of sovereignty and all political programmes were based on the wish to remain outside the great power blocs. This desire was reflected in two interrelated demands: the withdrawal from the Warsaw Pact and the proclamation of Hungary's neutrality.

Contributing greatly to the general popularity of the notion of neutrality was the seemingly rational (though it too turned out to be erroneous) premise that the Soviet Union would not see any increased security threat in a neutral Hungary. It was also a generally held belief that since the Soviets had assented to a negotiated withdrawal from Austria then they might very well consider doing likewise in Hungary. The flaw in this logic was that whereas the Soviet withdrawal from Austria had come about as a result of an intensely negotiated compromise between the great powers, similar action in Hungary would have required unilateral concessions on the part of the Soviet Union – a variable which was, naturally, not part of the great power equation.

FOREIGN POLICY OF THE IMRE NAGY GOVERNMENT

From the very moment when Imre Nagy became prime minister on 24 October, he was faced with increasingly radical demands not only with regard to the internal reorganization of Hungarian society, but also concerning the restructuring of the country's international status, namely its position within the Soviet alliance.

Though few people were aware of it at the time of the outbreak of the Revolution, Imre Nagy had circulated a theoretical treatise among his friends in January of that year (later printed in his book *On Communism*) which expressed support for the *pancha sila*, or the five basic tenets of the non-aligned movement with regard to peaceful coexistence – mutual respect for national sovereignty and territorial integrity, non-interference in domestic affairs, equality, reciprocal benevolence, and fraternal cooperation – identifying the totality of these principles with the notion of national independence. Nagy also expressed his conviction that national independence was not simply a question of achieving international autonomy, but also had a social dimension as well. In more specific terms, Imre Nagy believed that it was the Yugoslav model, that is a socialist domestic order coupled with a non-aligned foreign policy, which offered Hungary the greatest chances for achieving national independence. It is important to note that none of Imre Nagy's thinking was based on Hungary taking any sort of unilateral action; he hoped that the encouraging trends perceptible in international political relations would eventually lead to the dissolution of the contentious world power blocs, thus enabling the countries of eastern Europe to continue to build socialism on a new foundation of national independence and equality and non-interference in internal affairs.

Nagy considered the latter scenario to be all the more possible in light of the Soviet Union's apparently friendly disposition toward the non-aligned movement at that time; it was above all the Soviet Union's rapprochement with Yugoslavia that fed the general illusion that the Soviets were prepared to accept the principle that building socialism could be based on a model other than of their own.

It was Imre Nagy's thankless task as prime minister to reconcile his measured vision regarding the restructuring of Hungary's international relations with the increasingly radical demands of the Revolution. Nagy was always very aware of the fact that the fate of the Revolution was entirely in the hands of the Soviet Union and from the very outset of negotiations held with a high-ranking Soviet crisis-management delegation led by Mikoyan and Suslov, Nagy attempted to convince the Soviets that with adequate support he would be capable of stabilizing the internal situation.

The peaceful resolution of the Polish crisis probably strengthened Nagy's conviction that the Soviets were interested in finding a similar settlement in Hungary, even if they had to grant a certain number of concessions in order to do so. It was for this reason that on 25 October Nagy suggested that calling for Soviet intervention had been a mistake and that in the interest of calming unrest among the people it would be wise to announce the government's intentions to initiate negotiations regarding the withdrawal of Soviet troops from Hungary. Later on that day Nagy made this announcement, despite vigorous Soviet objections, in the course of a radio address. On the following day Nagy, playing up the extreme social pressures under which the Hungarian leadership was operating, attempted to convince the Soviet delegation that over and above suppression of armed resistance, the most effective way to bring the prevailing disorder under control would be to place the party at the head of the mass social movement which had materialized with the Revolution.

The events of the following days seemed to vindicate Imre Nagy's policy toward the Soviets; his pledges to consolidate the situation in Hungary were designed to extract further concessions from them: on 29 October, Soviet military units began withdrawing from Budapest and the Soviet government's declaration of the following day included an explicit promise that it would lay new foundations for relations between the Soviet Union and other socialist countries based on equality and non-interference in domestic affairs; in addition, it promised not to reconsider the decision to withdraw Soviet troops from Hungary.

At nearly the same time, however, signs of the Soviet Union's real intentions began multiplying at an alarming rate: as already mentioned, beginning at 31 October came reports that fresh Soviet troops were entering the country, occupying all important strategic locations. It was at this point, when it became clear that the Soviet invasion, with the obvious aim of overthrowing and abducting the legitimate Hungarian government was imminent, that the cabinet decided to make an heroic last-ditch effort at rescuing the Revolution: Nagy announced Hungary's withdrawal from the Warsaw Pact and declared the country's intention to be neutral. At the same time he sent an appeal to the secretary-general of the United Nations requesting that the four great powers help defend Hungary's neutrality (see Chapter 4) and that this question be urgently placed on the agenda of the upcoming General Assembly.

The Imre Nagy government had therefore turned to the great western powers and the United Nations – always with the ideal of Austrian-style neutrality in mind – in a last-ditch effort to stave off the increasing threat of a Soviet invasion. Nagy himself was nevertheless quite aware of the extreme improbability of vigorous assistance from either the great western powers or the UN; he was also quite familiar with Soviet imperial politics and thus recognized that within the existing inter-national political context it was likewise very improbable that the Soviet leadership – for whom the suppression of the Revolution was never really more than a logistical question – would relinquish one of its strategically important dominions just because the government there had declared its independence.

Thus, even as Nagy launched a further appeal for UN action on 2 November, he continued to work desperately behind the scenes to try and work out some kind of an agreement with the Soviets. In the first days of November, Nagy summoned the ambassadors of the socialist countries, first of all Soviet Ambassador Andropov, in order to try and persuade them of the correctness of his policies. Moreover, Nagy informed Andropov that he was willing to rescind his appeal to the UN in exchange for a Soviet pledge not to engage in further military intervention; Nagy also requested an immediate audience with the highest-level Soviet leadership – a request which the Soviets promptly denied. Finally, in discussions held in Budapest with a Romanian party delegation on 3 November, Nagy attempted to coordinate a plan whereby Gheorghiu-Dej would petition Khrushchev for a Soviet-Hungarian summit meeting. On the very same day, however, the Soviet leadership was holding a summit meeting of a very different nature in Moscow with János Kádár in order to coordinate the violent overthrow of the Hungarian revolutionary government.

THE SOVIET BLOC AND THE REVOLUTION

As already mentioned, on 23 October the Soviet leadership only reluctantly agreed to comply with Gerő's request that Soviet troops assist in the dispersal of the mass demonstrations in Budapest. However, the next day they sent a crisis-management delegation to Budapest consisting of Mikoyan, Suslov, KGB leader Serov and the deputy chief of staff, I. Malinin. For several days after the outbreak of armed conflict, Khrushchev and the rest of the Soviet leadership continued to maintain hope that the newly appointed prime minister, Imre Nagy, would effectively quell the reigning disorder and that the Hungarian crisis could ultimately be resolved within the same framework of compromise and negotiation which had proved successful in Poland. In negotiations conducted with Nagy and the rest of the Hungarian leadership of 26 October Mikoyan and Suslov defined the outer limits of possible Soviet concessions in their expression of a willingness to allow some people who had previously belonged to non-communist parties into the government (the possibility of a multiparty system was not even considered) and a return of Soviet troops to their bases after the restoration of order, similar to what had occurred in Poland. They also warned the Hungarian leadership that further concessions might very well lead to the overthrow of the communist system, an eventuality which the Soviet delegation quite clearly suggested would evoke a vigorous response from Moscow. The Soviet leadership never entertained the slightest notion of allowing the restoration of a parliamentary system in Hungary for fear that it would lead to the disintegration of its vitally important east European security zone.

There were also significant ideological factors motivating the Soviets to suppress the Hungarian Revolution. As previously mentioned, during these years Soviet attempts to enlarge the world communist empire centred on the Third World; the Soviet leadership could well imagine the damage that might be done to these expansion efforts if Hungary were to be seen restoring multiparty democracy by way of an anti-Soviet uprising nearly ten years after the institution of communism.

The Soviets regarded the following elements to be of paramount importance to the maintenance of the communist system in the eastern European satellite states: a competent and unified Communist Party leadership; a potent and resolute state security apparatus; a loyal and disciplined armed force and military leadership, and a strict party control of all media. Any hint of unrest in any of these three institutions immediately set off warning bells within the Soviet decision-making mechanism; the breakdown of all four of them at once, as happened in Hungary in 1956, left the Soviets with only one option: armed intervention.

However it was in the short-term interests of the Soviet Union to exercise this radical option only if all possible peaceful means of resolving the crisis had already been exhausted; the Soviet desire to preserve communist bloc unity and the process of rapprochement with Yugoslavia, to improve the standing of communist parties in the west and propaganda efforts in the Third World, as well as to find a peaceful resolution to the Polish crises all weighed in against the option of armed intervention.

Tactical considerations also compelled the Soviets to make further concessions: On 28 October, they assented to a cease-fire, agreed to withdraw their military units from Budapest – without having first eradicated the groups of armed rebels – and did not take official issue with the passage in the new government communiqué pertaining to the initiation of negotiations over the eventual withdrawal of Soviet troops from Hungary. The Soviet government pronouncement of 30 October contained further pledges to examine the possibility of troop withdrawals from Hungary.

The developments of the days following the government's acceptance of the Revolution's essential demands on 28 October convinced the

Soviet delegation that the Leninist-Stalinist-type communist system was in jeopardy of collapsing in Hungary. They concluded, correctly, that Imre Nagy – whom they already held to be opportunistic and irresolute – was unable, and worse yet, unwilling to restrain those forces which were threatening to break up the entire Soviet system.

This on-the-spot assessment of the situation in Hungary led the Soviet leadership to the conclusion that the possibilities for peaceful resolution of the crisis had been exhausted; accordingly, on the second day of its session of 30 and 31 October, the presidium of the Central Committee of the CPSU reached a decision in favour of armed intervention and took the steps necessary to set Operation Whirlwind in motion.

On 1–2 November Khrushchev held talks with the leaders of the east European socialist countries and China (who just happened to be in Moscow), all of whom assured the Soviets of their continuing support. Though the leaders of Poland and China had earlier endorsed the revolutionary changes which were taking place in Hungary, more recent developments – above all the withdrawal from the Warsaw Pact and declaration of neutrality – implied for them a repudiation of the entire post-Second World War European geopolitical structure; for the Polish this geopolitical structure constituted the foremost guarantee of its border with Germany and as for the Chinese, Nagy's abolition of the single-party system amounted to conclusive evidence that he was a traitor. In the course of negotiations which took place during the night of 2–3 November on Brioni Island, the Soviets and Yugoslavs were able to come to an agreement regarding steps to be taken in response to the Hungarian Revolution, which the Soviet leadership found particularly reassuring since Tito had publicly expressed his solidarity with the Nagy government at the beginning of the Revolution. Recent developments in Hungary had greatly disappointed Tito, who had hoped that the Hungarians would look toward Yugoslavia for their new social, political and economic model. Therefore, to the great relief of Khrushchev and Malenkov, the Yugoslav leadership not only agreed that intervention was necessary, but also promised to help eliminate Imre Nagy and his adherents from political life.

WESTERN REACTIONS

Western governments – unlike their public opinion which expressed vivid solidarity with the Hungarian uprising from the beginning – were acutely aware of their limited room to manoeuvre within the existing

European status quo and reacted with extreme caution to the uprising in Hungary from its very beginning and, in most instances, went so far as to give explicit public endorsement of the principle of non-intervention. Behind the western response to the Hungarian Revolution was the realization that under the prevailing international political circumstances, any sort of western military intervention in Hungary contained the implicit threat of war with the Soviet Union, quite possibly to be waged with thermonuclear weapons, which would likely lead to the obliteration of the very eastern European peoples which intervention was designed to liberate.

Especially on the part of the three great western powers there existed the possibility of taking certain political steps between the two extremes of armed intervention and total passivity which might have encouraged the Soviet decision-makers to find a more constructive resolution to the crisis.

United States

The events which took place in Poland and, particularly, Hungary in October 1956 caught the US government completely by surprise, even though it was extremely well informed about the political changes which were taking place in these countries. Secretary of State John Foster Dulles had already publicly distanced the administration from the possibility of armed intervention during the Polish crisis, though this information never did reach those most affected by the crisis. In an appearance on the popular television political programme *Face the Nation* on 21 October, Dulles stated that the United States would not send troops to Poland even in the event of Soviet armed intervention. The US government was exceptionally pleased with what it deemed to be positive developments in the Polish crisis during the following days, for they had come about without any kind of American involvement whatsoever. Moreover, contrary to all the pessimistic predictions, the Soviets had not intervened militarily and had ultimately agreed to accept the new Polish leadership.

The Americans thus found the news of the uprising in Hungary to be all the more disturbing, especially since the US government had no previously prepared strategy for dealing with such an unlikely occurrence. It was at this time that the Eisenhower administration was confronted with the fact that, contrary to one of the predominant themes of the massive liberation propaganda it aimed at eastern Europe, even the United States, the world's greatest military power, had only very limited options regarding any sort of intervention within the Soviet sphere of influence. It was none the less very important for the United States to conceal this impotence in order to preserve its international prestige: it was for this reason that on 24 October, Dulles suggested to President Eisenhower that the issue of Soviet intervention should be broached in the Security Council (which indeed happened on 28 October after the three great western powers requested that the issue be placed on the Council's agenda).

On 26 October, the United States' highest level advisory body, the National Security Council, sat for the first and last time during the period of the Hungarian Revolution in order to evaluate the events taking place in eastern Europe and to plan what kind of official message to communicate regarding US policy on the region. Among the general confusion which reigned during the session there was one intelligent proposal made by Harold A. Stassen, the president's adviser on disarmament: Stassen suggested that it would be expedient to offer assurances to the Soviets that the United States would not seek to exploit the possible independence of the satellite countries in any way that could threaten the security of the Soviet Union. Although this suggestion was promptly rejected by the National Security Council, the next day proponents of the plan succeeded in getting the president to endorse an expanded version of Stassen's original proposal. According to this plan, the United States, either through Tito or some other diplomatic channel, would attempt to convince the Soviets that a zone of strictly neutral, non-NATO countries, politically akin to Austria, would offer them just as much security as the existing buffer of satellite countries. The essential logic behind the proposal was that during negotiations regarding the Austrian State Treaty it was precisely the Soviets who had insisted that Austria remain strictly neutral and not be allowed to join NATO. Of course the same possibilities for compromise didn't apply to the east European Soviet satellite countries as had applied to Austria, but within the strict confines which circumscribed the United States' room to manoeuvre, a plan offering the possibility of mutual concession, such as the plan then being proposed, was preferable to complete passivity. Ultimately Eisenhower instructed Secretary of State Dulles to build the message to the Soviets into the presidential campaign speech Dulles was to deliver in Dallas on 27 October. However Dulles, who had opposed the proposal from its very inception because it offered the Soviets exaggerated ideological concessions, watered it down – partly with the president's assent and partly on his own initiative – dropping any reference to both neutrality and prohibition on NATO membership. In the end, the US secretary of state's message to the Soviets consisted, in all, of the following celebrated sentence: 'We do not look upon these nations as potential military allies.'

This fundamentally modified version of Stassen's original proposal did not achieve its original aim of pacifying the Soviets, or perhaps more precisely, achieved it to an exaggerated degree. Whereas the original idea had been to try to induce concessions from the Soviet Union through explicit recognition of its security interests, the revised version was of a distinctly defensive tenor which the Soviets logically assumed to mean that the United States was not going to take any action whatsoever on behalf of the independence of eastern Europe. The US leadership none the less went to great lengths to make absolutely sure that the message reached its addressee: on 28 October, Henry Cabot Lodge, the US representative to the United Nations, quoted the passages from Dulles's speech which concerned the satellite countries during a session of the Security Council; on 29 October the US ambassador in Moscow received instructions to confidentially reiterate the germane points of the speech to the Soviet leadership, including Zhukov; and on 31 October Eisenhower himself reiterated the previously cited passage in the course of a televised address.

At the end of October a Special National Intelligence Estimate, prepared jointly by the CIA, the State Department and organizations of military intelligence, determined that the Soviets had only two options: either accede to Hungary's desire for independence and risk unleashing similar forces throughout the satellite countries or to forcibly reinstate their supremacy over the country. The authors of the report none the less left no doubt as to which option the Moscow leadership would choose in an emergency. Regarding possible US policy toward the crisis, the report of the National Security Council's advisory committee analyzing the recent events in Eastern Europe, completed by 31 October, basically expressed the view that prospects for concrete action were extremely limited, although it did contain one well-founded proposal for compromise with the Soviet Union according to which, if the Soviets withdrew their troops from Hungary, the Americans would, in exchange, make proportional reductions in the number of its troops stationed in western Europe.

The agenda for the 1 November meeting of the National Security Council called for deliberation over this document; however, before the meeting got under way, President Eisenhower, at the urging of Dulles, decided to postpone discussion on eastern Europe until a later date so that the Council could devote its entire time and energy to examination of the Suez crisis, which had degenerated into armed conflict on 29 October. The US leadership was not again inclined to occupy itself with the events taking place in Hungary until the time of the second Soviet intervention on 4 November. Eisenhower and Dulles had decided that since the United States really didn't have any effective means of exerting its influence inside the Soviet sphere, its energies should be concentrated on resolving the Suez crisis where it was faced with the task of laying down the law not with a rival superpower, but with its own military and political allies. In spite of its complications, this was a much easier and more feasible undertaking and within just a few days the resolute actions taken by the United States, particularly its economic arm twisting of Britain, had borne fruit.

Thus the sole international political forum which was apparently willing to give worthy consideration to the Hungarian crisis was the United Nations. However, the previously mentioned conflict of interest which arose among the great powers at the time of the simultaneous outbreak of the two international crises began to play itself out in the UN as well, just a few days after the Hungarian question had been placed on its agenda.

Britain, France and the Suez adventure

The governments of Britain and France, which were already preoccupied with preparations for an attack on Egypt, were likewise caught off guard by the developments in eastern Europe. Indeed, due to their paramount desire for success in the Middle East, the reaction of the British and French to the Soviet intervention in Hungary was even more cautious than the habitually restrained response of western governments to events in eastern Europe.

Contrary to the renown of the US secretary of state's previously cited Dallas address, it is a little known fact that representatives of both the British and French governments delivered similar messages to the Soviet Union which implied a recognition of Soviet security interests in eastern Europe. On 26 October French Foreign Minister Christian Pineau, in a speech delivered before a gathering of journalists, stressed that although the western powers welcomed the developments which were taking place in eastern Europe, it would be ill-advised to try to exploit them for their own military and political profit; Pineau furthermore insisted that raising the issue of relations between the west and eastern Europe was still dangerously premature and that, as for France, it would not intervene in Poland or Hungary under any circumstances. The British were even more adamant about avoiding even an inadvertent provocation of the Soviets and, furthermore, not giving them grounds for accusing the west of having in any way instigated the outbreak of the Hungarian Revolution. According to the memorandum of 27 October, written by Deputy Under-Secretary of State Sir John Ward, top secret sources had informed the British that the Soviets were preparing for western intervention in Hungary. Accordingly, on 1 November, the government declared in Parliament: 'It is not our slightest intention to try and exploit the events taking place in Eastern Europe in order to undermine the security of the Soviet Union'.

The striking simultaneity of the Suez and Hungarian crises inevitably raises the question whether the outbreak of the Hungarian Revolution had any bearing on the timing of the attack on Egypt which was planned during secret British – French – Israeli negotiations held at Sèvres between 22 and 24 October. Recently published monographs and primary source materials reveal that the date for the Israeli attack on Egypt (29 October) was almost certainly set during the first day of the Sèvres talks. When this conditional timetable was established, the foreign ministers of Britain and France immediately made it clear that they would have liked the Israeli attack to be fixed for an even earlier date. The rationale for this was not the presumption that the Soviet Union would be preoccupied with the crisis in Hungary, as is commonly assumed, since the Hungarian Revolution broke out only on the next day. However, the Polish crisis, which broke out a few days earlier on 19 October, may have exercised some influence on the timing of the attack – a suggestion which appears in various Israeli sources. But the most important reason for the haste of the British and French was undoubtedly that their expeditionary forces had been in a state of full preparedness – a condition which could not be maintained indefinitely – for quite some time simply waiting for the political green light to begin the attack on Egypt.

The official protocol containing the results of the secret Sèvres negotiations was finally signed on 24 October. In this protocol the day of the Israeli attack is permanently fixed for 29 October; thus the fact of the outbreak of the Hungarian uprising did not cause the slightest change to the existing strategy and, contrary to earlier suppositions, did not serve to bring forward the date of the military action in the Suez. Available sources even raise doubts as to whether the subject of Hungary even came up during the final day of negotiations on 24 October when news of the Budapest uprising could very well have reached the negotiating partners. However, according to Ben Gurion's diary, he learned of the outbreak of the Hungarian Revolution and the alleged Soviet suppression thereof only after his return to Israel, sometime during the midday of 25 October.

THE HUNGARIAN QUESTION IN THE UNITED NATIONS

The US administration, primarily for reasons of prestige, decided on 25 October that, in concert with its allies, it would initiate discussion in the United Nations on the subject of the Hungarian uprising. The British and French initially expressed reluctance when Dulles proposed on 26 October that the three countries launch a joint initiative to convene a meeting of the Security Council. With the Suez action having already been definitely decided upon, the British and French leadership was worried that if the question of Soviet intervention in Hungary were put on the agenda and discussed in the UN, it might serve as a precedent for a similar procedure regarding the joint Israeli – British – French attack on Egypt which was to take place at the end of October. But since they had not informed the United States of their plans, they were forced to accede to American pressure and on 27 October the United States, Britain and France submitted a joint request that the Security Council be convened to examine the situation in Hungary.

From this date until 3 November the representatives of these three great powers met continually behind the scenes in order to work out a UN strategy which all could agree on; the comportment of the United States, Britain and France during the three Security Council sessions which dealt with the Hungarian question on 28 October and on 2 and 3 November was completely planned in advance during these secret negotiations.

In the days preceding the Israeli attack on Egypt the UN representative of the three great western powers agreed that it was imperative to voice emphatic public condemnation of the Soviet intervention and that beyond this action they would employ a wait-and-see policy until the confused situation in Hungary became more transparent. The consequence of this policy was that the three western powers which had placed the Hungarian question on the agenda did not even introduce a draft proposal during the 28 October session of the Security Council. After the widening of the armed conflict in the Middle East with the engagement of Britain and France on October 31, the tenor of the negotiations among the great western powers regarding Hungary changed completely. Eisenhower and Dulles, who had placed increasing importance on establishing good relations with the Arab world with the aim of expanding US influence in the Middle East, reacted angrily to the actions of its European allies. Not only did they publicly condemn the Suez action, but also they instructed the US representative to the UN to submit a draft proposal calling for the immediate cessation of all military operations in the Middle East, a motion which brought about a circumstance which had no precedent in the history of the UN with the representatives of the United States and the Soviet Union voting in concert against Britain and France.

As a result of the sudden deterioration in relations between the western powers, subsequent discussions between them regarding the Hungarian question were conducted in an increasingly icy atmosphere in which the negotiating partners were not really interested in condemning, much less impeding, Soviet intervention, but wanted rather to exploit the Hungarian crisis in the name of their own, in this case drastically conflicting, great power interests. Beginning at this time, the British and French undertook to get the Hungarian question moved from the Security Council to the emergency session of the General Assembly – which had been convened to discuss the Suez crisis – where they hoped that the simultaneous treatment of two issues would lead to a mitigation of the censure they had been receiving. Transfer of the Hungarian question to the General Assembly would have been of incidental benefit to the forces of change in Hungary, for in the General Assembly there is no veto power, which left at least the theoretical possibility that the UN would pass a resolution having a positive influence on the outcome of events in Hungary. The sole objective of the US leadership under the existing circumstances was to resolve the Middle Eastern crisis; therefore they did everything within their powers to frustrate the afore-mentioned strategy of the British and the French: until 4 November the Americans succeeded in preventing them from submitting a draft proposal concerning the Hungarian question in the Security Council and further blocked them from referring the question to the emergency session of the General Assembly via the 'uniting for peace' procedure.

After the second Soviet intervention the US representative to the UN, Henry Cabot Lodge, unilaterally implemented the British – French strategy without asking for the cooperation of his European Security Council allies, with whom he had broken off negotiations regarding Hungary the previous day as a means of punishment for British and French actions in the Suez. When the Security Council was subsequently convened upon the arrival of the news regarding renewed Soviet intervention on 4 November, the US representative initiated a measure which effectively circumvented the Soviet veto and referred the Hungarian question directly to the emergency session of the General Assembly. On the afternoon of the very same day a large majority of this body voted to adopt a draft resolution – likewise submitted unilaterally by the US representative – which condemned the intervention of the Soviet Union, called for it to withdraw its troops from Hungary, and recognized the right of the Hungarian people to a government which would represent its national interests.

At the same time, this resolution – which the British and French supported despite its unilateral submission by the United States – made no reference to the recognition of Hungary's neutrality, for which Imre Nagy had so emphatically appealed in his messages to the UN secretary-general on 1 and 2 November. This may be due in part to the fact that there was much disagreement within the US leadership regarding whether Hungary's neutrality served the interests of the United States. The concept of Hungarian neutrality engendered a good deal of support in the State Department where it had already surfaced as a topic of discussion days before Nagy launched his appeals to the UN. President Eisenhower himself sympathized with the idea of establishing a zone of neutral states in central and eastern Europe but he hoped to achieve this aim through negotiations with the Soviets in a general framework of general reconstruction of east – west relationships. However Dulles, who had sharp misgivings regarding the increasingly powerful non-aligned movement, and was therefore generally ill-disposed toward the idea of neutrality, not surprisingly came out against the idea with regard to Hungary. Dulles firmly believed that if, perchance, Hungary were to succeed in its struggle to free itself of Soviet domination, the United States should not rest satisfied with the country's neutrality when there existed the real possibility of incorporating it into the western sphere of influence. And although Dulles was hospitalized on 3 November and did not return to his office until mid-December, it was his way of thinking which ultimately determined the conduct of the United States vis-à-vis the Hungarian Revolution during the critical first days of November.

In the early hours of the morning of 4 November, the United States none the less fervently condemned renewed Soviet intervention in Hungary – Eisenhower even sent a personal message of protest to Bulganin – and in this way succeeded in leading the world to believe that it had, from the very outset, played a constructive role in attempts to settle both the Suez and Hungarian crises.

The real clash of conflicting viewpoints in the United Nations, contrary to earlier interpretations, took place not between the western powers and the Soviet Union during meetings of the Security Council where what was said on both sides was primarily for public consumption, but behind the scenes, in the course of secret negotiations between the representatives of the United States, Britain and France.

The result of the discord which arose in relations between the great western powers over the Suez crisis was that the UN was unable to take firm steps toward the resolution of the Hungarian question at a time (1–3 November) when the circumstances in Hungary, such as Nagy's request for UN mediation, made such steps feasible.

However, one should not overestimate the potential influence of any UN resolution by the Emergency Session of the General Assembly condemning Soviet intervention, a measure which remained a distinct possibility right up until 3 November. The Soviet Union, in light of its status as a world superpower and the reassuring pledges it had received from the United States, was by no means disposed to let the moral authority of UN resolutions prevent it from intervening militarily, if necessary, to restore order in a country within its own sphere of influence.

The discord among the western powers which came about as a result of the Middle Eastern conflict no doubt made things easier for the Soviets, though it is fairly certain that even without the Suez crisis they would have pursued a similar policy, just as they made the same decision regarding Czechoslovakia in 1968. Similarly, western passivity was not caused by the Suez crisis, but by a limitation to its range of options in eastern Europe implicit in the prevailing status quo and the notion of spheres of influence. The Suez crisis simply served as a convenient excuse, especially for the United States, in order to explain why, after years of liberation propaganda, it was not capable of extending even the smallest amount of support to an east European nation which had risen in arms in an attempt to liberate itself from Soviet domination.

CHAPTER SIX

Rearguard Struggles

Early on the morning of 4 November, Imre Nagy and other members of the government who had remained in the Parliament building did not at first believe that the Soviets had broken their word, that the Soviet army was marching against Budapest. When the sound of artillery was heard clearly in the building, Nagy, Ferenc Donáth and Zoltán Tildy composed a statement, which Nagy then read from the broadcasting station in the Parliament building at 5:20 a.m.:

> This is Prime Minister Imre Nagy speaking. Today at daybreak Soviet troops attacked our capital with the obvious intention of overthrowing the lawful democratic Hungarian government. Our troops are in combat. The government is in its post. I notify the people of our country and the entire world of this fact.

In this address, repeated in various languages, Nagy did not call for armed resistance. That would have been pointless in view of overwhelming Soviet strength and the limitations of the Hungarian People's Army. But the possibility that individual military units might offer resistance on their own, though not expressed in the address, was not excluded. At the time of the broadcast, the government was still at its post, but soon the prime minister and his close associates, fearing arrest by Soviet occupation forces, took refuge in the Yugoslav Embassy in Budapest. They had lost contact with Pál Maléter and his delegation, who had gone to Soviet headquarters for negotiations on the withdrawal of Soviet troops; it was to be assumed that they had been arrested by the KGB. It was likely that Soviet units were on their way to the Parliament building to detain the remaining members of the government.

As the last broadcast of Free Kossuth Radio, Julius and Éva Háy, on behalf of the Writers' Union, turned to the intellectuals of the world for support in a dramatic appeal, repeated over and over again in several languages.

THE FIGHT AGAINST SUPERIOR SOVIET FORCE

The forces that were unleashed against Budapest and the other industrial cities by the Soviet army would have easily defeated the Hungarian national army in full battle readiness. But the Hungarian army was, in early November, anything but combat-ready.

Aside from a few despairing attempts, the regular troops did not even take up arms against the Soviet forces moving from Uzhgorod against Budapest along two march routes (see Map 2, p. 82). The Soviets proceeded from garrison to garrison disarming the still intact Hungarian forces, so there was no possibility of armed resistance by the army. Wherever the slightest attempt was made, it ended with shooting and loss of life. On their march through the country, the Soviets had taken many prisoners: the leading figures of the workers' councils and other organizations in Miskolc, Debrecen and Veszprém were arrested and sent off to the Soviet Union. At some places in the provinces, strenuous fighting occurred involving individual Hungarian soldiers. The sound of artillery barrage continued for days in Budapest, and Soviet tanks and armoured vehicles moved in all directions through the city. The people were gripped by fear and the feeling of hopelessness. Twelve years after war's end, people again sought protection in the air-raid shelters, no one went to work, and traffic was entirely still.

But the armed insurrectionist groups did not bow to the Soviet army without a fight. Because the Soviet forces entered the capital from several directions, the main centres of resistance developed at their points of entrance. Larger armed groups continued to fight in Corvin Passage on the Pest side, in the south-eastern suburb of Pesterzsébet, and at several points near Üllői Street, at Széna Square in Buda, and also in places around the main railway station (Baross Square) and in the strategically located Palais Schmidt in Buda (see Map 1, p. 56). While the numbers of fighters changed constantly, we know that in the Corvin Passage there were some two thousand, and the groups at Széna Square and in Pesterzsébet numbered about a thousand each on 4 November. At other places the strength of the more important resistance groups oscillated between 300 and 600. In Kilián Barracks, for a while regarded as the headquarters of the National Guard during the Revolution, only a small group of fighters held out and opened fire on the Soviet tanks that were moving from Üllői Street into the city centre. The response was heavy artillery fire that destroyed the entire block.

The invading forces caused extensive damage in Budapest. The rows of buildings along the invasion routes and on the circular boulevard were fired upon at second-storey level by the tanks, and the destruction left behind reminded of the fighting during the siege of the city toward the end of the Second World War. Only because the populace retained something of those war memories and fled to the cellars was it possible to avoid loss of life in the thousands.

After the invasion the capital was placed under military administration. The commandant in Budapest, General Grebennik, the deputy of the KGB chief, General Serov, released his first instruction on 6 November, a curfew from seven o'clock in the evening until seven o'clock in the morning. The populace was called upon to follow the commands of military patrols without resistance. Those armed rebels, but also unarmed citizens, who crossed paths with the patrols were sent off to the Soviet Union, and held for several weeks, mainly in the Carpatho-Ukraine.

Organized struggle against the powerful opponent lasted only a few days. In the Corvin Passage, at Baross Square, and at the Schmidt Palais it ended on 8 November; in Kispest and Pesterzsébet on 10 November. Resistance on the Danube island Csepel lasted the longest. That place was particularly important because an anti-aircraft unit had joined forces with the fighting workers to delay for several days the march of Soviet troops from the south to the inner districts of Budapest. The streets were effectively defended with a dozen anti-aircraft guns, and on 7 November a Soviet plane was actually shot down over the harbour. When Soviet troops took Csepel, and also the industrial city Dunapentele (the former Sztálinváros), one of the major provincial centres of resistance, on 11 November, the uprising was broken – even though there were still isolated skirmishes in Budapest and elsewhere.

After the invasion, the insurrectionists had installed new broadcasting stations, or continued the use of their old ones, calling upon the populace to resist the occupation and appealing to international public opinion for support. Their broadcasts, received by foreign stations, remained on the air for a few more days.

It is not known even now how many dead and injured were sustained by Soviet forces in putting down the Hungarian Revolution. The pictures of burned-out tanks and soldiers' corpses, along with later reports from resistance fighters, suggest substantial losses in men and material. It is very possible that the military command preferred to minimize the losses and failed to report all the dead and missing.

Recently declassified Soviet documents report the losses as 669 dead, 1,450 wounded and 51 missing.

The number of Hungarian losses in the armed uprising between 23 October and 11 November was set at a minimum of 2,700 dead with ten times as many injured in a secret report of the Statistical Office compiled in 1957. Of the dead, 1,330 were workers, 44 were students and 196 were children under 14 years of age. Yet this figure can by no means include all those who fell in battle or were shot in the streets, many of whom were buried in public parks and gardens. Even less reliable is this figure for the casualties in the countryside, to say nothing of those shot or injured during the second intervention of the Soviet Army. Neither are there trustworthy figures for those who died while trying to flee the country. Perhaps a thorough study of local records, now underway, will produce a more reliable information on the loss in human life.

As it became obvious that further armed resistance was pointless, many fled the expected retaliation. Thousands who feared – rightly, as would become evident – the restoration of communist dictatorship, even if under new names and in modified form, headed for Austria or Yugoslavia. Flight was not hopeless, for the minefields on the western border (the notorious 'Iron Curtain') had been largely removed earlier in 1956 and the border police had in part dismantled itself. The borders, impassable after 1948–49, were practically open from the end of October until late November. But even after the western and southern frontiers were again closed by Soviet or new Hungarian patrols, the people in border areas found ways to guide thousands through no man's land. Many were captured during flight; others lost their way and froze or drowned as they crossed rivers. There were many young people among those who were fleeing, people who had little to lose and who were confident of finding a new life abroad. But there were also many who had been victimized by the Rákosi regime, their freedom and basis of existence stolen from them, and others just liberated from prison by the Revolution, who chose flight. Students and young professionals, many of whom had been active in the Revolution, naturally formed a significant part of the exodus. But all sectors of the population produced refugees and in 1957 there was hardly a Hungarian family that didn't lose at least one relative or a friend. According to the figures of the UN High Commissioner for Refugees, by the end of 1956, 200,600 people had left the country. This number amounted to 2 per cent of the country's total population, a very high proportion for a mass migration. However, in certain parts of the country – mainly in western Hungary and the capital – the ratio was certainly much higher.

The difficulties of refugee life caused a small number, maybe some 16,000 to 18,000 – most of them in the first months after the Revolution's defeat – to return, especially when the Kádár regime offered amnesty for participation in revolutionary actions. Several freedom-fighters, who took this announcement at face value and returned to Budapest paid with their lives for their trustfulness.

INSTALLATION OF THE KÁDÁR GOVERNMENT

The group around Imre Nagy took refuge in the Yugoslav Embassy, hoping that they could go from there to Yugoslavia and continue their political activity on behalf of a free Hungary. Today we know that the 'asylum' offered by the Yugoslav government was the outcome of an agreement between Tito and Khrushchev concerning the 'elimination' of Imre Nagy.

At almost the same time, a radio station, probably from Szolnok or from Soviet Ukraine, reported that a 'Revolutionary Worker and Peasant Government' had been founded that would take up the 'fight against counter-revolution' with the help of Soviet forces. This report was purported to have came from Budapest and was signed by János Kádár, Ferenc Münnich and two other old communists. In the manifesto, entitled 'Open Letter to the Working People of Hungary,', Kádár and his comrades explained the need for this formation by the absence of any room for activity 'within the increasingly reactionary and ineffectual Imre Nagy government to oppose the growing counter-revolutionary threat to the People's Republic, the worker–and–peasant power, and the accomplishment of socialism'. Further, they had decided 'to fight against the pressing danger of reaction and fascism and their mass murdering followers with all their strength'. The open letter closed with an appeal: 'We call upon all loyal sons of our People's Republic, all true socialists, especially communists, workers, and miners, the best sons of the peasantry, and working intellectuals to support all measures of the Revolutionary Worker-and-Peasant Government and its struggle for popular liberation.'

When Soviet tanks encircled the Parliament building on the morning of 4 November, an agreement was reached with the troop commander, for the sake of avoiding bloodshed, specifying that the building would be evacuated voluntarily and that civilians within would be assured safe exit. Following Minister of State Zoltán Tildy those within then left the building, in accordance with the agreement. Only Minister of State István Bibó remained behind. As representative of the legal Hungarian government, he had on that very morning framed the following declaration:

> Hungary has no intention of pursuing an anti-Soviet policy. It desires truly to live in the community of east European peoples, of free nations that wish to organize their lives in a community ruled by freedom, equality, and freedom from exploitation. I reject before the entire world the slanderous claim that the glorious Hungarian Revolution was stained by fascist or anti-semitic excesses. The Hungarian people only opposed the alien army of the conqueror and its own units of executioners. The rough and ready justice that we experienced for a few days in the streets was brought under control just as the new government brought to a halt the unarmed reappearance of old conservative forces. The assertion that this need justified calling or, better, recalling a large alien army into the country is cynical and irresponsible. On the contrary, the presence of this army on our soil is a principal cause of unrest and disruption. I call upon the Hungarian people to regard neither the occupation force nor the puppet government it may install as a legal authority but rather to employ every means of passive resistance against it, excepting only the interruption of public services and water supply in Budapest. I am not in a position to command armed resistance, for . . . I do not know the military situation and it would be irresponsible of me to decide about shedding the blood of Hungary's youth. The Hungarian people have sacrificed enough blood to demonstrate to the world their commitment to freedom and justice. It is now the turn of the powers of the world to demonstrate the force of the founding principles of the United Nations and the power of the peaceloving peoples. I beseech the Great Powers and the United Nations to intervene wisely and courageously for the freedom of my subjugated people. I declare that the only authorized representative of Hungary abroad and the legal head of its diplomatic service is Minister of State Anna Kéthly.
> May God save Hungary
> Dated in the Parliament building, 4 November 1956.
> István Bibó, Minister of State.

A few days later, Bibó delivered copies of his statement to the more important western diplomatic representatives, and that proved to be the last official act of the legal Hungarian government. Still in the morning of 4 November, Bibó sent a cable, through the United States legation in Budapest, to President Eisenhower, urging him to act as mediator in both the Middle Eastern and Hungarian crises. Bibó suggested that a compromise might be reached by which the Soviet troops would leave Hungary in return of the British and French troops' withdrawal from Egypt.

The 4 November, when Soviet troops began their march toward Budapest, was a Sunday. On the next day, according to decisions by revolutionary committees and workers' councils, work was to resume throughout the country. But in reaction to the Soviet invasion, the country was gripped by a general strike.

People did not want to yield to the facts. They did not want to believe that the Revolution, generally regarded as the high point of Hungarian history, could be destroyed by naked force. They waited for a miracle, kept their hopes alive for a long time, and offered active and passive resistance in diverse forms. One rumour had it that Generals Maléter and Király had withdrawn into the Bakony Mountains and would resume the armed struggle. The intervention of the UN was expected daily. Even pragmatists who denied themselves such hopes could not believe that the occupation force would find, after such a unanimous expression of the national will, enough people ready to enter into their service, organize a party, and betray the Revolution and the sacrifices brought for the country's liberty.

And in fact the Soviets did not entrust the 'normalization' to anyone. Together with Kádár, three leading men of the CPSU presidium came to Budapest: Malenkov, Suslov and Aristov. They, together with General Serov of the KGB, remained in Budapest for about a month – of course, unknown to the public – in charge of establishing the political, military and police power of the new regime, of 'making order'.

János Kádár and his colleagues returned from Szolnok to Budapest in Soviet military vehicles on 7 November, the anniversary of the Russian Revolution. Together with additional newly designated ministers – including two former Social Democrats, György Marosán and Sándor Rónai, who learned of their appointments over the radio – the members of the new government took the oath of office, administered by István Dobi, head of the Presidial Council, and thus regarded themselves as legitimized. The Kádár government withdrew executive authority from the revolutionary organs, restored the legal status of the pre-revolutionary state institutions, and called officials of the public service to resume their functions.

Although the armed struggle was still going on, the government began trying to gain the confidence of the people. The anniversary of the Russian Revolution, 7 November, was made a normal working day, and the Kossuth-arms of 1848 was adopted as the official state emblem. A wage increase of 8–15 per cent was announced and the 'childless' tax, paid since 1951 by single persons and childless couples, was cancelled.

János Kádár, in his first public address on 11 November, declared the uprising defeated and announced that work had resumed everywhere in the provinces. He emphasized that the rebels had not fought against the Hungarian People's Republic but only against the crimes of the Rákosi clique – although the insurrectionists included many who had sought the restoration of capitalism. In the same speech, he promised a thorough correction of past mistakes and declared 15 March, the anniversary of the 1848 Revolution, a national holiday.

THE ABDUCTION OF IMRE NAGY AND ASSOCIATES

Meanwhile, Imre Nagy and the others who had sought refuge in the Yugoslav Embassy could only wait, being effectively cut off from the outside world, to see what might happen to them. The embassy building was surrounded by Soviet tanks and sentries and no one, except for diplomats and embassy personnel, was allowed to enter. During his stay there from 4 to 22 November, Nagy was repeatedly urged to resign and recognize the Kádár government. Nagy rejected these urgings emphatically.

He was secure in this position because of the unqualified support of his political allies. Except for Kádár and Sándor Kopácsi, the police chief seized by the Soviets, Nagy had with him in the embassy the entire Executive Committee of the anti-Stalinist Hungarian Socialist Workers' Party (MSZMP) founded on 31 October. Had Kádár and his accomplices succeeded, at this time or even later, in persuading Nagy to relinquish power officially, it would have amounted to an acknowledgement that the Revolution had, under his leadership, abandoned the legitimate national and democratic goals, and that would have had unpredictable consequences. Not only would it have influenced the United Nations and other international forums negatively, but also it would have precluded the development of a broad solidarity in world opinion that survived the defeat of the Revolution and preserved for decades the sympathy accorded to Hungary's democratic independence movement.

The Hungarian politicians in the Yugoslav Embassy continued to demand the removal of Soviet troops, the acceptance of Hungary's withdrawal from the Warsaw Pact and neutrality, and the restoration of a multiparty system. Despite their isolation, they kept themselves informed. They followed closely the news on Hungarian and foreign radio and found other sources of information on the course of developments outside the embassy, above all on the continuing resistance of the workers. It became clear to them that the objectives of the Revolution now depended entirely on the workers' councils.

After two weeks at the embassy, the 'fugitives' realized that they could not continue to expect Yugoslav hospitality. The Yugoslav diplomats demanded guarantees from the Kádár government that those enjoying refuge in the embassy could return without hindrance to their residences. Finally, on 21 November Kádár and Münnich officially signed a letter of safe conduct requested by the Yugoslavs. However, already in December 1956, Kádár conceded before the party leadership that the Yugoslavs had been informed orally that the written guarantee they had received on this point would not be honoured.

On the evening of 22 November the politicians and their families in the embassy were persuaded to board a bus that would supposedly take them directly home. Instead they spent the night at the KGB compound on the outskirts of the city, in Mátyásföld, and were flown on the next day to Romania where they were held under strict security guard, completely isolated from the outside world, in Snagov not far from Bucharest.

The Kádár government circulated a great variety of lies about Imre Nagy's fate. Delegations from the workers' councils wishing to speak with the legal prime minister were told that Nagy and his compatriots had chosen to go abroad because of possible assassination attempts, or that they had requested political asylum in Romania. The abducted politicians protested constantly to Hungarian and Romanian party organs about their treatment but of course to no avail.

Those prisoners who were later tried were arrested in the spring of 1957 in Romania and transferred to Hungary. Their families, more than twenty women and children enduring steadily worsening conditions, could return home only after the trials were completed and the executions carried out. For months they knew nothing of the fates of their husbands and fathers, only to learn finally from the newspapers of their execution or prison sentences.

WORKERS' COUNCILS HOLD OUT

As the armed struggle ended, the workers' own organizations became the strongest and most effective centres of resistance. After 4 November they were still being formed in plants where no councils had been elected during the Revolution. A countrywide wave of strikes developed under the direction of the councils. Each new strike was proof that the population did not accept the Soviet-sponsored Kádár regime.

The inventories of demands of the workers' councils contained many common elements. Almost all of the resolutions and manifestos called for the immediate withdrawal of Soviet troops from Hungary, a free press and, in order to prevent the infiltration of the military by former state security personnel, worker control over army and police, as well as amnesty for military and civilian participants in the insurrection and the return of all those removed to the Soviet Union. At the head of the lists, of course, stood the requirement of preserving and strengthening worker self-governance, the reinstatement of Imre Nagy, and implementation of the neutrality declaration.

The development of workers' councils at the district level began in Budapest, with a view to achieving better coordination of the activities of the individual factory councils and increasing their effectiveness by means of joint actions. The Revolutionary Worker Council of Újpest, having taken the place of the district revolutionary council, proposed on 12 November the formation of a central workers' council for Budapest and called by leaflet for a meeting to this end on the following day. The leaflet stated among other things that 'the further path of the Revolution will be determined only by the Hungarian people and perhaps first of all by the Budapest workers'.

A government decision by way of response was published on 13 November recognizing workers' councils only as organs of worker self-governance at the factory level: 'The organs of worker self-governance in the factory are the councils. Their jurisdiction includes all aspects of life in the factory.' The main purpose of this decision was to exclude the councils from politics. The economically devastating wave of strikes had made abundantly clear that the government had no popular support and would therefore have to negotiate with the workers' councils. But before the first meeting of government representatives and council delegates, several members and the chairman of the revolutionary committee of Újpest were arrested. At the same time, the central delegates' meeting, scheduled for the city hall in Újpest, was disrupted by the passage of Soviet tanks. Nevertheless, on 14 November in the electric plant Egyesült Izzó, where ten days before the first workers' council came into being, a Central Workers' Council of Greater Budapest (KMT) was established. A number of writers took part in this founding meeting. István Bibó's 'Draft Proposal' of 6 November on a compromise solution of the Hungarian problem (see p. 115) was read and a resolution adopted calling for establishment of workers' councils at the district level.

Central Workers' Council of Greater Budapest

The KMT leaders were summoned to the Parliament building for discussions on the evening of 14 November. It is now beyond question that the government did not aim to reach an agreement but wanted only to sound out the KMT position and gain some time. The government wanted mainly to have work resume, but the KMT coupled a return to work with political conditions. The cooperative efforts of the workers' councils in KMT proceeded swiftly. Delegates from numerous factories met on 15 November at the headquarters of the Budapest streetcar works. Tibor Déry spoke for the Writers' Union and a government representative was also present.

Negotiations continued on the same night with the government, focusing on three basic topics. The first was the creation of a country-wide organization of workers' councils, against which János Kádár argued that nothing of the sort exists elsewhere and that it would in any case be superfluous in a people's democracy. The second point was the withdrawal of Soviet troops, concerning which Kádár maintained that only the government could negotiate this matter and then only under the conditions that work resume and public order be restored. The third concern was the right to strike, the KMT insisting that it was the workers' only weapon and that, if it were abrogated, there would be no assurance that demands would be met. Kádár argued that the worker-and-peasant government represents the proper interests of the workers and that a legal guarantee of the right to strike is therefore unnecessary.

Although the KMT continued to regard the right to strike as a legitimate means, the overwhelming majority voted to resume work, on grounds that the country's desperate economic condition and the hardships inflicted on the people by the strike were overriding. On 16 November the KMT addressed the workers as follows:

> Brothers! Filled with a sense of responsibility for our sorely tested country, we have come to the conviction, regardless of any outside pressure, that it is necessary, for economic, humanitarian, and social reasons, to resume production without delay.
>
> In this critical situation it is a requirement of reason and of healthy humanitarianism, of conscience and the heart, that you – without relinquishing the right to strike – return to work on 17 November.
>
> We assure you solemnly that this decision does not signify our willingness to give up one iota of the basic demands and accomplishments of the popular uprising. Negotiations will continue and we are convinced that the remaining unresolved issues can be settled by efforts on both sides.
>
> Be united and steadfast! Trust and support us!

That the ending of the strike was not seen as abdication of the struggle is shown by the replacement of the KMT chairman, viewed by the majority as too ready for compromise after the negotiations of 15 November, by the energetic and radical Sándor Rácz, a 23–year-old toolmaker from the Beloiannis Plant for Telephone Technology. The other new leading figure of the KMT was the toolmaker Sándor Bali.

As a result of the KMT resolution, by 19 November work resumed in most of the country's factories, but the plan to establish a nationwide workers' council remained on the agenda. The founding conference was set for 21 November, but the arriving council leaders found the National Stadium, the intended setting, surrounded by Soviet tanks. Although some of the delegates from Budapest and the provinces gathered in the headquarters of the municipal streetcar works and discussed the coordination of activities, the founding of a national workers' council failed. This was a major victory for the government. Kádár and his colleagues did everything possible to prevent the establishment of a nationwide umbrella organization, for they knew that they would have difficulty in dismantling such a strong organization. The 'worker and peasant government' feared worker solidarity.

Although it appeared that normality had returned when work resumed, the government was unable to count on popular support. On the initiative of the Revolutionary Council of Hungarian Intellectuals, which had endorsed the KMT position, on 23 November between two and three o'clock – commemorating the events of the Revolution one month before – the streets of Budapest were completely vacated, as if the city had died. The day was observed in the provinces with warning strikes.

On 23 November, as the KMT delegates negotiated with General Grebennik about the kidnappings and the ending of the curfew, Imre Nagy and his fellow prisoners had already been removed to Romania. At the same time, the attacks on the KMT by the government in the mass media made it clear that the negotiations would produce no significant results. But KMT refused to stop the struggle and continued its organizational efforts.

Appeals and leaflets were sent to the provinces by KMT, and organizers went to the larger plants to help with the establishment of workers' councils at the local level. On 27 November a letter went to local workers' organizations urging them to make contact with the organization in the capital and, in cases where councils had not emerged, to form new ones. An important feature of the letter was that it took a position against both the Rákosi regime and any capitalist restoration. The KMT also announced in the letter the wish to make contact with Imre Nagy because one could not believe the official explanations of his group leaving the country. The possibly most important sentence read: 'The factories are in our hands, the hands of the workers' councils.' The government knew this too and wanted, above all, to terminate it.

The KMT never recognized the official trade union organization (SZOT) of the pre- and post-revolutionary period, and it spoke out against the formation of units of the MSZMP or any other political party in the plants. It also protested that the government would not approve publication of its own press organ. Nevertheless, on 30 November there appeared the 'Bulletin of the Central Workers' Council of

Greater Budapest' in mimeographed form. There was regular contact between KMT and the various groups of intellectuals. KMT published a dramatic appeal by the Writers' Union in its 'Bulletin' on 5 December.

Although the KMT demanded the suspension of those leaders who had compromised themselves in the Rákosi years, the Kádár regime insisted on its right to designate leadership cadres and reinstated factory directors who had been deposed for professional or political reasons by the workers' councils. And yet at the end of November the councils were still the actual 'owners' of plants and enterprises. In the constant, almost daily negotiations between government and KMT, the leaders of the workers were always more determined, holding firmly to their original positions. The government tried to divide the other side by favouring the less steadfast worker-leaders, those more inclined to compromise.

Toward the end of November the number of arrests increased and many council members who had not played leading roles were arrested. This led the KMT to consider a nationwide general strike in protest against these police measures. At a meeting on 8 December the decision was made to stage a warning strike on 11–12 December. The delegates learned during the meeting that, on that same day, miners had been fired upon in Salgótarján when they demonstrated against the arrest of workers' council members, and thirty-nine people were killed. This news provided the final impetus for the KMT to declare a 48–hour strike in protest against the government's terrorism and repression.

Final wave of strikes

It was no secret in the central council that the government wanted to suppress it, so it seemed appropriate to show the strength of the KMT. The underground paper, *Október Huszonharmadika* (23 October), published on 10 December, under the title 'Strike', both the KMT strike decision and the government decree dissolving KMT. The decree stated: 'The government declares the central workers' council and the community and city councils throughout the country illegal and forbids them as of this date any further activity . . . instructions are going simultaneously to all the ministries . . . and public administrations to offer the workers' councils within the factories all possible support.' The objective was to put a stop to the central coordination of local council activities that was essential to the political struggle. At this point the government did not dare as yet to proceed against the councils at factory level. That had to wait until later in 1957.

As soon as the prohibition was announced, the arrests of KMT members began. Sándor Rácz and Sándor Bali were summoned to the Parliament building on the pretext of new negotiations and were arrested there. A state of emergency was declared on the same day signifying the threat of death sentences for certain offences, and the jurisdiction of military tribunals for armed resistance and all other active forms of resistance. It was symptomatic of the general situation that the Soviet commandant issued a special order to the population on 8 December, one month after a similar order had been issued, to relinquish all 'hidden' weapons.

Despite the arrest of KMT leaders, the strike was observed nationwide on 11–12 December. The Kádár government now employed every means to restrict the power of the workers' councils. The arrest of Rácz and Bali triggered new strikes in a number of plants, but the government would not yield and some factories were even occupied by Soviet military units. Legal activity on the part of the councils was virtually excluded, yet the illegal or semi-legal councils continued their frustrating struggle for months against the new seizure of power by the party bureaucracy. A wave of solidarity swept the country, mainly evident in material support for the families of those arrested or kidnapped. But there were reprisals even for such help. In several towns across the country (Miskolc, Eger, Zalaegerszeg, etc.) security forces fired on peaceful demonstrators who protested against the arrest of council leaders and expressed solidarity with the general strike. Dozens fell victim to these atrocities and hundreds were injured.

The government issued an order on 5 January 1957 assigning the death penalty to the refusal to work and 'provocation to strike'. This so circumscribed the activity of the workers' councils that the workers had to give up hope of any independent representation of their interests in the factories. In the iron and metal plant in Csepel, the largest industrial factory in the capital, the workers' council dissolved itself in protest. The council justified that step as follows: 'In present circumstances we do not feel able to implement the demands of the workers and we do not want to raise false hopes in our fellow-workers by our mere existence.' Two days later the central workers' council of Csepel dissolved itself. The workers responded the next day with a strike and demonstration. The government could put down the demonstration only with the help of Soviet tanks, resulting in numbers of dead and wounded. Several council members and the chairman of the workers' council in the Csepel factory, Elek Nagy, were arrested on the same day.

The government replied to the workers' resistance on 13 January with a decree invoking the death sentence for practically all forms of critical expression. The 'fall of the fortress' Csepel signified the end of the workers' councils. Although the KMT remained illegally active for a time, its last appeal of 15 January was the last gasp of the council movement. Although there were various forms of passive resistance, some acts of sabotage, and occasional small strikes throughout 1957, the centrally designated management and the old trade union system under the control of state and party were restored in the factories.

'IN MARCH WE START AGAIN!'

A last sign of resistance was the appearance of the slogan, 'In March We Start Again!' In abbreviation MUK (Hungarian: *Márciusban újra kezdjük*), it was repeated from person to person and frequently turned up on the walls of buildings. Behind the slogan was no longer any serious movement or organization. It embarrassed only those in power and was used with a vengeance by them for propaganda purposes. One referred to this 'threat' to justify stronger repression and harsher measures. The government was concerned that the youth would observe 15 March by turning against the regime (as would occur in the 1970s). In order to dampen any enthusiasm for an observance of 15 March, the government responded to the underground slogan MUK with preventive measures.

Already in February it issued a decree on the formation of a 'workers' militia', and in March such groups were actually assigned tasks formerly performed by special police units. At first these armed paramilitary formations, which trained on Sundays and during paid work time, could not attract members from among the workers. The volunteers came from the ranks of party functionaries willing to take up weapons on behalf of the Kádár regime. These workers' militias, armed protectors of the ruling party, continued to exist until Kádár fell in 1989.

On 15 March 1957 these fighting groups kept a close watch on all public places. The real message of that day was that Hungary's fate had been sealed for decades to come.

SEARCH FOR A COMPROMISE: THE DEMOCRATIC PARTIES

Since it was not possible after the Soviet invasion to maintain a functioning multiparty system, political activity was confined to attempts by the leaders of the parties that had emerged or been newly founded in October to negotiate with the Kádár government in search of a compromise that would save the multiparty system. In the first half of November, János Kádár put out some feelers toward a few leaders of the former coalition parties, plainly seeking to give the impression that he was not totally opposed to a somewhat limited multiparty system. In an article of 15 November in the new organ of the MSZMP *Népszabadság*, he had renounced any claim of his party to a monopoly of power, promised a multiparty system and 'clean' elections, favoured the withdrawal of Soviet troops, and stated his desire to negotiate with Imre Nagy when the latter emerged from the Yugoslav Embassy. But since Kádár and the MSZMP did not want a real multiparty system, they sought contact with those political leaders they judged to be available for collaboration. The non-communist politicians who remained true to their principles and committed to the restoration of parliamentary democracy were treated as enemies and forced out of public life.

István Bibó's 'Draft Proposal'

István Bibó, the most distinguished representative of a democratic orientation, fashioned on 6 November (finalized a few days later) a detailed exposé entitled 'Draft Proposal for a Compromise Solution of the Hungarian Question'. In this 'Draft Proposal', Bibó emphasized that the Soviet occupation, contrary to the claims of the Soviet-supported government now in power, did not represent the restoration of order but rather the intensification of tensions. Proposing a reasonable compromise, Bibó detailed the manner in which the achievements of the Revolution and the security interests of the Soviet Union could both be protected (e.g. by substituting a bilateral treaty for the Warsaw Pact), and at the same time the anxieties of the communists could be assuaged (e.g. by an amnesty for transgressions in the Stalin era). Finally, he suggested how a withdrawal of Soviet troops in stages might be prepared. Bibó was of the opinion that the intervention of UN forces would be necessary only if the withdrawal of Soviet forces from Hungary could not be managed comfortably. Bibó's presupposition was that socialism would remain the social system of Hungary after the departure of Soviet troops. He proposed the convening of a national constitutional assembly to deal with the reconfiguration of internal politics; in this forum the delegates from workers' councils and revolutionary committees would decide about the nature of the state structure on the basis of the parliamentary system won in 1848 and the republic established in 1946. Bibó envisaged the retention of the land reform of 1945, the nationalization of large industrial concerns, and workers' self-management in cooperatively organized enterprises, while preserving the possibility of private enterprise, as he put it, 'with prohibition of exploitation'.

Bibó's 'Draft Proposal', more than any of the other conceptions in circulation, achieved widespread notice despite the difficulties of the time. There was general sympathy for Bibó's measured approach to the achievement of peace, and it would have been consonant with the early pronouncements of the Kádár regime had the latter not aimed in actuality at the reinstatement of a single-party monopoly and close dependence on the Soviet Union. Although the author did not intend it, his text appeared on handwritten posters and was extensively discussed both in the KMT and in the Writers' Union.

The 'Draft Proposal' seemed to offer representatives of the non-communist parties a possible basis for seeking contact with the government. But the preparation of a 'multiparty declaration' rooted in Bibó's ideas took some time. It was finally approved by representatives of the Petőfi Party, the Smallholders, the Social Democrats, the Revolutionary Council of Hungarian Intellectuals, the Writers' Union, the Peasants' Union and the Central Workers' Council. In mid-December, this proposal was presented to the Indian ambassador in Moscow, K. P. S. Menon (not the same person as the well-known Indian statesman), who was also accredited in Budapest and was then visiting Hungary, with the request that it be conveyed to the Soviet government. A copy was sent to the Kádár government. But this effort was without result, for the government had meanwhile succeeded in its police measures and had gone on the offensive politically. At this point it had no interest in compromise.

In a meeting of the Central Committee of the MSZMP on 2 December 1956, János Kádár spoke vehemently of 'counter revolution' in Hungary, arguing that the attack on the victorious proletarian revolution could only be counter-revolutionary, aiming at a capitalist restoration and reinstatement of the power of the capitalists. Although the 'multiparty declaration' referred explicitly to the possibility and desirability of securing democratic socialism in constitutional terms, the ruling party and government paid no attention to this fact. In the same Central Committee meeting, a 'correct' interpretation of events was determined which then remained the party line on 1956 for over thirty years. According to this explanation, what had happened in Hungary in October 1956 was counter-revolution from the very beginning even though some of the demonstrators protested rightly against the Rákosi regime on 23 October. Counter-revolutionary forces were already present and infiltrated the 'healthy' protest right away. There were, according to the resolution, four reasons for the counter-revolution: the anti-Leninist line and the crimes and faults committed by the Rákosi group since 1948; the destabilizing activity (a few month later this became 'organized conspiracy', and 'treacherous attempt at overthrowing the socialist system') of the inner-party opposition; the activities of reactionary forces in the country; and subversion by western imperialist agents.

WRITERS AND ARTISTS IN RESISTANCE

After the suppression of the Revolution, the members of the former inner-party opposition were the principal persons among the intellectuals who remained active. They regarded the defeat of the uprising by alien military force as a betrayal of socialism. The Soviet invasion had conclusively compromised their original goal of socialist order without terror. These circles had in fact only at this time identified with the Revolution in its full extent, from armed struggle to multiparty system.

People active in the revolutionary organizations and especially in the recently freed press had soon to recognize that open activity had become impossible, even life-threatening. Some of them tried to continue their efforts underground. The newspaper *Igazság* (Truth), founded during the Revolution by Gyula Obersovszky and József Gáli, appeared on 5 November and then, for the last time, on 7 November. The editors then went underground and operated illegally thereafter. The paper appeared irregularly until 4 December under the title *Élünk!* (We live!). The greatest success of the underground paper was a memorial march on 4 December, one month after the Soviet invasion, for the victims of the revolutionary action. This peaceable demonstration at Heroes Square, involving hundreds of women and girls dressed in black and with flowers in their hands, was broken up by the Soviet military. Ambassador Menon, after watching this march, reported with strong emotion on this silent expression of grief and solidarity.

Some of those allied with Imre Nagy since 1953 decided after 4 November to organize a mass movement. They were joined by members of the Petőfi Circle, former NÉKOSZ activists, and a number of students. The initiator and intellectual leader of this group, which took the name Hungarian Democratic Independence Movement (MDFM) on 13 November, was Miklós Gimes. After the Soviet occupation, the group established close contact with the non-communist parties with the aim of achieving a unified platform and the necessary organizational cooperation to advance national resistance and the revolutionary cause. Gimes's newspaper, *Október Huszonharmadika* was edited in the most dangerous circumstances and appeared for almost a month starting on 15 November; it was circulated from hand to hand, mostly by young insurrectionists.

The stand of the Writers' Union

The executive committee of the Writers' Union published an appeal in the name of the Hungarian intelligentsia on 12 November, asserting that the Revolution had expressed so unambiguously the will of the Hungarian people that only a new, freely expressed declaration by the people could supersede it. On this point there could be no bargaining. The Soviet troops must depart. Beyond that, the appeal protested against official terrorism and persecution.

Various organizations joined the appeal, including the Hungarian Academy of Sciences, the Union of Musicians, the Union of Actors, the Union of Visual Artists, the Union of Architects, the clandestine Revolutionary Councils of Hungarian Radio, and of the Hungarian Press Agency. On 21 November the Revolutionary Council of Hungarian Intellectuals was founded. This central organization sprang from the Revolutionary Committee of Intellectuals that emerged during the Revolution. The composer Zoltán Kodály was elected chairman and György Markos, old communist and anti-fascist resistance fighter, was chosen as secretary. The founding members included the best minds of Hungary. The Council was also among the organizations banned on 11 December under the emergency decree.

The full membership meeting of the Writers' Union on 28 December adopted a statement entitled 'Sorrow and Confession' written by Áron Tamási, a universally admired writer of Transylvanian origin. This statement of principle by all the writers included the following:

> National independence and the development of a democratic social order is the desire of all Hungarians; that is what moves us and in which we wish to participate. We want to address everyone with the message that fills our hearts and in the way that our lives as writers will unfold in future. Moved by our common sorrow, we extend our hand to the worker, offer farmers and the youth our heartfelt greeting. We should persuade the political leaders that politics is not an end in itself but only a means to serve the wellbeing of the people, and we want to move them to use this means in accordance with the wishes of the Hungarian people. We pledge our loyalty to that flag that shows the nation born again out of the revolutionary unity of the people. We want to defend and care for the spirit of Hungary in loyalty and conviction. Morality should be the foundation of our work, and our works should lend purpose and form to the creative power of the people, humanity, and the ideals of this era.

Tibor Déry spoke to this gathering of 'the greatest, purest, and most unified revolution' in Hungarian history and the Hungarian workers' movement, reflecting the viewpoint of most of those in attendance as he noted that it had been 'put down because of an abysmal shortage of statesmanlike wisdom'. The assembly greeted the declaration with enthusiasm and committed itself to the goals of the Revolution. By way of response, the government banned the Writers' Union on 17 January 1957.

With the passing of time and as state terrorism increased, more and more people abandoned resistance. A majority of the writers fell silent, many choosing passive resistance, for the arrests of writers and journalists continued. By the end of January, all artists' unions and organizations were placed under the supervision of the interior ministry, which amounted to prohibition.

Those intellectuals who remained true to Imre Nagy and his ideals and who saw it as their task to redeem the honour of socialism reacted decisively against the policy of restoration and the increasingly brutal official terror. One of these, Sándor Fekete, formerly associated with *Szabad Nép*, began work on an analysis of the situation, writing under the pseudonym 'Hungaricus'. Following discussions with like-minded people he produced a booklet containing a comprehensive account reflecting the shared viewpoint. The first part was ready by the end of December and circulated, illegally of course, in intellectual circles. The second part, entitled 'The New Socialist Path', began to circulate in February 1957. The work dealt with the history of the Hungarian communist movement from its beginnings to the outbreak of the Revolution in 1956, defining the October rebellion as 'a national uprising'. Hungaricus emphasized that 'the people wanted independence above all, for they saw in the loss of autonomy the source of all their misery and hardship'.

Not surprisingly, this work aroused the anger of the government, and the author and his associates were sentenced to lengthy prison terms. The booklet was soon smuggled out of Hungary and circulated in the west. It was the first Hungarian study to provide a critical analysis of the Revolution and, beyond that, the whole system of Soviet socialism.

Around the same time, in April 1957, István Bibó formulated an analysis of the events of 1956 and a proposal for a peaceful solution of the 'Hungarian question', more detailed than his 'Draft Proposal' had been. He opened his study with these words: 'Hungary's predicament has become the scandal of the world.' He then proceeded to demonstrate that the Soviet intervention was a scandal of the western world (placing the honesty of liberation propaganda in doubt), of the communist camp (disappointing all those who hoped for de-Stalinization), and also of the adherents of a 'third road' (questioning its feasibility in the face of naked violence). But Bibó continued to offer the other side of the coin, by proposing that the Hungarian Revolution also represented hope for the west (proving the indomitable wish for freedom in eastern Europe), for the world communist movement (if the fatal decision of intervention is recognized as a grave mistake), and even for the 'Third Road' and 'world peace' (if the Soviets understand the possibility of establishing a friendly, but not oppressed Hungary). Finally, he concluded by sketching the tasks of the west, the Soviets, the believers in a 'Third Road', and closed with these words:

> As for the Hungarian people who presently bear all the glory as well as the burden of a historical role, they must continue to reject any accommodation to lies and violence, even if this means reducing their existence to a vegetative level for a certain period of time. It is not their task to initiate a new uprising and thus provoke repeated reprisals; however, it is their task to honour and safeguard − against slander, forgetting, and fading − the banner of their Revolution, which is also the banner of a freer future for mankind.
>
> ('The Hungarian Revolution of 1956: Scandal and Hope', in I. Bibó, *Democracy, Revolution, Self-Determination*, ed. by K. Nagy, Social Science Monographs, Atlantic Research and Publications, Boulder, Highland Lakes New Jersey, 1991, p. 352)

He, too, obtained his 'reward' for this writing − among other utterances of his during and after the Revolution − in the form of a life sentence for 'subversion of the people's democratic order' in 1958.

FIRST MONTHS OF EMIGRATION

The politicians and intellectuals forced into emigration tried to keep alive the ideas of the Revolution, chiefly in western Europe and the United States. But in truth they had little hope of influencing events in Hungary. Anna Kéthly, minister of state in the Nagy government, was, as István Bibó announced on 4 November, designated as the official representative of the overthrown Nagy regime. On 4 November she had been attending the meeting of the Socialist International in Vienna and could not return to Hungary after that.

Béla Király, commander of the National Guard, had also fled abroad. In Strasbourg, seat of the Council of Europe, there was a meeting in January 1957 chaired by Kéthly, Király and József Kővágó (who had been mayor of Budapest in 1945–47 and for a few days in October 1956) to form the Hungarian Revolutionary Council. This Council represented Hungary at the United Nations and was also the organization of political emigrants recognized by the Council of Europe as representing the Imre Nagy government. It was this Hungarian Revolutionary Council that published Nagy's writings in a collection titled *On Communism: In Defence of the New Course*. The manuscript had been smuggled out of Hungary in an adventurous way; it was organized by László Kardos, former leader of NÉKOSZ and the agrarian engineer and former FKGP politician, Árpád Göncz.

The members and associates of the Council delivered the most important eyewitness accounts for the UN special commission assigned in January 1957 to investigate the events in Hungary. But developments in Hungary could in no way be influenced from the west; they were again controlled from the east.

UNITED NATIONS REPORT

As long as the UN special commission existed, Hungarian politicians and their organizations in exile concentrated on supporting its investigation. They also attempted to persuade other UN members outside the bloc to condemn the Kádár regime and to protest the political arrests and reprisals.

The commission's report on the Hungarian issue was presented in the summer of 1957 and was considered by the General Assembly in September. The commission consisted of representatives of Australia, Ceylon (now Sri Lanka), Denmark, Tunisia and Uruguay. The most active member of its staff was its second secretary, the Danish diplomat Povl Bang-Jensen, who had great sympathy for the Hungarian Revolution and may have paid for it with his life. (He was dismissed from the UN while trying to protect the anonymity of the Committee's witnesses, and was found dead in a New York park a few years later. The mystery of his death was never unravelled.)

The report plainly condemned the Soviet intervention and described the Revolution as a justified expression of the Hungarian people's aspiration for freedom. The report's conclusion included the following:

> What took place in Hungary was a spontaneous national uprising, caused by long-standing grievances. One of these was the inferior status of Hungary with regard to the USSR. . . . The few days of freedom enjoyed by the Hungarian people provided abundant evidence of the popular nature of the uprising. A free press and radio came to life all over Hungary, and the disbanding of the ÁVH was the signal for general rejoicing, which revealed

the degree of unity achieved by the people, once the burden of fear had been lifted from them . . .

This democratic achievement of a united people was indeed, threatened by a form of 'counter-revolution' and it was to this that it succumbed. However, the 'counter-revolution' consisted in the setting up by Soviet armed forces of Mr Kádár and his colleagues in opposition to a government which enjoyed the overwhelming support of the people of Hungary.

(*Report of the Special Committee on the Problem of Hungary, General Assembly Official Records: Eleventh Session*, New York: UN, 1957, pp. 12, 138)

The report closed with the pronouncement that what had happened in Hungary was an aggression by the Soviet Union's own definition and thus a serious violation of the principles of the United Nations. But despite the harsh wording of the condemnation, the UN could do little to change things in Hungary. In relations among the great powers the Hungarian question arose again and again, but the Soviet Union and its satellite states were able to prevent any action, even a visit to Hungary by the investigating commission.

On behalf of the Revolution and the imprisoned writers, intellectuals and freedom fighters, many personages raised their voices worldwide but with little effect. The only success registered by international protest was the reduction in the sentences given the writers József Gáli and Gyula Obersovszky, from the death penalty to many years in prison.

The regular and frequent attention to the Hungarian situation did represent a threat to the international image of the Kádár regime. The old/new party machinery did all that it could to stage protests in Hungary against 'intervention in the internal affairs of the country'. By means of threats and promises, such as the intimation that the imprisoned intellectuals might be treated better or even freed, it proved possible in September 1957 to get a goodly number of writers to sign a protest against the activities of the UN special commission. Many of them thought they would save friends and colleagues from the gallows by signing a statement so obviously dictated from above, one that would be recognized for what it was abroad. And it was true that the west saw the document as evidence of the unrestrained terror applied by the regime. Such machinations thus gained very little even if they did hurt the solidarity among the intellectual supporters of the Revolution's aims. In the United Nations, the Hungarian issue remained on the agenda for another five years.

CHAPTER SEVEN

Aims and Programmes

Having surveyed the events from reform through uprising to the defeat of the Revolution and the ensuing passive resistance, the question arises: what was this all about? The problem goes directly to the character of the movement itself. Analysis of the demands, appeals and declarations is the only way to imagine how matters could have developed further, for in the political issues of the moment the public displayed an astounding (or, better, in revolutionary times, a natural) unanimity. This was, surely, not the outcome of some fiendish conspiracy – as Kádárist propaganda wanted to have it – but rather the fact of common sufferings on the one hand and the discussions on reform that did not stop ever since 1953, on the other. Then, once the free expression of opinion became possible in the press and on the radio, contacts multiplied and viewpoints were exchanged. The Free Kossuth Radio and local transmitters spared no effort to see that the revolutionary organizations, the committees and parties in Budapest and elsewhere, could give voice to their views. It was typical in the first revolutionary days to hear on the radio: 'Place your radios in the window!' (Portable radios were not available in Hungary and television did not exist, so it was the living room receivers that could reach the most people with the revolutionary demands.) Yet it seems appropriate to distinguish between the articulated objectives and those that were never formulated in written form.

To begin with the latter, people could most easily reach agreement about what they did not want. Everybody was fed up with the communist regime's watchfulness over every detail of daily life; with the imposed, alien and irritating regulations and rituals; with the anxieties and boredom of daily existence; with the very low wages and daily obligatory 'press analysis' at the workplace; with Soviet films, the political seminars, and so on. People had no patience any more with the constant invocation of 'the example of the fraternal Soviet Union'. They wanted to travel, also to the west, and to listen to American hit songs. But it was not a question of antipathy, still less of hatred, toward the Soviet Union – provided only that the occupation force would disappear and leave other people in peace.

COMMON PROBLEMS, DIFFERENT EXPECTATIONS

After several decades it is not easy, at bottom it may even be impossible, to reconstruct the positive ideas that animated the 1956 uprising. Yet it is worth the effort to try to understand what was in the minds of thousands of people as they framed appeals and resolutions or eliminated the old authorities in order to replace them with their own revolutionary organizations. If one were to reduce these goals and ideals to a single formula, such as 'Liberty, Equality, Fraternity' of the French Revolution, one might find the suitable words in the address given by Imre Nagy on 31 October to the throng gathered at the Parliament building. The prime minister spoke of a free, independent, democratic Hungary, determined – as he added a few days later – on a neutral course. Nevertheless, one must consider that the content of individual slogans meant different things to different people already during the Revolution, and that contemporary analyses assessing the understandings of that time are still less consistent.

The most important positive aim of the Revolution was the reinstatement of democracy. Since the regime called itself a 'people's democracy' – a tautological term that masked the shortage of authentic democracy – it was only appropriate to demand the democracy that was inscribed in the constitution. Central elements in the political thought of the Revolution were a parliamentary system grounded in free elections and freedom of expression in speech and writing. The main demand of the Revolution, as we have seen, was liberation from Soviet tutelage as prerequisite for the removal of the party dictatorship. On these matters, all participants in the Revolution were agreed. But the conception of a democratic order in detail underwent major changes after the 1953 reform programme and during the Revolution. There were divergent opinions about true democracy and various models of democracy existing alongside each other. But the time was too short for the unfolding of a competition among the assorted ideas.

In the few days of freedom, four major strains of thought appeared in embryo, displaying divergent conceptions of the political system and of the socio-political model. First, there were the adherents of a reformed socialist order, the former inner-party opposition, most of the workers' councils, many of the Social Democrats and others who trusted in Imre Nagy as a person able to renew the country in a socialist framework. However, there soon appeared a second trend, by no means clearly separated from the first, which was a 'national-democratic' one, represented by the leaders of the peasant parties (NPP, FKGP), above all, by the outstanding political thinker István Bibó, by some other politicians of the 1945–48 coalition era, and in exile by many non-communist Hungarians, such as the writer and commentator Zoltán Szabó in London.

Both of these directions were in agreement that the new Hungary should be built on the basis of the reforms of 1945–47, on the democratic platform of the wartime anti-fascist alliance, and rejected a restoration of the pre-war system. Both favoured a socialistic orientation in the broadest sense, even if the latter favoured different emphases in their social and economic programme and had a different base in terms of social support.

Third, in the last revolutionary days, a conservative, mainly Catholic group centred on Cardinal Mindszenty took shape, oriented to an older historical model and accepting the post-1945 reforms only with reservations. This group stood for a quite different socio-political programme in contrast to the first two strains. The most important difference between the 'leftists' of all types and the conservatives appeared in their judgements of the events themselves. The anti-Stalinists among the communists as well as the democrats and populists were in agreement that it was revolution that had occurred on 23 October and that the ensuing struggle against the Soviet forces was fought for the possibility of a fundamental social change. In keeping with their intellectual tradition, Cardinal Mindszenty and his group refused the notion of a revolution and emphasized only the national aspect of the fight. In his radio address of 3 November, the Cardinal said: 'Everyone in the country should know that this fight was no revolution but a fight for freedom.' In his eyes no revolutionary change or experiment was needed, rather a return to the 'legitimate' tradition disrupted by 1945.

The conservative tendency undoubtedly had a broad base in the populace and especially among the insurrectionists, but their representatives fell into, and remained in, disarray. By the time the erstwhile middle class supporting the Cardinal had overcome its fear, recognized its possibilities, and begun to act, the country had already been overtaken by Soviet tanks. The rear-guard fighting was not animated by Cardinal Mindszenty, who had found refuge in the US legation, but was conducted rather by the young freedom fighters, the workers' councils, and other small groups that continued resistance beyond 4 November.

As mentioned before, there were also voices representing an aggressive, radical, partly extreme right-wing, undifferentiated anti-communism. These rather diffuse political sentiments, maintaining that Stalinist excesses must be immediately avenged and that all communists – Imre Nagy and his associates included – must disappear from public life, found expression in the streets but never coalesced into a political programme.

FOR A JUST SOCIETY

The demands that touched the existence and daily life of the people could be found mainly in the manifestos of the factory and workers' councils. These resolutions and lists of demands contain a plenitude of details about the hated piecework, the unjust work quotas and low wages, the minimal social accomplishments, and the miserable supply of foodstuffs from a ruined agriculture. All these details show that the most active fighters of the Revolution struggled not only for freedom and independence but also for a humane mode of life and appropriate conditions of work. Such demands were reflected in the programmatic campaign for what many believed to be a 'genuinely socialist' society.

The workers' councils in the factories and the revolutionary committees in offices and institutions expressed not only the political aims of the constituents but also their status as responsible owners of the plants. The roles of political representation, defence of interests, and proprietorship had blended together. As often happens in revolutionary times, the tasks of direction in plants and factories accrued to the councils, for the former directors, chosen according to political norms and knowing that they lacked the trust of the workforce, had mostly fled, leaving a vacuum that had to be filled.

The assumption of control over production was, at the same time, part of the socio-political programme of many leaders of the uprising, especially those from the workers' councils. The goal of that programme was to place the country on a new basis whereby short-term political objectives and envisaged long-term independence would constitute the foundation for a new 'socialist order' in the classical sense. The intended economic order would place decision-making in industry, mining and transport in the hands of the producers (workers, technicians and other staff); the tasks of individual plants, setting of wage rates, and the designation of supervisors would no longer be determined from outside, either from banks and factory owners or from central institutions such as ministries or commissions organized according to party requirements. As we know from the Soviet economic model of 'actually existing socialism', the new model was clearly not what communist parties understand as 'social property', 'worker power' or 'socialism'. The notions of the workers' councils were much closer to the classical socialist programme of the nineteenth and early twentieth centuries, and were filiated with those social democratic programmes implemented in our time in some western, e.g. Scandinavian, countries.

AGAINST RESTORATION OF THE 'OLD ORDER'

People of all tendencies and localities were agreed that the great social and economic changes of 1945–48 had to be preserved in their essence. This conviction embraced the fighters in cities and countryside, the revolutionary councils and national committees, whatever emphasis they gave to their party programmes in other respects. 'We reject any attempt to restore the dominance of large landowners, factory owners, and bankers' was a statement endorsed by representatives of many persuasions.

Béla Kovácas, former chairman of the FKGP, who had returned only shortly before the uprising from many years in a Siberian camp of the Gulag, spoke on 30 October in Pécs as follows: 'No one should dream of the old order. The world of counts, bankers, and capitalists is gone for good; anyone who sees things now as if it were 1939 or 1945 is no authentic Smallholder.' Kovács used the two cited years to suggest that the pre-war political system and the socio-economic order of pre-land-reform vintage were consigned fully to the past. His view was that the policies of 1956 had to build on the social and economic reforms of the post-war years, before the communists forced the introduction of state socialism and a set of policies ignoring the needs of working people.

The writer László Németh, a highly regarded figure of the interwar populist-nationalist intellectual circle who had been silenced in 1946, expressed his concerns about possible future developments in an article of 1 November: 'We must be vigilant, while the people in arms are focused on the withdrawal of Soviet forces, to assure that new opportunists do not make a counter-revolution out of the Revolution and set the Hungarian struggle for freedom on the course of 1920.' This was a clear warning against the followers of Regent Miklós Horthy who had led the counter-revolution and White Terror of 1919 and against the so-called Christian course of 1920s that followed. In an article of 2 November in the new paper of the Petőfi Party, *Új Magyarország* (New Hungary), Németh described that 'historically significant' political system for which the Revolution fought, in his opinion, as 'a multi-party system of shared principles able to join the ideological strength of socialism with the flexibility of the parliamentary system'.

A THIRD ROAD

While time did not permit the development of a detailed social and political programme, all of the relevant political forces of the Revolution favoured the division of the lands that were the pre-war basis for large landowner domination and the conversion of banks and large industry into social property. The protest was aimed at 'social property' in the hands of a party bureaucracy. In this sense, the Revolution adopted socialist ideals. There were many of course who knew from experience that the healing of a ruined economy was impossible without a more or less free market. But such views were seldom expressed in 1956. One must remember that the problems of the welfare state that emerged everywhere in the recent decades and the failure of all the reforms of 'existing socialism' were not yet known.

At that time most people nursed a solution, possibly utopian, the so-called 'Third Road', that promised to bypass both of the existing, counterposed systems in favour of the building of a just society. The concept of a Third Road, advocated in the interwar period by Wilhelm Röpke, had had a favourable response in Hungary already. It was also known that elsewhere in Europe – in Britain, France and the Scandinavian countries – the economic systems of the 1950s combined private property and nationalized enterprises, while recording significant social achievements at state initiative. Though the ideas about a third alternative were not free of inconsistencies, they seemed to fit the country's international situation. Just as one wished Hungary to be free of both power blocs, so it seemed that an intermediate position in politics and in terms of the social and economic system should also be possible. Zoltán Szabó described the contradictory programme in one of his London radio commentaries: 'For the socialists the Revolution was much too liberal, for the liberals much too socialist.' The notion of 'private property limited by social considerations', along with the welfare state as protector of workers and self-management by workers, was a normal part of European thought in the 1950s. Even if Hungarian people knew little about the different existing schemes, including the workers' self-management of factories introduced at this time in neighbouring Yugoslavia, these economic and social models were simply 'in the air', so to speak. Nor should one underestimate the old Social Democratic and trade union traditions that were not forgotten even though their organizations were destroyed in 1948. Although the Social Democratic Party appeared relatively late on the political scene during the Revolution and, understandably, remained suspicious of the 'revisionist' communists, there were many old trade unionists in the workers' councils and they had not first learned of socialism in a perverted form. They upheld the old values of struggle against exploitation, worker solidarity and trade union organization, even in the time when free trade unions were repressed.

Many participants in the Revolution outside the ranks of workers were also motivated by the tradition of a free and just society, what they held to be an authentic socialism. One can be sure that this did not correspond to the ideals of all of the society, but it was characteristic for the situation in 1956 that no significant force or personality defended the alternative, which appears today as the only possible one, namely a capitalistic economic system with unrestricted market and comprehensive privatization. As a matter of fact, a group of economists met on the last days of freedom and discussed possible future steps. They, too, agreed that during the hectic days of freedom fighting no decisions should or could be made on the economic system. This should be left to the hoped-for freely elected parliament. However, in their circles several variants of complete or limited marketization were discussed. (Actually, the complete restoration of the Soviet type command-style planned economy was delayed for quite a few months even after the restoration of the Moscow-supported communist system.)

Cardinal Mindszenty, whose office and personal convictions inclined him to conservative standpoints, spoke in his famous radio address on 3 November of the will of the entire Hungarian people: 'we live under the rule of law in a classless society, we are developing further our democratic accomplishments, and we hold to the principle of private property limited by social concerns'. Thus, even the Cardinal, who rejected socialist viewpoints in all questions of the social order, did not explicitly oppose some form of socialistic order. The notion of a just limitation of private property was developed at the end of the nineteenth century by the Roman Catholic Church as a counter to the objectives of Marxist Social Democracy. Parenthetically: what the Cardinal understood under 'classless society', basically a Marxist formulation, is not quite clear. In any event, he was not advocating in so many words a return to the hierarchical social order of the pre-war period.

UNITY OF AN ENTIRE NATION

The most important trademark of the days of the Revolution was that the entire nation stood united, beyond all differences of opinion or ideology, for freedom. The whole people rose up on behalf of the realization of a more humane and ethical programme as embodied in their own and Europe's best tradition. All the details may not have been known by every freedom fighter, but the essential programme was upheld by the majority of the population. An exception was the dwindling minority that was itself a part of the regime and dependent on it ideologically or materially.

In the street language of the Revolution, national unity was expressed in the slogan: 'Whoever is a Hungarian is with us!' It did not mean that anyone was to be excluded from the new Hungary; rather the opposite: whoever is with us is a true Hungarian, an upstanding human being. Many non-Hungarians fought against the Stalinist dictatorship, though unfortunately there are no exact numbers. Many refugees who had found asylum in Hungary, foreign students from the people's republics of Europe and Asia (Poles, Chinese, Koreans) and even some Soviet soldiers whose homelands had been subjugated by the Bolshevik dictatorship joined the ranks of the freedom fighters and were received with open arms. (Some of the fifty-one Soviet soldiers reported 'missing in action' may have been among those who joined the fighting and/or escaped to the west.)

The slogan also contained no distinction among Hungarians, neither of nationality nor of religion nor of origin. When long-suppressed national animosities did surface, it was the revolutionary organizations that opposed discrimination. In County Baranya, for example, where post-war expulsions and resettlements produced tension between the remaining Germans and Hungarian newcomers from Slovakia and Bukovina, there was open antagonism in several villages. The local National Committee, in which both groups were represented, put a stop to the attempted 'reparations' and called for an early formal investigation of all charges, but time did not allow the Committee to accomplish this.

In the light of Hungary's modern history it is necessary to mention that very few anti-semitic voices were heard during the Revolution. In a few remote hamlets there were demonstrations against 'Jews and communists', for example in an eastern Hungarian locality where it was believed that two Jews returning in 1945 from a German death-camp were of assistance to the Soviets in abducting Hungarian civilians and sending them to Siberia.

That such occurrences were rare is a 'surprising' feature of the national unity, surprising because it was not rare in central Europe that anti-semitic tendencies emerged in critical moments and because this centuries-old form of seeking scapegoats was skilfully exploited by Hungarian governments of the interwar period. It was surprising also because, as mentioned in Chapter 1, it was no secret that several leading figures of the Stalinist regime toppled in 1956 came from Jewish families. That the freedom fighters did not fall into the trap of the slogan about Judaeo-Bolshevism testifies to their moral and political maturity. Eyewitnesses have reported how a man recognized in the street belonging to state security was let free because someone remarked he looked Jewish 'and we don't want to be known as Fascists'. Typical of the mood of the time is the fact that not even the only known – and otherwise uninteresting – manifesto reflecting national socialist thinking, stemming from a politician of the 1940s, contained anti-semitic or chauvinistic slogans.

It is hardly surprising that in the brief period when freedom reigned and the state monopoly of force was broken, representatives of extreme or entirely unrealistic demands should appear. But the populace in its overwhelming majority remained sensible. It is doubtless natural that, once the common goals had been reached, national unity began to show fissures. Many of the older generation, convinced conservatives or right-leaning opponents of every sort of socialism, excluded from political affairs since 1948–49, now saw a possibility of becoming active. They also had sympathizers among the youth. It is certain that, had the invasion not occurred, the ideological and political contradictions would have sharpened and emerged into the open.

It is highly probably that, in the absence of the cohesive force generated by the threat to the nation, unity would not have endured for long. Hints of different political viewpoints were heard in the last days before 4 November. Such was the aforementioned radio address of Cardinal Josef Mindszenty on 3 November in which the language was more revealing than the actual content (he called the government 'heir of the fallen system'). This suggested a shift away from national unity toward the emergence of a distinct Catholic-conservative bloc. Another direction was embodied in the developing political leadership of the coalition partners of the re-formed Communist Party. These groups had supported Nagy during the Revolution, but it remains an open question whether this cooperation with anti-Stalinist communists would have lasted for long.

However, all these reflections are conjectures. Decisive for the Revolution was the unanimity during the days of struggle and the weeks of subsequent resistance. The uprising of 1956 belongs to the series of great popular movements loyal to the ideals of the French Revolution and the Rights of Man, and it was the first in east-central Europe in which members of society, wishing to become citizens, rose against the tyranny of totalitarian power. The most fitting formulation was perhaps that of István Bibó, when he referred to 1956 as a 'Revolution for human dignity'. Just this universality, in which the realization of individual freedom and freedom of the nation are joined in unusual harmony, may explain why the remembrance of the uprising survived defeat, merciless vengeance and decades of defamation.

CHAPTER EIGHT

Repression and Reprisal

The vengeance of the Habsburgs after the defeat of the revolution of 1848–49 and the resulting grief and dismay were deeply moving experiences retained permanently in the national memory. People remembered the death by firing squad of the first prime minister, Count Batthyány, the execution of thirteen generals in Arad, the officers and politicians imprisoned in the citadel of Kufstein, and the forced recruitment of soldiers of the Honvéd army – not only during the open dictatorship that followed but also in the decades after the settlement of 1867 when authority and society were again at peace.

The reprisals that followed the defeat of the 1956 Revolution far exceeded the terror ensuing after the 1848–49 revolution and war of independence. The victorious Kádár regime not only was concerned to erase with greater or lesser success the memory of the Revolution, but also tried to spread the cloak of silence over its own acts of retaliation. For decades one could not mention the names of the executed Prime Minister Nagy or Defence Minister Maléter, nor could one speak of the young rebels who ended on the gallows or of the thousands who landed in prison. Their memory was kept vivid only by the emigrants in the west and, after the 1970s, the Hungarian underground opposition. At the end of the 1980s, as the communist power was crumbling and the details of the reprisals of 1956–57 began to emerge, young people reacted to the disclosures with horror.

The Kádár regime tried to conceal its vengefulness with the same hypocritical politicizing that was characteristic of its initial activity. In the first official announcement, for example, the government promised freedom from prosecution for participants in the Revolution even as the delegation from the Nagy government at Soviet headquarters in Tököl was arrested by a special unit formed from Soviet and Hungarian state security personnel. At the very same moment, when the newly established Kádár government announced this freedom from prosecution, the same special unit moved on to Budapest to arrest the remaining members of the Nagy government in the Parliament building. Had they not been held up by Honvéd units, and had Nagy and his colleagues not found shelter in the Yugoslav Embassy, all of the Hungarian leaders would have fallen into the hands of the occupiers and their lieutenants in the first hours of the Soviet invasion.

PURPOSE AND INTERNATIONAL CONTEXT

Reprisal was only one aspect, albeit the most important, of the post-revolutionary history of Hungary. The period from November 1956 to the beginning of 1963 was a time of repression and persecution. The ruling group sought above all in this period to break the resistance of a society decisively opposed to it, to defeat the remaining organizations and resistance groups, and, in a word, to accustom the society to its own defeat. There were many and varied means available for this purpose. Any sort of political resistance was met by forceful measures, the revolutionary political and social organizations were disbanded, and the still significant surviving remnant of private farmers was subjected to forced collectivization in 1959–61 and thus eliminated as a social force. At the same time, concessions were made to those who were disposed to obedience: wage increases, elimination of forced deliveries in agriculture, and modest improvement in living standard. In the subsequent years, there were also accommodating gestures toward the erstwhile middle class and, later, signs that the authorities would remove themselves to some extent from the private lives of the people.

Reprisals were aimed primarily at those who were politically aware and who attempted to organize resistance. The scope of the retaliation was determined in part by the interests of the regime, in part by the vengefulness of the executive power; but there were also foreign policy considerations that influenced developments.

The cautious reform programme initiated in the Soviet Union in the spring of 1956, after the Twentieth Party Congress of the CPSU but before the outbreak of the Hungarian Revolution, soon faltered. The Soviet leadership was alarmed by events in Poland, by the strength of reform movements within the communist parties, and then by the Revolution in Hungary, and that fortified the still strong Stalinist tendencies in the Soviet presidium. These were the forces that were in alliance with the leaders of the GDR, Czechoslovakia, Romania, Bulgaria and China, encouraging the Hungarian state and party leaders to undertake a mass retaliation ending with an unprecedented bloodbath. At first, however, Kádár and his colleagues held in check the lust for revenge on the part of the repressive apparatus, without leaving room for a charge that they were 'soft' on the 'class enemy'. They oscillated between two dangers: that of a resurgence of popular rage against them and, on the other hand, the possible danger posed by the intrigues of Rákosi allies in Moscow. Mátyás Rákosi and the other communists who had fled to Moscow during the Revolution used their connections to the orthodox Stalinists, showering the Kremlin leaders with indictments of the 'moderate' policies of the new Hungarian leadership. Only when the initial reign of terror had put an end to any kind of resistance and when the old Stalinist group around Molotov, with whom the Rákosi group maintained good relations, was removed from the Soviet leadership in the summer of 1957, could the Kádár regime make its own decisions freely and unleash the retaliatory apparatus without fearing a Rákosi restoration.

PHASES OF REPRISAL

The retaliatory process in its narrow sense divides into four phases. They were of variable duration, depending on the particular priorities of the regime in setting its political goals.

The main goal of the first phase, from 4 November to the beginning of December, was to defeat the armed insurrection. Since the Hungarian leadership was entirely dependent in the first weeks, the 'restoration of order' was directed, as mentioned earlier, from behind the scenes by the Soviet emissaries. The measures taken by way of implementation were mainly the business of the occupation army at this stage. It sometimes happened that fighters captured in skirmishes were immediately shot by Soviet soldiers. Usually, however, those captured were placed in barracks or prisons under Soviet direction. At first there were no courts martial, and both Soviet commanders and János Kádár conducted negotiations with unarmed resistance leaders, such as the representatives of the Central Workers' Council. On the other hand, twelve members of the Borsod workers' council, who made their recognition of the Kádár regime conditional on negotiations in person, were arrested on 5 November and sent off to the Carpatho-Ukraine. There were also instances when measures were quickly retracted if they proved unhelpful in breaking the resistance. Thus a group of young rebels was brought back from the Soviet Union at the end of November. In the provinces things were a bit different where commandos of the newly formed machinery of repression had begun their own brutal destruction of the revolutionary organizations and their active members.

The second phase began early in December with the ruling party's determination that the uprising had been simply a counter-revolution. By this time the reorganization of the police power (consisting mainly of officers) and of the Interior Ministry was complete. Since the armed resistance was virtually eliminated, it became possible to relieve the Soviet military and security forces of their role in the reprisals – though they remained of course as 'instructors'. New tasks came to the fore at this point: the overcoming of unarmed resistance and the discouragement of any sort of peaceful protest. The workers' councils and revolutionary committees that had survived at the regional level were prohibited and some 200 leaders of the councils were arrested in the first days of December. Martial law was imposed and further waves of arrests followed. Now began the expansion of the apparatus of repression and the creation by decree of the legal basis for massive court and other proceedings to follow in the next phase. This, the intimidation phase, concentrated on retaliation for armed resistance. The prisons filled gradually and the internment camps, dismantled in 1953, were reopened, although no decision had yet been made on the ultimate fate of those imprisoned. Dozens of young people, found in possession of weapons, were executed. József Dudás, leader of a National Revolutionary Committee, and János Szabó, the legendary 'Uncle Szabó', commander of the freedom fighters at Széna Square, were among the first to be sentenced to death in a secret trial before a military tribunal and executed. Yet in general the process was lethargic, for which the government held prosecutors and courts responsible. The close of this period coincided with János Kádár's visit to Moscow in March 1957, where he reached agreement with the Soviet leadership on speeding up the massive programme of reprisal. It was also agreed that it should all occur behind closed doors with the public excluded. The worldwide protest that had developed may have been a factor in this decision.

At the beginning of April, after Kádár's return, the Executive Committee and Central Committee of the MSZMP ratified the programme of mass reprisal. They also determined that Imre Nagy should face trial, along with his associates. By this time, apart from a few minor incidents, there was no longer any resistance worthy of the name, and the reorganized party cells in the factories had effectively crippled the still legal workers' councils.

The third phase, lasting from April 1957 until spring 1959, can be characterized as the period of massive reprisal. The people's courts formed according to party directive saw not only those who had been active in the resistance after 4 November but also masses of individuals who had participated in the Revolution or in its 'preparation' (i.e. members of the inner-party opposition). As of May 1957, the police renewed the massive arrests and began gathering evidence against thousands of people in custody. Although military tribunals were still handing out sentences until autumn 1957, the investigative processes lasted for months, sometimes more than a year. Prosecutors and courts were constantly overburdened. In 1957 alone, more than 20,000 political cases were initiated, but the system produced sentences in only some 6,000 of them. The period ended in 1959 with a partial amnesty. Many factors contributed to the political leadership's awareness that it was necessary to moderate the terror. Since the society had capitulated, any continuation of the repression would have damaged the international standing of the regime excessively. The leaders could well have been made uneasy by the 'efficiency' of an unrestrained machinery of repression. And there were new tasks on the agenda, such as collectivization of agriculture. None of this meant that forcible measures were being abandoned altogether, however. Alongside the 'small' amnesty of 1959, a group of intellectuals involved in resistance after the Revolution was sentenced. And there were individual political trials also thereafter.

The concluding phase lasted from spring 1959 to spring 1963. Proceedings against 'counter-revolutionaries' became isolated instances and in general the number of political sentences dwindled. Nevertheless, this period saw a series of important political trials of Catholic priests and laymen. The emergency laws of spring 1957 and their implementing organs were abandoned: the internment camps were closed in April 1960 and the people's courts were dismantled in April 1961. Most of the former state security officers were dismissed from the state police service in 1961–62, because of the offences against the law perpetrated before 1953 against the old communist leaders. Of course none of these offenders was ever called to account for those transgressions, not to mention those that they perpetrated after 1956. It was just that the old apparatus of the interior ministry seemed dangerous for the intensified 'de-Stalinization wave' of the early 1960s and as a potential resource for a possible attempt at restoration by the Rákosi clique.

The relaxation of repression was helpful for the external policies of the Kádár regime. At US initiative, the Hungarian question remained on the UN agenda uninterruptedly after 1956. Neither the termination of arrests nor partial amnesties in 1959 and 1960 sufficed to bring a change in that situation, especially since the latter affected only a few well-known intellectuals and those serving light sentences. Only in the autumn of 1962 did secret negotiations between the United States and the Hungarian government induce the UN to remove the Hungarian question from its agenda, whereupon a general amnesty was declared in Hungary in March 1963, effecting the release of most of the victims of reprisal. Those armed fighters sentenced for murder and the so-called repeat offenders were omitted from the amnesty, but the international public was beset by new problems and Hungarian society was so apathetic that the omission was barely noticed. For years, however, the individuals released at this time suffered the most various disadvantages: many remained under police surveillance, they could not practise their professions, and they could not reclaim the apartments and belongings that hat been confiscated.

COMMANDERS AND EXECUTIONERS

After December 1956 the arrests and interrogations were no longer conducted by members of the Soviet army. In their place appeared Hungarian units of the emergency police, called 'quilted jackets' (*pufajkások*) in popular parlance because of their characteristic Russian uniform. This new police force was formed from former state security personnel, army officers and party functionaries driven from their positions during the Revolution. Although directly subordinate to the party, the leaders of this machinery of repression had a good deal of independence. Early in 1957 the 'specialists' of this formation, the entire spy network, were transferred to the reorganized Main Department of Political Investigation in the Interior Ministry.

The old guard of state security remained almost untouched. They were under the command of party functionaries seconded to the Interior Ministry for this purpose. These were ordinarily functionaries of DISZ who had demonstrated their party loyalty in 1956. However, the political leaders attempted to foster the appearance of the rule of law. The methods of the old ÁVH that were customary in the 1950s were forbidden, yet beatings and torture continued everywhere outside the capital, and there as well except with prisoners who were well known.

At the end of 1956 and early in 1957 there were purges of judges and prosecutors. Those among them who had learned from the lawlessness of the 1950s and from the review of the earlier sentences found themselves in a moral dilemma and refused openly to participate in the new wave of trials. All of them who expressed their reservations were fired; many were unable to practise their profession for years thereafter. Attorneys were also screened and a secret list prepared, from which defendants had to accept a 'trustworthy' defence attorney. The reprisal campaign was under the direct personal control of the minister in charge of the police forces: Ferenc Münnich, as Minister of All Armed Forces from November 1956 to March 1957, then the ministers of the interior. The political police delivered the indictments directly to the prosecutors, who then had little difficulty determining the appropriate punishment to demand. But the interior minister was actually responsible mainly for operations, and real control rested with the relevant Central Committee secretary (first György Marosán, then Béla Biszku) and, ultimately, with the Executive Committee or Politburo of the party. These party organs considered the 'reprisal issue' dozens of times in 1957–58. Their competence embraced everything, from questions of principle down to decisions in particular cases. The Central Committee was also involved in the more important decisions. Such was beyond question the case of 'Imre Nagy and Co-defendants', which dragged on for a year and a half.

TRIAL OF IMRE NAGY

The fate of Imre Nagy and his associates was clearly related to the individual phases of the reprisal. But because of the exceptional importance of that proceeding, it is appropriate to consider it in some detail. Already in November in the Yugoslav Embassy, it was clear that, since Nagy and his comrades were unwilling to accept Kádár's betrayal and the second Soviet invasion, let alone to lend their support, any return to political activity was out of the question. Nagy and his associates had been abducted on 22 November 1956 and sent to Romania. That Nagy should be held to account was first discussed in January 1957 at the conference of eastern bloc party leaders that convened in Budapest.

In that same month, Gyula Kállai, acting for Hungarian and Soviet authorities, sought out the prisoners in Romania. It was also Kállai who suggested in the party's executive committee that Nagy be brought to trial. The presidium of the CPSU considered this Hungarian initiative in March 1957. And when Kádár visited Moscow at the end of the month, the course of action was approved by the Soviet leaders; on 2 April 1957 the Executive Committee and Central Committee of the MSZMP decided on the initiation of a judicial proceeding. Imre Nagy and his comrades were then arrested in Romania, taken secretly to Budapest, and subjected to imprisonment and an investigative process that was to last nearly a year.

Already in the second phase of the repression, the Kádár leadership had arrived at a political conception whereby Nagy and his colleagues were to bear the principal burden of guilt for everything that occurred in Hungary in October 1956. As the indictment read, they had sought already before the Revolution to seize power, to 'pave the way for reaction' by their betrayal, and, before and during the events of 1956, to 'lead the country out of the socialist camp'. By December 1956, this interpretation was being voiced in increasingly harsh formulation by Hungarian and other leading politicians of the communist orbit, thereby supplying the investigating officials in advance with a kind of framework for their charges.

Although he was unsuccessful, the Polish party leader Gomułka was the only one to speak against the death penalty threatening Nagy and his comrades when the communist leaders met in Moscow in May 1957. It is not surprising therefore that the bill of indictment was made ready fairly quickly – by August 1957. From this point on, the opening of the proceedings hinged on internal and external political considerations. Béla Biszku presented the indictment personally in Moscow and it was approved by the presidium, with the help of party secretary Andropov, in summer 1957. The Soviet leaders also took note of the Hungarian announcement of intended death sentences. (At this point the candidates for the death penalty included Imre Nagy, Géza Losonczy, Pál Maléter, Miklós Gimes, József Szilágyi, Ferenc Donáth and also Béla Király, who was not in their hands.) There were no Soviet objections to the trial, but the leaders urged the Hungarian party to schedule it at a time after the UN meeting of September 1957 and after the planned conference of communist leaders in Moscow in November of that year. The Soviets were concerned to resume the reconciliation with Yugoslavia, which had been marred partly by the Hungarian Revolution and the treatment of Nagy and his comrades. For that reason, the version of the indictment discussed between Moscow and Budapest made no mention as yet of the charge concerning 'Imre Nagy's Yugoslav connections'.

Moscow's request was fulfilled in Budapest: at Kádár's initiative, the Central Committee resolved on 21 December 1957 'to give the green light for the proceedings as provided by law against the instigators of the counter-revolution'. In February 1958 the proceeding began but was broken off the next day at Soviet request. The reason for this was certainly that the expected death sentences would be disadvantageous for the Soviet Union in the preparations for the great powers' summit conference and the arms control treaty. Kádár and the Hungarian party leadership dismissed the notion of passing milder sentences and preferred to wait. Palmiro Togliatti, the Italian Communist Party chief and erst-while critic of Moscow's domination of the communist movement, urged Kádár to postpone the trial of Nagy because of the forthcoming Italian parliamentary elections.

The trial began again in June 1958. Imre Nagy, Defence Minister Pál Maléter and the journalist Miklós Gimes were sentenced to death and executed on 16 June. Another member of the group, József Szilágyi, had already been sentenced to death in a separate trial. And Géza Losonczy, for whom a similar fate was intended, died in prison before the trial began following a hunger strike. The remaining defendants – Sándor Kopácsi, Ferenc Donáth, Zoltán Tildy, Ferenc Jánosi and Miklós Vásárhelyi – were sentenced to long prison terms.

Already during the investigative detention and throughout the proceedings, Imre Nagy had disputed the legal basis for the trial and declared himself not guilty. In his last words after the announcement of the verdict, he maintained that he had to the last been true to the pure socialist idea and to the Hungarian nation. He voiced confidence that the charges against him would be recognized as untrue and that 'the international working class and the Hungarian people' would judge him justly. His final words were: 'I do not appeal to the court for clemency.'

TRIALS AND VERDICTS

The trial of Nagy and colleagues was the most important event of the period of repression, and was also altogether characteristic, for hundreds of similar proceedings were conducted throughout the country in 1957–58. The first of these, as already mentioned, occurred in January 1957 when Dudás and Szabó were hanged.

A number of trials began in February 1957 with the public admitted and with full reports in the press. Public trials were conducted for the commander of the Tűzoltó Street freedom fighters, István Angyal (and the poet István Eörsi alongside him), for the resistance group active in the hospital in Péterffy Sándor Street – Ilona Tóth, medical assistant, and her co-defendants – and for others charged with the lynching of security personnel following the massacres in Miskolc and Monosmagyaróvár. In these trials the courts tried to present the defendants as ordinary criminals. But the draconian sentences, particularly in the trial of 'Ilona Tóth and accomplices' involving death penalties for the medical intern Ms Tóth, charged with murder, and also for the writer József Gáli and the journalist Gyula Obersovszky, unleashed worldwide protest. Thereafter, all of the important political trials were conducted behind closed doors. Thus, the public did not learn of the death sentences and executions of the three delegates from Győr – theatre director

Gábor Földes, protestant minister Lajos Gyulyás and high school teacher Árpád Tihanyi – who had tried to pacify the crowd aroused against the security personnel in Mosonmagyaróvár. The public was likewise excluded from the proceedings against the writers and the executive committee of the Writers' Union charged with preparing the way for the uprising; among those found guilty and sentenced were Tibor Déry, Julius Hay, Tibor Tardos and Zoltán Zelk.

The death penalty was the result in most of the cases against leaders of the armed groups. Among those sentenced and executed were the leaders of the National Guard in Csepel: István Angyal of Tűzoltó Street, and János Bárány, leader of the armed group in Tompa Street. Péter Mansfeld was still a minor when he was found guilty of participation in the fighting at Széna Square and of 'armed conspiracy'; his death sentence was carried out in 1959, three days after his eighteenth birthday. In a few cases, the death sentence was reduced to imprisonment by a higher court or by a pardon, a procedure that saved the lives of Imre Mécs, Jenő Fónay and some of their co-defendants.

The leading members of the workers' councils and revolutionary committees, which were still legal for a time after 4 November, did not escape the reprisals. In March 1958 the leaders of the Central Workers' Council of Greater Budapest were sentenced, Sándor Rácz to life imprisonment and Sándor Bali to twelve years. The head of the revolutionary committee of Veszprém, Árpád Brusznyai, was executed in January 1958. The death sentences pronounced after more than a year of proceedings on the leaders of the revolutionary committee of Újpest, the cabinet-maker Pál Kósa and his six co-defendants, were carried out in August 1959. Without exception, all members of workers' and revolutionary councils active in larger cities and more important factories were subjected to trial. And the wave of reprisals did not spare the smaller communities either.

Long prison sentences were meted out in July–August 1958 to the 'Imre Nagy group', members of the former inner-party opposition and those active in the resistance after 4 November, including Gábor Tánczos, secretary of the Petőfi Circle, and a number of social scientists and followers of Imre Nagy. The trials of army officers who had sided with the Revolution and sought to maintain order also took place in this period. Colonel János Mecséri, commander of the tank brigade stationed in Esztergom, who later served in the staff of Maléter, was executed along with six other officers. Minister of State István Bibó was brought before the People's Judicial Council of the Supreme Court in August 1958 and, along with him, Árpád Göncz, who had exerted himself, through the mediation of India, to bring about negotiations between revolutionary forces and the Soviet government. The sentence for both was life imprisonment. As late as spring 1959 there were still political trials. The journalist Sándor Fekete was tried because of his analysis of the Revolution under the pseudonym Hungaricus, and with him the last resistance group from the former inner-party opposition, including the psychologist Ferenc Mérei, the historian György Litván, the folklorist Jenő Széll and the economist András B. Hegedűs.

It seems to have been a principle of the repression to 'provide' each of the larger communities and each major workplace with its own special trial, or at least the discovery of a couple of 'counter-revolutionaries', so that the populace could not miss the message of intimidation. Everyone who tried to enlist foreign assistance or appeal to world public opinion because of the draconian sentences had to reckon with lengthy imprisonment. Such was the case of Domokos Kosáry, the respected professor of history, of Tibor Pákh, the Christian-Democratic politician who dared to investigate the Soviet-Hungarian economic and technical ties, and Péter Földes, the journalist. Földes was sentenced to thirteen years by a military court as late as 1960.

HOW MANY VICTIMS?

Although we have still no exact figures on the full extent of the reprisals, it is a reasonable estimate that, from the end of 1956 to 1959, at least 35,000 people were subjected to police or prosecutorial investigation because of political crimes. Even in the cases that ended with the police investigation, the victims were assured of several weeks in jail. Those subjected to court proceedings numbered 26,000, and some 22,000 received sentences. In the great majority of cases, the sentences were based on participation in the uprising or on resistance to state authority in the period after the Revolution. A smaller number of 'political' cases involved illegal frontier crossings, i.e. those apprehended while fleeing.

Between 1957 and 1960, some 13,000 people landed for a longer or shorter time in the newly developed internment camps (Tököl, Kistarcsa), and many thousands were placed under police surveillance. More than 100,000 people were directly affected by the repressive measures, and family members of those affected should be added to the total. Although a goodly percentage of the active participants in the uprising had left for the west by the end of 1956, the reprisals against those remaining in Hungary assumed a massive scale. The death sentences and prison terms formed the pinnacle of the pyramid; the rest, down to the base of the pyramid, consisted of those who experienced the 'milder' forms of repression.

Next to its sheer magnitude, the most important feature of the reprisal was its brutality. From December 1956 to summer 1961, when the last death sentence in a 1956 case was carried out, the number of death sentences brought to their conclusion can only be compared with the murders in the gloomiest years of the Rákosi regime. According to our best information to date, some 350 people were executed, including at least 229 people sentenced to death in political trials because of their participation in the uprising. Nearly three-quarters of them were young workers around 20 years of age who had engaged in the street fighting. The merciless quality of the reprisal is shown by the severity of the sentences: half of those charged before the people's courts were sentenced to more than five years' imprisonment. Official information about the closed trials fostered the claim that death sentences were reserved for cases of 'murder and involvement in lynching', as the official historians of the Kádár regime echoed years later. But the facts that have come to light since contradict that claim. On the strength of extorted and false testimony, the death sentence was imposed on persons who happened to be in a place where an atrocity was committed but were regarded by the court as accomplices, or on individuals who had participated in the armed struggle but without committing any violent act.

TARGET GROUPS FOR RETALIATION

The repression of the period following the Revolution differed in one fundamental respect from the vengefulness of the Rákosi regime. Rákosi and his lieutenants found themselves in a virtual state of war with the entire Hungarian society. The array of their 'enemies' extended from the 'class enemy' to the highest levels of the party leadership. The repression after the Revolution, on the other hand, had relatively definite objectives. The 'target groups' display a fairly homogeneous character with respect to occupation and age: the majority were workers 20–30 years of age. But they can also be classified according to the nature of their participation in the uprising and their putative standing in the emerging assessment of the Revolution by the Kádár regime. In this sense, we can distinguish three groups that were principal targets of the reprisals.

First, there is a group consisting of 18–20 year olds, mostly unskilled workers and apprentices, who took part in the armed struggle or were associated with insurrectionist groups. Their representation among those sentenced was relatively small in number, but most of them were found guilty by the courts and given harsh sentences. Most of those sentenced to death came from this group, as did those left out from the general amnesty. This group had chosen the most radical form of fight against the prevailing political system, and the regime may well have supposed that its most committed opponents would emerge from its ranks. This assumption was proved by the fact that even after the end of armed struggle, the insurrectionists had played important roles in the resistance groups of the underground. At the same time, the number of those fighters who had fled the country was relatively high, with the result that the full force of reprisal frequently fell on the more gullible among them, often on individuals whose involvement in armed resistance was marginal.

Second, the group that contributed the greatest number of those sentenced consisted of the members of the workers' councils and revolutionary committees from factories and local institutions. Most were workers and farmers of 28–35 years of age; a smaller number, often teachers and principals, came from the intelligentsia and enjoyed respect in their immediate surroundings. From this group came the organizational talent that rose overnight to become the local leadership elite of the Revolution. Equal to the demands of the extraordinary situation, they were ready and able to act within the direct democratic control obtaining in their sphere. It was characteristic that most of those who were elected to the provisional councils during the Revolution were confirmed in their positions by the new elections later in November. It also appears that most members of this group stood for socialist principles, their political views having been formed early in the post-war period in the workers' parties. Many members of this group had come into conflict with the regime during the Stalinst era. Workers' council members who were charged ordinarily appeared before regular courts and received milder sentences than the youths of the first group. Quantitatively, however, this group was hardest hit, both by judicial sentences and by extra-legal measures of repression. This was no accident, for it was clearly a major goal of the repression to eliminate this politically active segment of the society. It could properly be said of this group that it contained the moral and human capability of leading new democratic movements.

The third target group, numerically smaller but important and characteristic for the repression, was the intelligentsia, the circle that figured before 1956 as the inner-party opposition and the intellectuals associated with it, all of whom identified with the democratic and national objectives of the Revolution. Many of them participated actively in the resistance after 4 November. Not a few of them had some experience of resistance work under a dictatorship, before 1956 or even before 1945. A central objective of the Kádár regime was to obliterate any basis for such activity, which is why the intellectuals as defendants all received such harsh penalties.

BALANCE SHEET OF REPRESSION

The Kádár regime had goals for its programme of repression that went beyond the immediate ones of intimidation, overcoming resistance, and appeasing its own lust for revenge. One such objective was to find an 'explanation' for the Revolution, an answer to the question why the regime collapsed in October 1956. The ruling elite of the new regime knew from personal experience of the spontaneous and popular nature of the Revolution, and some of them had publicly acknowledged these facts in the October days. A number of them had originally shared the democratic, anti-Stalinist and national aims of the Revolution. But in the course of the repression, the Revolution was portrayed as agitation, conspiracy and deliberate destructiveness on the part of a small and consciously anti-communist group.

Accordingly, the investigating authorities and the courts did not, as was done in the show trials of the 1950s, invent horror stories – though their experience in such matters was not totally forgotten. The central aim was an 'interpretation' of the events that was comfortable for the regime, in other words their criminalization. Thus, the indictments and justifications of verdicts transformed inner-party criticism into 'organized anti-state activity', membership in revolutionary councils into 'partici-pation in a subversive movement', armed struggle against the invader into 'murder' and 'distruction of public property.' In the same manner, other defendants became 'clerical and reactionary elements' on the grounds of their family background or even without any such basis. Those workers and farmers who joined the Revolution and who had, in the 1950s, been charged with invented crimes, such as 'industrial sabotage' or 'avoidance of mandatory deliveries', were now called 'hard-ened criminals', 'kulaks' or 'rabble'. It is difficult to say what audience was intended with this 'explanation to the world'. In any case, the Kádár regime propagated this as official ideology for the outside world, especially the Soviet Union and other allies, but also for internal con-sumption in the at first small but by no means unimportant camp of followers. The regime did not assign great importance to the acceptance of this explanation by the general population, which would at all events have been difficult to accomplish.

Aside from initial uncertainties and occasional actions in the provinces, the reprisals did not touch all citizens or permeate everyday life. The press reported briefly or not at all on the court verdicts. The 'show trials' took place behind closed doors. The pamphlets dealing with the 'crime of counter-revolution' circulated early in 1957 but then ceased to appear; they did not have to be studied in hundreds of political seminars. Anyone who had been active in 1956 could be certain of retaliation, but anyone who had been inactive and remained so was left in peace. That sums up the most important goal and the saddest result of the repression. The best elements of the society, engaged in the Revolution, were broken and deprived of all hope, groups as well as individuals, while the majority were rewarded for their silence, their readiness to forget, and their compliance, first by being left alone and later by the prospect of a modest prosperity.

The farmers remained free of the mandatory deliveries that had been abolished during the Revolution. There were significant wage increases at the end of 1956 and through foreign credits the government was able to assure that there was something to buy with the larger incomes. In the renewed collectivization, the most brutal methods of the Rákosi era were avoided. In fact those methods were not necessary, for people now accommodated to the inescapable. Private plots were left to the farmers, allowing for some private production and, thereby, economic improvement.

At the June conference of his party in 1957, János Kádár had declared that most people worry less about larger issues of politics and more about their own material advancement. And it was true that the shattered society responded to signs of modest liberties and possibilities: the improved availability of goods as compared to the 1950s, later the permission to travel that could be had for $70, and the elimination of the certification as to social origin in admissions to higher education.

Furthermore, the state intervention in private affairs abated noticeably. The formerly obligatory political seminars, the newspaper-reading hours, and the required parades accompanied by slogans and clapping became things of the past. The regime gave up the effort to elicit demonstrations of public acceptance. Kádár's cynical remark of 1961, 'Whoever is not against us is with us', became the political rule of this period. The mentality that emerged was characterized by the psychologist Ferenc Mérei as a 'national amnesia'. Hardly anyone spoke any more of the Revolution or its defeat. Not only when someone was arrested, but also when someone was released, the fact was merely noted.

The social 'peace' thus achieved opened certain paths of advancement for individuals, but it also meant the dissolution of the social solidarity that had appeared so strongly during the Revolution. The tragedy of this historical period, from the repression through 'consolidation' to 'collective suppression', was that for nearly two decades, until the appearance of a new generation, all political activity of a democratic nature was impossible.

CHAPTER NINE

Resonance and Memory

In the west as in the eastern bloc, the human reaction to news on the brutal defeat of the Revolution was one of profound shock. Soon after the outbreak of the uprising there were already mass demonstrations, in Rome, Paris, London and elsewhere, in support of the revolutionary movement and against Soviet intervention. Among the first to protest were the Hungarians living in exile in the west as well as exiles from other communist countries. As it became clear that Moscow was employing armed force against a national movement and that there was more at stake than the removal of one communist regime in favour of another of similar sort, there were expressions of sympathy from many quarters. The organization of help – money, foodstuffs and medicine – became a worldwide affair.

REACTIONS IN EAST AND WEST

Among the east European countries, solidarity with Hungary was most pronounced in Poland. Besides the traditional friendship of the two nations, the Poles felt that the Hungarians were fighting for the same objectives, with the difference that Hungary had not been able to achieve reform of the regime by peaceable means.

By 27 October a dense network of spontaneous actions in support of the 'Hungarian brothers' had developed in Poland. Lines formed at the blood donation stations, and the collection of food, medicine and money was well underway. Beginning with workplace collectives and on through students, soldiers and passersby on the street, people contributed generously and, in thousands of petitions, declared their solidarity with the Hungarian Revolution. According to Polish sources, Poland had provided, from voluntary contributions, the equivalent of some $2 million by 19 November 1956, placing it at the head of the list of supporters of the Revolution in Hungary, the US supplying roughly $1 million. All other countries offered help in the amount of $3.8 million. The Polish press, comparatively free at this stage, reported quite objectively on events in Hungary. More than ten Polish reporters were in Budapest during the Revolution and wrote sympathetically about what they witnessed. Upon their return home, they continued to report on their experiences, not only in print but also in numerous gatherings.

Poland received with outrage the report of intervention on 4 November, and a not insignificant number of party members urged the Polish leadership to protest officially against the Soviet aggression. When the Polish ruling party refused and then voted along with the other satellite states against the US-sponsored UN resolution condemning Soviet intervention, the outrage grew until Gomułka was charged with betrayal of the Hungarian Revolution. By December 1956 the Polish censorship forbade any mention of the Hungarian Revolution, though Poland did not for a time join the other socialist states in applying the term 'counter-revolution'. By means of its repressive policy on the press, the Polish leadership succeeded in dampening the positive public attitude toward the Hungarian cause. But after Imre Nagy and his co-defendants were executed and Gomułka adopted the official Hungarian line in this connection, the 'pacified' Poles again gave vent to their anger. Many protested by resigning from the Communist Party. And for many more the executions destroyed all hope that socialism could be reformed.

In Romania also, especially in Transylvania and Timișoara, students and lecturers arranged demonstrations in many places, presented demands similar to those that had appeared in Hungary, and applied pressure on the ruling powers. Dozens of students and young intellectuals were arrested and imprisoned or sent as forced labourers to the infamous camps in the Danube delta; the noted poet Paul Goma, who later emigrated to Paris, was among them. The Romanian party leadership used the protest as the occasion to rid itself of some of the party cadres of Hungarian nationality, although Romanians as well as Hungarians had participated in the protests. It was also a convenient excuse to restrict the autonomy that had been granted to the million-strong Hungarian minority.

In Czechoslovakia, on the other hand, and especially in Slovakia, the loyalty of the Hungarian minority to the party leadership was emphasized in the propaganda and the expressions of solidarity with the Hungarian Revolution were ridiculed, while the recalcitrant Slovakian writers were discredited. At first the Czechoslovak leadership did not support the hard line advanced by Ulbricht and the SED at the Warsaw Pact conference in Moscow on 24 October, the call for immediate intervention, but that changed in a few days. Thereafter even Tito was criticized for the reservations he had about the Soviet invasion. Already in the spring of 1956, the Czechoslovak leaders had succeeded in repressing the acclaim unleashed by the Twentieth Congress of the CPSU, particularly in the Writer's Union, and by October there was no significant potential left for a positive response to events in Hungary. By recalling the interwar conflict between Czechoslovakia and Hungary, the press and radio were able to portray the Hungarian uprising as a nationalistic-revanchist movement And yet hundreds were arrested in October and November 1956 because they had, in some form or other, expressed sympathy with the Hungarian Revolution.

The party leadership in the GDR also managed, by all appearances, to stifle any public expression of solidarity. Yet Otto Spülbeck, Catholic Bishop of Bautzen/Meissen, sent a pastoral letter to be read in all the churches of his diocese, openly condemning the use of force and quoting the Papal Encyclical *Datis nuperrime* in which Soviet aggression against Hungary, as well as the Anglo-French attack on Suez, was denounced. There were protests among young workers and students, and state security records (which have now come to light) suggest that the intellectual ferment reached east German universities as well. Handwritten leaflets appeared on bulletin boards demanding a MEFESZ-type independent student union, others referred to the events in Poland and Hungary as signs of hope for the success of a struggle for German freedom and unification. We know a bit more today about the way in which certain rebels within the inner circle of the SED were encouraged by the anti-Stalinist movement in Hungary – though nothing came of it at the time. The arrest and trial of well-known intellectuals (such as Wolfgang Harich and his friends) in 1957 was clearly connected with the events in Hungary; the defendants were expressly accused of 'subversive contacts' with Hungary, especially with Georg Lukács.

Even now we are not well informed as to the reaction in the Soviet Union, including the camps of the Gulag, to the Hungarian Revolution and the Soviet intervention. Among the documents that have come to light so far is a set of leaflets and underground newspapers dealing with the events in Hungary and Poland. In Leningrad (now St Petersburg), seven students were tried for expressions of solidarity with the Hungarian Revolution and sentenced to years of hard labour. In Moscow too there were arrests and sentences for expressions of sympathy. It has only lately become known that the Soviet response to events in Poland and Hungary, contained in a bulletin from the CPSU in December 1956, was not received in local party units with the usual silent acceptance. Hundreds were expelled from the party because they did not agree with the views of the Khruschev Politburo and because they criticized the slow pace of de-Stalinization. From memoirs and the occasional personal recollection we know that the news of the Hungarian uprising was received with excitement in the Baltic republics and in the Caucasus (especially in Georgia), where people held their breath for weeks, whether a revolt against Soviet Russian oppression – what they, too, had to suffer – would succeed.

The other side of the coin is that those communist leaders who felt threatened by a radical dismantling of Stalinism – from the GDR to Czechoslovakia to China – were shocked by the Hungarian Revolution and tried, while invoking the Polish and Hungarian events, to erect barriers to any sort of reform. For decades in China, every move of a critical, democratic or reformist sort, and every corresponding idea, was labelled 'Petőfi-Circleism'!

People in the west, who already felt a certain degree of guilt over the plight of eastern Europe, generally felt extremely sympathetic toward the Polish people and, even more so, the Hungarian attempts to regain a certain degree of independence in October of 1956. Protests and demonstrations of varying size and fervour expressing support for the Hungarian Revolution took place not only in Europe and North America, but also over the entire world. Foreign journalists and film crews operating freely in Budapest provided the world with its first images of the armed rebellion which had broken out in a country inside the Soviet empire. Whereas people in the west felt sympathy and admiration for the Hungarian rebels they saw battling overwhelming Soviet firepower using Molotov cocktails and small arms, they continued to harbour reservations regarding the Imre Nagy government all the way until the decisive turning point of the Revolution on 28 October. From this date until 4 November, people in the west generally felt a good deal of optimism regarding what had so recently seemed to be an utter impossibility – that a satellite country would succeed in freeing itself from the Soviet orbit without external assistance.

After the Revolution was put down, the dominant concerns in the west were the provision of aid and the wave of refugees that continued unabated until mid-December. Austria, only recently freed from the four-power occupation, was scarcely in a position to care for the masses of refugees from Hungary. In less than a month's time, over 180,000 people arrived into the camps and temporary quarters set up at the eastern border and elsewhere in Austria. No international machinery was in place to cope with such a situation, and most governments were confronted in 1956 for the first time since the end of the Second World War (and the mass expulsion of Germans and others) with the political and social problems of mass migration. It was the unrewarding task of the Hungarian refugees to place these problems on the agenda in western Europe and beyond.

The majority of the refugees found sanctuary in North America (*c.* 80,000), Britain (*c.* 22,000), the Federal Republic of Germany (*c.* 16,000), Switzerland (*c.* 14,000) and France (*c.* 13,000). After some initial hesitation, all the western states were ready to accept the refugees. Around 10,000 students were enabled through government and private scholarships to continue their studies in the countries that received them.

BUDAPEST AS SYMBOL OF STRUGGLE FOR FREEDOM

As in 1848–49, Hungary in 1956 became the worldwide symbol of freedom and of the tragic defeat of a people rising up in the cause of freedom. A whole series of poets and writers concerned themselves with the Hungarian struggle for freedom. The Italian poet, Alberto Mondadori, wrote a poem of 100 lines entitled 'An Angry and Tender Song for Hungary', the first line of which read: 'Since the fourth of November I hear only screams'. The Polish poet, Zbigniew Herbert, underscored the helplessness of the neighbouring people:

> We are standing at the border
> we stretch out our hands
> and knot a great rope of air
> for you brothers
>
> just standing at the border
> the name of which is reason
> we watch the conflagration
> we gawp amazed at death
>
> (Translated by George Gömöri and Clive Wilmer)

The French poet, Julies Supervielle, also stressed the isolation that characterized the Hungarian struggle in a poem entitled 'To our Hungarian Friends':

> moving the earth's moving
> with such relentlessness
> dragging nation after nation
> not round five continents
> around Hungry it goes
> where hills and valley bleed

> ours the fault that you there
> must live and die this way

(Translated by Kenneth McRobbie)

It tells a great deal about the worldwide response that the Hungarian writer, Tibor Tollas, was able to gather an anthology entitled *Gloria Victis* (Honour to the Defeated) consisting of hundreds of poems celebrating the Hungarian October, sent to Tollas from all over the world.

Albert Camus, the French Nobel laureate, wrote a commemoration of the Revolution's first anniversary in which he castigated the political indifference of contemporaries:

> I am not one of those who wish to see the people of Hungary take up arms again in a rising certain to be crushed, under the eyes of the nations of the world, who would spare them neither applause nor pious tears, but who would go back at once to their slippers by the fireside, like a football crowd on Sunday after the cup final.
>
> There are already too many dead on the field, and we cannot be generous with any but our own blood. The blood of Hungary has re-emerged too precious to Europe and to freedom for us not to be jealous of it to the last drop. . . .
>
> Hungary conquered and in chains has done more for freedom and justice than any people for twenty years. But for this lesson to get through and convince those in the West who shut their eyes and ears, it was necessary, and it can be no comfort for us, for the people of Hungary to shed so much blood which is already drying in our memories.
>
> ('The Blood of the Hungarians' (1957), quoted from T. Tollas (ed.) *Gloria Victis*, Munich, 1966, pp. 9–10, translator unknown)

On the first anniversary of the Hungarian Revolution, John F. Kennedy, then US Senator from Massachusetts, said in a speech (now engraved on the memorial to 1956 in Boston):

> October 23, 1956, is a day that will live forever in the annals of free men and nations. It was a day of courage, conscience, and triumph. No other day since history began has shown more clearly the eternal unquenchability of man's desire to be free, whatever the odds against success, whatever the sacrifice required.

In the eyes of the world the Soviet tanks destroyed a popular uprising whose goal was, as many were persuaded, the building of a free and democratic society. And that happened only a few months after the Twentieth Congress of the CPSU at which the Stalinist dictatorship was revealed, the cult of personality condemned, and only days after the Soviet leadership had assured the states in its sphere of the right to choose their 'own path to socialism'. On 4 November Moscow made it clear that it was either unable or unwilling to forgo its hegemony and its military system of repression.

Recognition of this fact was a turning point for many people in east and west alike, people who thought of themselves as socialists and regarded freedom as being compatible with socialism. Many thinkers and politicians who later acted to prevent a continuation or reinstatement of Stalinism were able to recall that their eyes were opened to the true character of the regime by the Hungarian and Polish events of 1956.

With the execution of Imre Nagy and co-defendants two years later, the 'blood of Hungary', of which Camus had spoken, flowed again. On 20 June 1958, the Indian statesman Krishna Menon wrote: 'Whoever remains silent today about the suffering in Hungary not only helps in the acceptance of what has happened but also becomes an accomplice in the suppression of the Hungarian people'. Alas, the logic of great power policy made accomplices of many otherwise honourable western politicians.

1956 AND THE WESTERN LEFT

Western intellectuals who were most keen to follow the fate of the Revolution and were open to its ideals belonged mostly to the left end of the political spectrum. Many of them had known for years that Soviet Russia, which had been the hope of many for the creation of a new world, was actually a land of terror, a great power specializing in the repression of other peoples, but tried to nurse their earlier illusions. Many of them had been members of one of the western communist parties or were sympathetic supporters. The events of 1956 in Poznań, Warsaw and Budapest finally convinced them that they had been led astray from the ideals of their youth. The French actress Simone Signoret, who had been a guest along with Yves Montand at the 1957 New Year's celebration in Moscow, expressed the sentiments of many others in Paris and elsewhere about the situation in Budapest when she addressed her hosts, saying that the Soviet soldiers 'in one short week stopped being only the heroes of 1917 and the victors of Stalingrad . . . but had transformed themselves into imperial troops invading a colony. Those who condemn such acts when they occur elsewhere cannot close their eyes to these'.

The tanks in the streets of Budapest had demonstrated that the Soviet turn away from Stalin's horrific legacy was merely verbal. Precisely for the leftist sympathizers among the western intellectuals, so far as they could tell from the fragmentary news from Budapest, it seemed that the struggle of the Hungarian revolutionaries centred on a renewed 'social-ism' unblemished by mass murders in Moscow. That many former communists inscribed Fifty-Six on their banners, regardless of the extent to which the Revolution was a true harbinger of the renewed socialism they desired, was of course, less the result of precise analysis of the events than a form of wishful thinking on their part – and a symptom of the deep crisis of western leftist movements.

It is no exaggeration to say that the events of 1956 greatly hastened the decline of the large and influential western communist parties. A French historian spoke of the Hungarian Revolution as 'the beginning of the long twilight of the western communist parties'. The British Communist Party lost the best of its intellectual leaders. The Swiss party's membership was reduced by half. The Danish party split after 1956. The Italian CP, one of Europe's largest, lost 200,000 or 10 per cent of its members even though its First Secretary Palmiro Togliatti hesitated for a few days before endorsing the Soviet intervention. One hundred and one well-known Italian communists signed a letter of protest directed to the party leadership, condemning in the sharpest terms the Soviet intervention. The Italian trade union CGIL also con-demned the invasion and the Communist Party's endorsement thereof. The other large western party, the French, proved sufficiently disciplined that it lost few members. Maurice Thorez and the other Stalinists in the leadership persuaded the workers that the events in Poznań, Warsaw and Budapest were mere deviations organized by unruly intellectuals. Although the Soviet intervention was condemned by the unions (CGT and Force Ouvrière) and by many French workers of anarchist leaning, the party leadership, relying on references to the intervention in Suez and the traditional disparagement of intellectuals, was able to regain the trust of the workers.

But with the French intellectuals, largely inclined toward communism from the time of the Resistance, it was a different story. The Soviet invasion alienated many of them from the French CP. In November 1956, such prominent individuals as Simone de Beauvoir, Albert Camus, Aimé Césaire, Pablo Picasso, Jean-Paul Sartre and Vercors signed protests against Moscow and its Stalinist representative, the French party leader-ship. It is true that not many members turned in their party books, mainly because the CP leaders cleverly manipulated slogans such as 'the lessons of the Suez adventure of imperialism' and 'international worker solidarity'. And quite a few of the protesters of 1956 returned to the fold only a few weeks or months later – at least until 1968.

Besides these emotional attitudes, there were several authors among the anti-Stalinist left that turned to the Hungarian 1956 as an 'example' of what they had hoped for. In 1976 appeared *Hungary 1956* by the English political scientist, Bill Lomax, who had focused his investigation on the workers' councils and the organs of grassroots democracy, based not merely on sympathy but also on much new research. He, even more than Hannah Arendt, saw these spontaneous initiatives as the trademark of 1956, even though he did not overlook the emergence of very different political forces (which appeared to him as being reactionary and right-wing) either. Lomax's book not only had a great success in the west, but also was soon translated into Hungarian and circulated in Hungary as a clandestine (samizdat) publication as well.

ORGANIZATIONS AND AUTHORS IN EXILE

As soon as the tens of thousands of refugees had established themselves in the west, they formed a whole group of new Hungarians emigrant organizations and devoted themselves to preserving the legacy of 1956. Already existing Hungarian organizations acquired new members all over the world. Although there were significant differences in viewpoint between the new exiles and the earlier ones, all Hungarians united in the most basic cause of memorializing the Revolution.

The organization of Hungarian students in exile had an important role to play, with its 7,000 members by 1957. Many student organizations in Africa, Asia and Europe at that time still sympathized with the 'anti-imperialist' Soviet Union and supported the communist-led International Student Organization. On the strength of their personal experiences, the Hungarian students were able to unmask Soviet imperialism and its apparently democratic front organizations without being branded as 'agents' of the western powers. The Hungarian members of the international student movement functioned as catalysts in the formation of a genuinely free and democratic student organization (ICS) that is still of international importance.

There had been several major waves of emigration from Hungary in the twentieth century – of those fleeing the White Terror of the Horthy regime, the unemployment of the Depression, the persecution of 'Jews' in the 1940s, the advance of the Red Army and the Communist take-over in 1945–49 – but the country had never lost so many professionals, university students, athletes and artists all at once. Complete school classes, the entire student body of certain faculties (for example, of the famous forestry college in Sopron) and whole athletic teams along with coaches and trainers decided to gamble on the hazards of a new start in the west rather than accept the new Soviet domination. The profound loss that the stream of refugees of November-December 1956 meant for Hungary was a gain for the destination countries. Exiled musicians founded the Philharmonia Hungarica in Stuttgart and enjoyed world-wide success under the direction of Hungarian conductors living abroad. The student refugees became professors and researchers in all fields; they obtained posts at hundreds of universities and research institutions of western Europe and North America.

Emigrant circles also attended to the intellectual significance of the Revolution, above all by the creation of a free Hungarian press in the west. *Irodalmi Újság*, the weekly that had been the most influential voice of reform before the Revolution, was re-established, first in London and then in Paris, by exiled Hungarian writers. *Nemzetőr* (National Guardsmen), the journal founded and edited in Munich by the poet Tibor Tollas, who had been imprisoned for years during the Rákosi era, has preserved the spirit of 1956 for over three decades. Other Hungarian newspapers with a long tradition abroad found new contributors among the exiled writers, professors and students. These publications provided for years regular theoretical and programmatic treatments of the Revolution. The organ of the populist writers, *Látó-határ* (Horizon) in Munich, published numerous literary studies, poems, novels and essays on the Revolution and the ensuing reprisals.

As soon as the emigrants became more familiar with the political life of their new homelands, and as the relative stabilization of the Kádár regime made it evident that their exile would last for a long time (or forever), they began to search for allies in the cause of circulating on the international level the intellectual legacy of the Revolution. In 1958 György Heltai, a close associate of Imre Nagy, in cooperation with Balázs Nagy, former secretary of the Petőfi Circle, Béla Szász, and Zoltán Sztáray, who had spent many years in the Recsk forced-labour camp, founded the Imre Nagy Institute for Political Research in Brussels. They published a journal in Hungarian (*Szemle*) as well as in English and French (*Review/Études*), and served for years as a gathering point for western sympathizers of the left, those who recognized that the lessons of the Revolution reached far beyond local Hungarian problems and who believed that a renewal of socialist ideas in the spirit of 1956 was possible. Similar 'workshops' of the emigration were established else-where too, varying among themselves according to theoretical orien-tation. These were gathering places for students and intellectuals from Hungary where they could also meet new friends, not all Hungarian, and discuss problems of the Revolution and the general situation in east-central Europe.

Besides western historians and political scientists, such as Melvin J.

Lasky or Paul Zinner, exiled Hungarian authors produced the first analytical works on the reform era and the uprising (see the bibliography). Based partly on their own experience, partly on the UN report and interviews with participants in the revolutionary events who had emigrated to the west, they attempted to go beyond the bare historical facts to establish the character of the October–December 1956 events and to place these properly in Hungarian and European historical context. It was typical of these works that they began with the crisis associated with the failure of reform, at the point when an abyss opened up and led finally to the uprising – as expressed in the title, *Rift and Revolt in Hungary*, of Ferenc Váli's book. The author's special interest lay in the motivation and goals of the insurrectionists and in their relationship to the documented political programme. Other themes were the relationship between the intellectual elite revolting against the holders of power and the 'masses', and the special features of the Hungarian uprising, particularly in comparison with Poland. They tried to explain the unforeseen eruption, as expressed in the title of the book by Paul Kecskeméti, once a liberal Hungarian journalist and then an American political scientist: *The Unexpected Revolution*.

In response to the smear campaign against the Revolution's prime minister in Hungary, Miklós Molnár, former editor of *Irodalmi Újság*, joined with László Nagy to produce a book about Imre Nagy, which appeared in French just after Nagy's execution. Then came Tibor Méray's biography of Nagy, copies of which were smuggled into Hungary to become one of the most read of the forbidden books. These authors and others prepared the documentation *The Truth about the Nagy Affair*, published by the Petőfi Circle in Exile in Brussels in several languages in 1959. Tamás Aczél and Tibor Méray also wrote about the literary segment of the inner-party opposition, explaining the importance of the 'writers' revolt', discussed in Chapter 2. It is a noteworthy coincidence that Miklós Molnár's history of 1956, entitled *Victoire d'une défaite* ('Triumph of a Defeat' published in English as *Hungary 1956*), appeared on 20 August 1968, one day before Soviet tanks began to move on Prague. The author wanted his paradoxical title to suggest that the Hungarian Revolution, despite being overcome by superior force, amounted to a victory in the moral sense and as a political example it set for the future.

François Fejtő, an acknowledged expert on the history of eastern Europe (who had left Hungary in 1948), published his first book on the Hungarian Revolution by the end of 1956 in Paris. The first volume of his *History of the People's Democracies* had appeared in 1953, to be followed by the second in 1962, providing an overview of Soviet policy in the Stalin and post-Stalin eras and, against this backdrop, an evaluation of the Hungarian and Polish developments of 1956. One of Fejtő's central themes in his many publications was the potential for conflict in the differences emerging after 1953 among the Soviet, the Yugoslav, the Polish and the Hungarian models of socialism. He inquired as to the possibility that communist policy could be compatible with national interest in an individual people's democracy and under what circumstances a communist politician might, even for a short time, become a national leader. On the basis of rich documentary material, Fejtő emphasized the special importance of the Soviet-Yugoslav conflict for the eastern bloc, and argued persuasively for the significance of the decision of the Khrushchev leadership in 1956 to set relations with Yugoslavia on a new footing.

On the conservative side, the programme associated with the name Mindszenty took on ever more precise shape in the emigration. Its spokespersons abroad did not offer any large synthetic works about 1956, for their interpretation – understood from a moral and political standpoint as that of an obviously anti-communist independence struggle of Christian Hungary – fit perfectly with the notion of 'enslaved nations' that prevailed in many western nations during the Cold War. The editors of the aforementioned journal *Nemzetőr* largely followed this conservative anti-communist line.

In the works treating the life and struggles of Cardinal Mindszenty, who had become a symbol of resistance, attention was of course given to his release in 1956 and the few days of activity that was possible for him. The conservative organizations, including the old émigré clubs and the Hungarian churches abroad, kept alive the memory of 1956 in this spirit and helped to assure that the generations growing up in alien circumstances would not lose sight of the national and antitotalitarian traditions.

Finally, those radical anti-communist groups, already present in the streets during the Revolution, created their own image of 1956. A good example was the book about the armed struggle *Corvinköz – 1956* published in the United States by Gergely Pongrátz before he returned to Hungary in 1990. Authors of this persuasion have been questioning the complex reciprocal relations and cooperation that existed between radical reform ideas of the intellectuals and the general dissatisfaction in the population, between a government representing democratic-socialist tendencies and the more or less likeminded workers' councils, and the armed fighters. For them, the armed struggle was all that counted.

DISTORTION AND CONCEALMENT

Although the Kádár government that took power on 4 November was prepared initially, for reasons of weakness or lack of legitimacy or tactical advantage, to negotiate on certain points, it completely overturned the ideals of the Hungarian Revolution, refused all reasonable compromise, and invoked terror as its response. Nevertheless, one still frequently hears the statement: 'Kádárism did realize one or another of the Revolution's demands'. But if we hold that the basic goals of the Revolution were freedom, independence, neutrality, democracy and genuine national unity in a just social system, then the Kádár regime realized none of them and could realize none of them. It is true that a milder form of repression replaced the open terrorism of the first years, giving rise to a kind of black humour that labelled Hungary 'the merriest barracks in the socialism camp'. The regime had, thus, learned something from the Revolution: to observe the limits of what the society could endure and to rest content with merely formal loyalty on the part of citizens.

Striving for legitimacy, the Kádár regime sought for a time to discredit the Revolution, to depict it as a 'fascist counter-revolution'. A whole series of so-called White Books appeared in 1957–58 describing the 'counter-revolutionary events' that ostensibly took place in the towns and villages, claiming to be based on documents but in fact relying on distortions and falsifications. Many official propaganda publications tried to depict the leaders of and participants in the Revolution as fascists, criminals, US agents or adherents of the 'old regime'. This smear campaign, however, lasted for only a short period, then gave way to the tactic of concealment that continued for decades.

The silence that ensued, attempting to conceal the truth about 1956, was well-nigh all pervasive. Yet, it was never completely successful. A telling detail: even in the 1970s, the typewriters and copying machines in factories and offices were locked away by the authorized persons before 23 October in order to forestall the production of leaflets on that anniversary. In that way, many people who had heard little about 1956 within their families were informed by colleagues why the heavy office machines had to be dragged to the safe of the security officer.

Further, although the reprisals could not be discussed, there were in schools, plants and villages the relatives of persons who had been abducted or sentenced, of those who were missing or killed in the fighting or fled into exile. Those left behind never forgot the human casualties, even as they were unable to evade repression and penalties. About these things, 'everyone knew' even though they did not speak of them. As discussed before, the general depoliticization of society and the provision of a relatively comfortable way of life were in return for the required silence. However, the memory of the Revolution remained a 'smouldering fire in the ashes'. In the 1980s a sociologist came across the fact that people had not forgotten that 23 October 1956 was a Tuesday. Although the Revolution had been taboo for decades, the fact was clearly remembered. Recollections of the 'October events' lived on in such seemingly unimportant fragments.

When it became possible to travel, Hungarian students, intellectuals and other interested 'tourists' discovered Hungarian bookshops abroad where they received books on 1956 as gifts; hundreds of volumes were smuggled into Hungary in this manner. As in the era of neo-absolutism that followed the revolution of 1848–49, some brave student group demonstrated each year on 15 March, outside the official commemoration, for the ideals common to 1848 and 1956 – freedom, independence and the removal of foreign repression. And many of these youths, just as in the 15 March observances after 1849, made the acquaintance of the less hospitable aspects of the local police station.

Films, stories and novels occasionally mentioned the themes of tragic loss, the shadows of disappeared relatives, or details that reminded of particular 'white spots'. Allegory proved again, as so often under tyranny, to be the best means of outwitting the censor. Miklós Jancsó's film, *The Roundup* (1966), dealt with the bandit Sándor Rózsa who had fought alongside Kossuth and was captured in 1850, but everyone understood that the film really referred to present chicanery by the police and to the persecution of thousands of innocent and honourable people. Medieval heretics pursued by the Inquisition also served handily for allegorical purposes. Gyula Illyés's drama *Tiszták* (The Untainted) was a memorial for the Albigensians and, at the same time, the contemporaries subjected to overseeing power. Peter Gothar's film *Time Stands Still* (1982), which achieved world renown, depicts 1956 and the ensuing contradictions using one family as example: the father fled abroad, his friend finds a place in the new regime after serving a term of imprisonment, and the sons struggle with the difficulties of accommodation.

Generations of young people were unable for decades to learn more about the Revolution than isolated fragments or falsifications, until they began to ask about the truth content of the information. Then, if they really searched, they could after many years find answers in the samizdat literature circulated by the opposition. In the 1970s it became possible – after János Kádár had set an example in a toast – to speak of 1956 as a 'national tragedy' in film and literature, but the intended bridge signified no basic change in the official assessment of the Revolution. The bridge was in effect a one-way street. The former oppositional journalist Peter Kende wrote about this in the Paris emigration: 'The double meaning of the notion of tragedy makes possible the apparent bridge-building. . . . Yet if the lament reads, your fight was in vain, that does not mean the same as when it reads, our fight is lost.'

BREAKING THE SILENCE

The oppositional underground press began in the 1980s to break the silence that had prevailed in Hungary about 1956 for decades. But this 'second public' was too restricted to allow for the development of a relevant discussion of the meaning of the Revolution before 1988–89. In the writings that were published in Hungary, the attempt was made to keep alive the memory of the uprising. The magnificent poem by Gyula Illyés, 'One Word on Tyranny', written in 1950 and first published during the Revolution, was circulated on audio-cassette in the 1970s as cassette-recorders became the favourite 'music instruments' of young people.

Among the first samizdat publications were the documents on 1956 collected by György Krassó and 'published' in *Napló* (Diary), a hand-copied 'journal' circulated among Budapest oppositional intellectuals in the late 1970s. (It was also he who had translated Lomax's book on 1956 and managed to circulate it in hundreds of copies in the underground.) In 1983, the most widely read underground newspaper in Hungary, *Beszélő* (The Speaker) devoted an entire issue to the memory of the executed prime minister, his fellow martyrs, and the ideas for which they sacrificed their lives.

Yet, still in 1984, as the journal *Új Forrás* (New Source) published the young Gáspár Nagy's poem which only by cryptic initials referred to Imre Nagy ('the grave Is Nowhere . . .'), the journal was banned and the editorial group disbanded. True, the last lines of this short writing, subtitled (P.S.) were explicit enough. They ran (in English translation):

one day he must be buried agaIN
and we must not forget him agaIN
we must call out the name of the assassIN.

(Translated by George Gömöri)

When in the mid-1980s, as 1956 became a central theme of the newly organized opposition and the discussions could no longer be halted, the downfall of the Kádár regime was, as suggested in the Foreword, already foreshadowed.

The discussions about the assessment of 1956 will certainly continue in Hungary for a long time, for it is not just an academic debate or an exchange of opinions but goes directly to the legitimation of the new order. The basic question is: on what historical tradition the new democratic republic can and will build. The reinstatement of the near-miraculous national unity of those days of four decades ago is scarcely possible amidst the daily business of laborious rebuilding. But it is also clear that the reconstruction of the manysidedness of the 1956 Revolution will not be possible on the basis of positions that carry heavy political and emotional freight. That can happen only through the disentangling of the thousands of strands of the events and the motives of participants, to which end research into the gradually more accessible foreign and Hungarian archives and the readiness of eyewitnesses and of victims still alive to publish their memoirs will be necessary to the forging of a secure foundation.

Afterword

P. Kende

The 1956 uprising of the Hungarian people belongs to those rare, truly epochal events the importance of which does not fade with the passing of time. Moreover, the past four decades, and especially the years since the collapse of the Soviet empire, seem only to have confirmed the assumptions made at the time by the more astute contemporaries. An inquiry into the fate of these assumptions lends itself quite naturally to reflections suitable for an Afterword. One only has to start out from the contemporary assessments, be they positive or negative, and ask whether the intervening forty years either verified or falsified them. Answers can be given now with much greater certainty than they could even in 1986, for the most decisive pieces of 'evidence' accumulated precisely after 1989.

Let us concentrate only on those most relevant features of the events that had struck the minds of contemporaries and the reverberations of which can still be felt. First, the Hungarian Revolution shook the seemingly unshakable Soviet empire. Second, it exploded the political (and philosophical!) fiction of proletarian socialism and with it a number of other dogmas of the European left. Third, it was an example of a revolutionary mass movement – including the armed uprising – that challenged the totalitarian system from inside with the aim to recover the elementary rights and freedoms abrogated by the dictatorship; hence, it could properly be called an 'anti-totalitarian revolution'.

In the preceding summary positive values were attached to these features, but this is merely a question of wording. They can also be formulated in the language of the Soviet political and imperial system, in which case they become features of a counter-revolution in the service of the west that endangered the achievements of 'socialism' and disturbed the development of the relations between the states of the

Soviet bloc. Its instigators then appear as traitors to the cause of socialism, reactionary adventurers who aimed at the destruction of the new society that was to be built under communist leadership. All this is accurate within the particular frame of discourse and does not contradict the meaning of the previous positive characteristics. Except for one significant difference: by implying that 'counter-revolution' is to mean the intent to restore the pre-1945 'old order', and not – what we demonstrated to have been its programme – the dismantling of the totalitarian system. It is worth considering this and – in the light of the events since 1989 – to ponder, whether an anti-totalitarian revolution, even if it starts out as a democratic movement, does not potentially include certain 'restorationist' elements. The use of the word 'counter-revolution' was, of course, not a choice informed by political science (in which the violent overthrow of a given government may equally be called 'revolution' or 'counter-revolution'), but was mere propaganda, aimed at denouncing the events of 1956 within the Soviet bloc and, above all, among the western sympathizers of Revolution. But leaving this aside for the moment, let us note that the Soviet leadership – in its own way – recognized the epochal significance of the Hungarian Revolution no less than did its convinced adherents and western admirers.

In what follows the significance of the explosion of 1956 will be examined in terms of the three striking characteristics mentioned above. Besides the more specific question about its place in post-Second World War history of international relations, it may be useful to test whether and in what sense the intervening four decades have verified the assessment made by contemporaries of the Hungarian October.

THE SHAKEN EMPIRE

The Hungarian – and, naturally, also the Polish – events that 'shook the Kremlin' hit the world as a surprise. As outlined in Chapter 5, the western chanceries were totally unprepared for such an event. Nor were political observers of the Soviet orbit better prepared, for they too believed that the empire was – even after the death of Stalin – unshakable. Berlin 1953 was in fact registered mainly by Germans on both sides of the wall. Nor was Poznań recognized as more than an isolated episode. Hence, it is fair to say that the anamnesis of the Soviet crisis began with the autumn of 1956. More precisely: the visible, audible, 'filmable' story began at that date, relegating all that might have prepared the explosion into the category of 'prehistory'. On the plane of palpable history, the one that is able to capture the attention of the public, Warsaw and

Budapest made it clear that the Soviet edifice was not that concrete block that it pretended to be, that there was life within this structure, where people moved, anger boiled, and – conditions permitting – forces could emerge that were able to rock the entire building. In a word, the message from Poland was that society is alive, and from Budapest that communism can be toppled.

These messages were clearly received in Moscow, and the subsequent thirty-odd years of the Soviet system could be described as a series of measures aimed at avoiding a repetition of 1956. But the messages also touched the hearts and minds of people in the farthest corners of the countries under Moscow's rule. The disobedience of an entire people – however unbelievable it may have appeared before – became a cherished example in the collective memory of oppressed people. (In this respect the fame of Budapest travelled farther than that of Warsaw.) It is well known that 1956 was very much on the minds of Czech reformers in 1968 and of Polish oppositional leaders in the 1980s, both as precedent and a strategic question. There are indications that the Hungarian uprising, as a badly handled challenge, had worried even Gorbachev, suggesting that the Hungarian question was still a 'question' in Moscow thirty years later.

In the context of contemporary history, the first and most immediate significance of the 1956 eruption was that it confirmed the Soviet supremacy over eastern Europe. This suzerainty developed in fact between 1944 and 1946, not because of some secret agreement between the wartime Allies (as has been believed ever since Yalta), but as a consequence of the actual balance of power at the end of the Second World War and western attitudes in the first years of the Cold War. This de facto tolerated, but de jure assiduously denied acceptance of Soviet domination of the region was for the first time tested – and subsequently tacitly 'codified' – precisely in 1956. Or to put it otherwise: the pact of Yalta was really written in 1956, when the western powers indicated both by their (in)action and their explicit diplomatic messages, that Moscow's tutelary position over the 'people's democracies' enjoyed international approval. This must have surprised the Soviet leaders most of all, who in the course of the Polish and Hungarian events feared that all their gains of 1945 might – with or without a military strike – be lost. The demonstrative passivity of the western powers made them realize that their domination of eastern Europe was final and unassailable. This recognition defined all their actions thereafter.

Another major consequence of the Hungarian Revolution was an accelerated change in the relationship between the Kremlin and the European satellite parties. (Actually, a revision began right after Stalin's death.) The new Soviet leaders, or at least the more innovative ones (Malenkov, Khrushchev), seem to have intended to change the role of these parties from mere agents and satellites into consulting partners. The courting of Tito also fits into this strategy, except that he insisted on the position of an equal partner as a minimum, and was not prepared to give up the slightest morsel of the independence he had won in 1948. Thus, the 1955 readmittance of Tito-Yugoslavia to the community of socialist states aggravated the thorny problem of partnership with the satellite communist parties, as Khrushchev, at least tacitly, approved of Tito's claim to 'sovereign equality'. This challenge became dramatic in the Hungarian Revolution. However, the concessions granted to Yugoslavia could not be explicitly revoked, and this fact seriously under-mined the 'ideological' foundations of Soviet intervention. That is why, even if in 1956 Khrushchev and company acted according to the later Brezhnev doctrine, that could not be pronounced in so many words at that time.

Looking at it in this way, the Revolution can be seen as an event that disturbed a kind of evolutionary process with which the first post-Stalin generation of Soviet leaders wanted to experiment. This trend was still reflected in the 30 October Moscow declaration. Not even the most radical reorganization of the alliance, as it may have been envisaged by Khrushchev, could accommodate the granting of a true sovereign status, as demanded by Hungary in the last days of the Revolution. The reformers in the 1956 Kremlin could only go as far as they did in Poland, but not to the stage of a multiparty system and neutrality. However, this limitation should not be taken as self-evident. In late October, before the decision to intervene against the Nagy government, the Soviet Presidium's deliberations did in fact include an option that would have meant Hungary's 'Finlandization'. There is no reason to subscribe to the – then and since generally accepted – tenet that the Soviets had no other choice but the brutal suppression of the Hungarian revolt. Maybe Khrushchev's position in the given power configurations within the Kremlin did not permit an alternative solution, but that should not mean that this was in the so-called 'interest' of the USSR. A look at the *longue durée* seems to prove the opposite – if the correctness of a choice in a historical dilemma can ever be proved. The decision to intervene in Hungary and the concomitant political conceptions sealed the fate of the Soviet empire. After the defeat of armed resistance, Hungary was 'normalized', that is, returned to the only accepted mode of communist exercise of power. The same was done later in Czecho-slovakia and, exactly a quarter of a century after the Hungarian uprising, in Poland. In the subsequent decade the reform-minded Gorbachev exerted himself in the Herculean task of changing the course of Soviet internal and foreign policy in the spirit of cooperation with the West. These efforts were in vain, but they disturbed the system to the point of collapse, first of the Soviet empire, then of the USSR itself.

This history in a nutshell – which disregards, among others, the economic parameters – may suggest that Khrushchev acted correctly in 1956, in that he postponed by thirty-five years that final outcome which was triggered by Gorbachev's reform experiment. However, a different reading is also possible. According to that, the 1956 decision placed the Soviets on a trajectory which allowed for no other outcome. But precisely in 1956 – or rather, in the period of post-Stalin rearrangement – there might have been an alternative. Let us explore this hypothetically.

In 1956 Moscow may have had the possibility for working out a compromise with Budapest just as Britain had in 1947 by granting independence to India or de Gaulle in 1962 by obtaining a vote for letting Algiers go. While revising Stalin's policies, the Soviet leadership could very well have opted for the solution – considered by Gorbachev thirty years later – to establish its western (central European) glacis with states that enjoy the support of their people while being attached to the USSR in terms of foreign policy. This arrangement would have surely demanded considerable adjustments in ideology, but in terms of security it would not have been less acceptable than the limited sovereignty granted Finland or the neutrality negotiated for Austria in 1955 in return for the evacuation of its Soviet-occupied eastern districts. Moreover, by allowing central Europe a free course of development, the Soviet Union, as the undisputed superpower in the region, would have gained enormous economic advantages (as it did in the case of Finland). It is worth noting that such a well-informed observer of the events as Henry Kissinger mentioned this possibility in his book, *Diplomacy* (New York, 1994).

To push this fantasy to the brink: assuming such flexibility for the Soviet empire, even the endgame could have been played differently. In an advantageous climate of Soviet liberalization, the 'Prague Spring' could have happened ten years earlier, and if the Kremlin had been able to handle that, the end of the Cold War and German reunification could have preceded Gorbachev by twenty or twenty-five years. With a signal difference from 1989: the Soviet economy would still have had huge reserves and the leadership of the USSR would not have been forced to accommodate itself with the west against the backdrop of total domestic collapse. In other words: a changed Soviet system could have joined the world powers as a much more viable partner.

Turning this imaginary scenario around, two other hypotheses could be proposed. Had the post-Stalin reorganization in the Soviet empire proceeded swiftly towards modernization and a certain reliability (legality, etc.) to the extent that no explosion occurred in Poland and Hungary in 1956, nor later in Czechoslovakia or Poland, the bloc might have arrived at the rosy ending sketched above, becoming a fair competitor on the world scene. The Soviet Union might have ended up as one of the leading powers at the end of the twentieth century. That this scenario did not happen is to no small measure due to the fact that the Hungarian Revolution threw sand into the machinery. And finally, one more mental experiment: the Soviet leaders could have reacted flexibly to the Hungarian uprising in 1956 (as hypothesized above) but this might not have been followed by a successful adaptation, rather the opposite. New revolts and challenges could have rocked the edifice, exactly as the Kremlin feared all along. Because of these conflagrations, the collapse of the system would have been hastened by thirty years or so. Would that have been different from the 1989–91 one? Among many other features, one major difference would have been that the blame for defeat could have been placed not on the proponents of inertia, but on those who advocated and granted concessions. Thus the political and military potential of the most restorationist elements in Russia would have survived intact and ready to act. Thanks to the immobility of decades, there remained little of such potential for the 1990s.

Of course, as we know, none of these things happened: 1956 remained an unused opportunity, or rather a source of fear from which the Soviet leaders and their allies, the east-central European party and state leaders, drew merely technical lessons. The men of the Kremlin understood that in the future their directives must be implemented in a differentiated way and not without consulting – or even bargaining – with the concerned local potentates. The latter, in turn, understood that it is not enough to build castles in Spain and pursue prestige projects, but that people must also be fed and given something in other spheres, such as culture, as well. But the prevailing ideological rigidity after 1956 barred even economic reforms, to say nothing of political ones. Therefore, the Soviet empire operated with ever decreasing efficiency. The standard of living could be improved only by getting into serious debt (or, as in Czechoslovakia, by keeping living standards stagnant for decades though without debts). While this is not to deny that the Soviet order managed to get stabilized for a long time after 1956, it paid a high price: except for a few, more conspicuous than relevant, modernizing gestures, the system proved unable to adapt to the challenges of the times. The consequence was the sudden collapse in the 1980s. In this sense, there is a deep connection between 1956 and 1989. In a word, the system's demise was a function of its reactions to the challenge of 1956, its attempts to re-establish its balance and avert any similar event.

THE END OF AN ILLUSION

Let us start with a chronological fact: the year 1956 lies exactly at the midpoint between the 1917–19 Russian communist revolution and the collapse of the Soviet system in 1989–91. This suggests a connection with the change of trend that must have happened at some point in time between the beginning and the end of that system. The following considerations may help to define this 'inflection point'.

In a certain way the Bolshevik revolution and the ensuing totalitarian communism was, despite all of its local (Russian, Eurasian, etc.) traits and historical-personal accidents (such as Stalin), part of that spiritual-political transformation that began with the European Enlightenment. Yet, it turned virtually all elements of the democratic and humanistic content of that secularizing programme into its opposite, placing it into the service of a tyrannical regime that strove to control every move and action of society totally. (How far it succeeded is another question.) Simultaneously, the communist ideology, while continuing to refer to those enlightened and progressive ideas that were its midwives, kept denouncing all the surviving variants thereof as fakes and distortions. Instead, it claimed that the Soviet social and political system was the fulfilment of these ideals and their sole true heir.

Remarkably, this claim was to a certain extent accepted also by people who had nothing to do with socialist or left-liberal concepts. It was accepted first of all by placing communism on the 'left' of the political spectrum, in contrast to Mussolini's Fascism or to Nazism, to which all mental kinship was denied. And it was accepted in the sense that Jean-Paul Sartre called revolutionary Marxism 'the unsurpassable horizon of our times'. Without the relative sympathy or at least benevolent patience of the European *progressiste* milieu and their political camp (Labour Party, French Radical Socialist, etc.) Soviet communism could not have become that powerful political force which it was in the mid-twentieth century. The role played by the Soviet Union on the side of the Allies during the Second World War had, of course, very much to do with this. But it could be asked whether this alliance – besides the unquestionable strategic necessity – wasn't due to an extent to the image of Soviet society held by a significant segment of western society. After the war, when sympathies for the Soviets generally declined, a fair number of western intellectuals flocked to the communist parties or expressed direct solidarity with the USSR. In several – peculiarly, mostly Latin-speaking – countries the pro-Soviet communist parties secured considerably more votes than the social democratic ones, which remained true to a western orientation and liberal democracy. For some reason which is still not quite clear, many western sympathizers of the Soviet system subscribed not only to the ideal aims of communism, but also to those terroristic methods – show trials, mass arrests – as well by which Stalin's communism silenced all its opponents and established a near-complete monopoly of power.

There is good reason to argue – and this is the main point here – that this political and spiritual influence of Soviet communism was fundamentally shaken by the Hungarian uprising. As discussed in Chapter 9, the decline of the western communist parties, and especially their support among the intellectuals, began in 1956. The fiction of dictatorial proletarian socialism came to be questioned if not rejected even by those who had cherished it at the height of Stalin's reign. But how could a series of events lasting for a relatively short time and in a far-away small country release such far-reaching waves? And was this impact an episode, or did it start a trend that lasted to the end of the collapse of the Soviet system?

The first question may be answered by pointing to the symbolic meaning of what happened in Hungary. To be sure, Hungary was by no means a priori the ideal venue for such a confrontation. It was one of the less significant countries in the Soviet satellite system, neither well known nor highly regarded in western public opinion. (Poland and Czechoslovakia, for example, always had a better press in the west than Hungary, infamous for its nationalities policies in the past and known as Hitler's ally from 1939 to 1945.) And yet, it was in this small country where for the first time an emblematic struggle between the Soviet Union and a revolutionary risen people – above all, its proletariat – took place. And 1956 was the historical moment when the Soviets appeared, if not the first time, but for the western sympathizers most openly and unequivocally, as mere oppressors, as naked military might. Their action had no other acceptable rationale than a superpower's imperial interests, denigrating all those principles which their frame of reference used to rely upon. For those familiar with the history of the USSR and the international working-class movement, the Soviet Union had long lost its claim to be a revolutionary workers' state. Some wrote it off after Kronstadt, some after Stalin's rise to power. But for the wider public – especially in the Euro-American world – 4 November 1956 became the moment of truth. By acting as they did, the Soviets presented incontrovertible evidence that they are not what they pretended to be but its exact opposite.

Besides the obvious joy and feeling of justification by all those who believed in the eventual victory of democracy among the 'captive nations', there were a number of particular reasons why the resonance of Budapest was as loud and wide as it was. One of these was the crucial role in the resistance by the workers' councils – and the fact that no 'anti-workers' councils' emerged that would have demonstrated the existence of a pro-communist working class. Another was the part played by the writers, some of whom were well known in the west, and particularly in leftist circles, such as Gyula Illyés, Julius Háy and Georg Lukács. A popular uprising in which such famous and left-wing writers and other intellectuals stood side by side with simple working people could not convincingly be described as the action of a misled, unbridled rabble. Additionally, the wide political spectrum of Imre Nagy's last government, in which men who rose during the Revolution (as Pál Maléter) sat next to well-known politicians of the post-war coalition period who had survived Stalinist jails and persecution (Tildy, Kovács, Kéthly), was more than impressive. Finally, there was the person of Imre Nagy. The nationally acknowledged revolutionary government was headed not by some suspect, power-hungry adventurer, not by an old piece of furniture taken out of mothballs, but precisely by that person whom the post-Stalin leadership had selected in 1953 to replace the badly compromised Rákosi and whose return to power was demanded on 23 October 1956 by hundreds of thousands of citizens but who was also accepted by the emissaries of the Kremlin themselves (see Chapter 4).

And one more aspect, very important in the western perceptions of the Revolution, should be added: that the non-communist or anti-communist masses were joined by a good number of former communists, in the workers' councils, in the Revolutionary Council of Hungarian Intellectuals, among the writers and in Nagy's immediate entourage. The formula of 1956 was thus not simply 'people *versus* communists', but rather the people along with a fair contingent of communists against the supporters of the Stalinist regime and their Russian allies. Numbers (which we still do not know precisely) are not important here, but rather the fact that quite a few functionaries of the fallen system supported the popular uprising. That made the slogan about 'counter-revolution' in itself problematic, while it certainly contradicted the image won by western observers. That many a western leftist might have personally empathized with those ex-communists who joined the uprising, whom they may have seen as similar to themselves marching down their road to its logical end, should also be mentioned parenthetically.

As to the long-term impact of 1956, a few caveats should be added before going into details. First of all, it could hardly be proved that the Hungarian Revolution was the very event that definitely terminated all the myths about the USSR, and finally led to the end of all illusions about socialism, including democratic socialism. Intellectual and political processes of this sort can never be precisely dated; neither their beginning, nor their end. Nobody can predict now what ideologies will prevail in the twenty-first century. Furthermore, the prevailing ideas in a society are simultaneously influenced by several intellectual and factual processes. Political events are only one of these, and to place a single set of events into the centre disregarding all other aspects would be more than immodesty. If we think especially of the 1960s, we remember that this was also the beginning of the 'environmentalist wave', and, as we know, in the subsequent decade the ideology of progress had the greatest trouble precisely with ecological standpoints. It is, therefore, better to limit our question to the *image* of the Soviet system and formulate it in the following way: did 1956 have a lasting impact on that image, or did it remain a mere episode?

The impact of the Hungarian Revolution seems prima facie to have been episodic. In a peculiar way, the ripple effect of its influence was interrupted by the launching of the first sputnik. This is an interesting addition to the psychology of 'Sovietophilia' in which the admiration of demonstrated force often played a role. Thereafter, the western world got mentally prepared for a long lasting coexistence with the Soviet system, which led to such things as the theory of convergence or an *Ostpolitik* that closed both eyes to the 'trespasses' of the communist police-state. This relative calm was broken by the troops of the Warsaw Pact marching against Prague, in a way a repetition of November 1956 (only now with Hungarian troops among them). Since much has been written on the parallels of the two invasions, let us emphasize the difference. While in terms of superpower behaviour the two were, indeed, quite similar, they were different in terms of ideological impact. November 1956 was the Waterloo of leftist thought. Not so 1968, or not in the same way. The preceding 'Prague Spring' evoked the impression that not all is lost in the Soviet orbit, communism may be redeemable, can receive a 'human face', and if so, the expectations attached to the Russian Revolution of 1917–19 may prove not to have been entirely unfounded. The Czech reform communism gave for a while a new élan to the western left; the short-lived success of the so-called Eurocommunism was also nourished by these illusions. Eurocommunists (and some other socialist parties in Europe and Latin America) faulted Brezhnev not primarily because of the brutality of military intervention, but because the action seemed to them politically and theoretically unfounded. The tanks rolled against comrades who – so they argued – did not endanger the cause of Soviet socialism, but, to the contrary, promised great moral and economic triumphs for it. This interpretation, besides being faulty in many factual details, disregarded all that was similar between the Czech movement and the Hungarian events of twelve years before. But it is worth mentioning, for it displays a certain frustration as well as self-justification. The European left experienced 1968 not as another discreditation of communism but rather as a missed great opportunity. The intervention of August 1968 was, therefore, a shock of a different type, in a certain sense even more profound than that of November 1956.

The ideas and concepts associated with the Hungarian Revolution surfaced again during the 1970s in Poland. In 1980–81 the Budapest formula appeared clearly – and now with lasting validity – for the whole world to see: on one side the 10 million workers of Solidarity, on the other the Soviet-communist power machinery. True, the latter was sustained in Poland by Poles, but the suzerain power made sufficient noise to reveal the 'domestic' actors as agents of the Kremlin.

Thus we do arrive at the signal date of 1989, when the Soviet system collapsed like a house of cards: after long years of fight in Poland, in a few months in Hungary, in weeks in East Germany, in days in Czechoslovakia, and finally in Romania and the Balkans. In a strangely paradoxical way, this did, and then again did not, surprise anybody. The end was (or could have been) foreseen; still the speed of collapse and the – in the last resort – 'smooth' demise of the system surprised everybody. But then the world took it for granted that the collapsed system would be replaced almost automatically by institutions of pluralist democracy. For the model had been prefigured in 1956 in Budapest.

In summary, then: 1956 was one, surely very significant, event among many others that changed the trend towards the downfall. It was not even the very beginning. As argued in Chapters 1 and 2, the Soviet system's crisis started in 1953 at the latest. Khrushchev's role should not be underestimated. His Canossa in Yugoslavia and the secret speech at the Twentieth Congress were necessary though not sufficient causes of the Hungarian uprising and its long-term consequences. The process seemed to be halting in the mid-1960s, and new, different impulses were needed – such as those of the emerging Soviet dissidents' ever more audible voice – to continue. The impact of 1956 was, thus, a long-term trend in this sense: not a linear progress but a halting and fluctuating process. (In certain contexts, reference to Hungary could strengthen opposite forces, supplying arguments for hardliners.) Nevertheless, it can be argued that 1989 was the continuation and fulfilment of 1956, the radical rejection of the entire system, for which the Hungarian Revolution was the primary historical precedent.

MODEL FOR COMING REVOLUTIONS

The recognition that the Hungarian 1956 was an 'anti-totalitarian revolution', and the first one of its kind, was made by two political philosophers of the stature of Raymond Aron and Hannah Arendt. Later, the notion was accepted by leading authors of the French 'new left', and it became the generally accepted interpretation in the French liberal-democratic thinking of the last three or four decades. In Anglo-Saxon (mainly North American) circles its reception was hindered by the stubborn – and, seen from an east European vantage point, quite absurd – reluctance of some Kremlinologists to recognize the totalitarian character of the Soviet system. The notion of a Soviet 'institutional pluralism', a strange offshoot of the convergence theory, was trying to hide in the magician's hat that very character of the Soviet system against which all liberation movements had fought. Without entering into debates on terminology, there can be no doubt that for all those opposing the Soviet regimes – from 1956 down to their final victory in 1989 – the enemy appeared 'totalitarian' in its intentions and, mostly, in its methods as well. True, the Kádár regime was, in comparison to the reign of a Brezhnev or Andropov, only 'three-quarters totalitarian', but this was sufficient to keep the majority of the people in a lasting state of fear and resigned apathy. That this statement is just as much an opinion as the one on institutional pluralism could be argued, had the events of 1989 not unequivocally proved the case of the totalitarianists. If the Soviet system had been any kind of pluralism, it might have managed gradually to transform itself into something 'more pluralist', and become a politically and economically viable competitor of the free market societies and democracies. But this did not happen: it collapsed or burst asunder the very moment that its leaders were forced to accept a modicum of pluralism. The mere fact that the Communist Party ceased to keep its absolute monopoly of power made the system fade away. Actually, in some Soviet republics the local ex-communist potentates tried to play institutional pluralism, and that sufficed to induce clinical death to the system.

The Hungarian 1956 was an anti-totalitarian revolution first of all in this sense. The massive – partly armed – uprising conspicuously and visibly swept away the power-monopoly of the Communist Party. For reasons that were to a great extent national, caused above all by the first Soviet intervention, the party apparatus and its police ran in panic, the army fell apart, or (in small segments) chose the side of 'the nation'. Thereafter nobody held sufficient power for decision-making or acting. In the suddenly materialized atmosphere of freedom new political forces appeared – and could have become organized, had there been time for it. (In fact, only plans and projects were formulated.) That the nominal central authority (for administrative power rested at most in the hands of local authorities) was headed by Imre Nagy, had great symbolic value. With him a man came to the helm, who – although risen in the previous regime and who needed time to overcome his own initial disorientation – finally chose decisively and unequivocally the side of 'the people' and 'the nation' over his Soviet communist past. The anti-totalitarian character was finally expressed in institutional terms when the one-party system was replaced by a multiparty cabinet that proposed parliamentary elections and was about to cancel the one-sided dependence on the Soviet Union.

In this sense, the Hungarian Revolution was a precursor of what transpired after 1989. It was an example and model that had no parallel between 1956 and the collapse of the Soviet system.

The 1968 Czech ferment was, of course, in certain respects a continuation of 1956. The processes that started to gain speed in the Czechoslovak society would have sooner or later certainly – but to an extent even in the short run – challenged the autocracy of the Communist Party. This aspect was correctly assessed by Moscow. The special feature of the 'Prague Spring' was that the tiptoeing popular revolt enjoyed the connivance of a significant segment of the communist establishment, in contrast to the Hungarian, which, with its violence and destruction, frightened the entire establishment. National aspects were not missing either, especially after the Warsaw Pact invasion, which humiliated the Czechs and Slovaks (maybe the former more than the latter) not only in their human and civic but also in their national dignity. Still, the 1968 sequence of events did not duplicate the Hungarian precedent, the replacement of the one-party state by a representative, pluralist government.

Something similar can be said about the Polish upheaval of 1980–81. Although it mobilized the great majority of the society and led to the establishment of such a representative trade union that it could be regarded as a veritable counter-government – and was popular enough to survive in the underground the years of martial law – it still did not overthrow the communist system. This statement is not meant to belittle the significance of the social and political movement surrounding Solidarity. Everybody agrees that it was the largest and most tenacious movement of disobedience and opposition in the entire history of the Soviet system. Moreover, if we consider that all that followed in 1988–89 (the round table, elections, the first non-communist government) was in effect a continuation and fulfilment of the movements of 1980–81, Solidarity will have to be recognized as one of the most significant factors in the collapse of the communist world. Nevertheless, the Polish 1980 proposed a more modest programme than the Hungarian 1956. No doubt, this was conscious self-limitation on the part of Solidarity's leaders; by not challenging the party's and the government's right to power, they wished to avoid the fate of the Hungarians of twenty-four and the Czechs of twelve years before. Therefore, they could aim at 'detotalitarizing', that is, at establishing pluralism, only in the social, not the political sphere.

The claim that the Hungarian Revolution was anti-totalitarian implies nothing more than that it replaced the Soviet-type system by something else, that it dismantled the monopoly of power in the hands of the Communist Party, and thus opened the way to expressing alternative social and political wills. An anti-totalitarian revolution is by definition libertarian, just as in Hungary, where the struggle was fought for the recovery of elementary rights of freedom as well as for national independence and dignity. By elementary we mean those which originate in the spontaneous needs of human dignity. In 1956 in Hungary the denunciation of lies and the will to speak the 'truth' were central features. (It may be recalled that the uprising in fact broke out around the right to free speech over the radio!) This aspect places the anti-totalitarian revolution into the neighbourhood of the democratic popular revolutions of the nineteenth century, as both Aron and Arendt had underlined.

However, the anti-totalitarian character of a revolution does not say anything about the kind of society and institutional system that it was hoped would emerge from its possible victory. As sketched in Chapter 7, the discussions about these matters began already in October-November 1956 and became more vocal after the defeat of the uprising. The dominant elements among the forces in the forefront of the revolution subscribed to some kind of socialist democracy, but it does not follow that they would have remained dominant after a consolidation, nor that they would have proceeded in the same direction. One has to consider the influence of pre-war traditions and ideas of Hungarian society on the one hand and the fact that the presence – or, after a hoped-for victory, the overpowering proximity and superpower status – of the Soviets engendered a kind of self-censorship of the words (maybe even thoughts) of the non-communist participants of the Revolution, on the other hand. According to the dominant ideas of the epoch, this self-censorship favoured socialistic and 'third roadish' prospects and refrained from the emphasis of capitalist methods of production and private property, except in the agrarian sector.

This trend was enhanced by the democratic, or rather egalitarian, climate of opinion that characterized post-1945 Hungary. While the communist take-over in all fields of life was rejected virtually by everybody, we have quoted (see pp. 127–8) influential statements against the restoration of the pre-war system. Maybe the one or the other feature of the interwar years appealed to some and a return to the multiparty system of the immediate post-war years was widely expected, but Hungarians would not have wished that the Revolution's demands appear in the world as a restorative attempt. (Hungary's image in the world was – just as that of several neighbouring small countries – always very important for the society. Hungarians are wont to watch, with great attention, how things in their country are seen abroad, especially in the 'civilized west'.) The actors of the Revolution chose, therefore, not only for practical reasons, but also as a matter of 'good form' the formulation of aims in the language of *progressiste*, left-leaning democracy. After the second Soviet invasion it became outright a question of honour to demonstrate that the intervention was both legally and ideologically unfounded. First-class minds such as István Bibó drafted manifestos which underscored the proximity of the revolutionary demands to the set of values of an ideal socialism. In April 1957 (as quoted on p. 120) Bibó went as far as arguing that a compromise between Moscow and Budapest would be advantageous for the Soviets by saving or even increasing their moral influence in the world.

All this does not, of course, supply much of a basis for imagining the possible development of Hungary after a victorious revolution. Besides the aforementioned uncertainties, it is well known that, to put it mildly, revolutions rarely accomplish what their participants – or initiators – envisage. How could the rather chaotic conditions of the first days of November 1956, however carefully analysed, offer reliable indications for a reconstruction of imaginary subsequent events? There is no real basis for such an extrapolation, not only because the Soviets drowned in blood the Hungarian Revolution, but also because we have no comparable data. There was no analogous situation somewhere in the region that might offer indications for such an exercise. The one closest in time and space, Gomułka's Poland, returned too quickly to the course of the 'normalized' one-party dictatorship to offer a comparison. The

'Prague Spring' occurred already in very different historical conditions and, as argued above, did not reach the stage that would qualify it as a parallel. Moreover, the forces active in Hungary in 1956 died out in the meantime, both figuratively and biologically.

That the question of 'what would have happened, if . . .' – an anathema or at least an object of derision for any serious historian – keeps recurring in our minds is nevertheless natural, because, by history's inscrutable logic, the Hungarian people seem to have achieved in 1989 what they fought for in 1956. Post-communism became, now not only in Hungary but in a dozen other countries at the same time, the sort of field of experiment which is most welcome from a scholarly position as well. These analogous processes can now offer relevant insights, much more than an isolated case. Moreover, with the collapse of the Soviet Union, that limiting factor that induced a certain restriction or self-control in 1956 (and 1968 or 1980) vanished. The now openly emerging trends are, however, not the same that were at work in the movements of the past four decades. Nor can they assert themselves totally free of control, as the people of the region are now dependent on the goodwill of the west, thus it appears wise to adjust one's actions and words to the expectations of the western democracies.

With these limitations in mind, the political constructs emerging in eastern Europe since 1989 can be regarded as the flourishing of trends that survived communism or had been engendered by it. The striking similarities in the region should not cover up the significant national differences. The discussion of these is beyond the purview of this Afterword. Still, let us note that the liberation from totalitarianism did in itself not define the political order following it. Also, there seems to be not insignificant social support for restorative forces who expect the solution of serious problems of today by returning to the condition preceding communism.

None the less, the political development of post-1989 Hungary can be said to have fulfilled, thirty-three years later, the anti–totalitarian programme of the 1956 Revolution. It led to the establishment of western-type democratic institutions and not to the return to pre-war conditions. Whether this would have happened in 1956, cannot ever be decided. Let me just state that by the end of the second millennium Hungary became an independent parliamentary republic. This may be a modest statement, but sufficient to justify a certain sense of satisfaction.

Chronology

1944
21 December   Provisional National Assembly in Debrecen.

1945
20 January   Armistice agreement with Allies.
17 March   Decree on land reform.
4 November   First parliamentary elections.

1946
1 February   Proclamation of the Republic.

1947
10 February   Peace treaty in Paris signed.
30 May   Prime Minister Ferenc Nagy forced into exile.
31 August   Manipulated multiparty parliamentary elections.
September   Founding of the Cominform.

1948
25 March   Nationalization of large enterprises.
12 June   Founding of the unity party MDP.
20 August   Beginning of forced collectivization.
23 December   Arrest of Archbishop József Mindszenty.

1949
15 January   Parliamentary elections with unity list.
24 September   Verdict in Rajk trial.
28 December   Nationalization of all major enterprises.

1950
17 June	Founding of the unified youth organization DISZ.

1951
2 March	Five Year Plan targets raised.
May-June	Deportation of 'class enemies'.

1952
14 August	Mátyás Rákosi prime minister.

1953
18–19 June	Negotiations in Moscow; critique of Rákosi by the Soviets.
27–28 June	Central Committee resolution on the 'New Course'.
4 July	Imre Nagy's programme speech in Parliament.

1954
24 March	Beginning of rehabilitation of incarcerated communists.
5 May	Negotiations on reform in Moscow.
1–3 October	Central Committee ratifies Nagy's reform plans.
1 December	Rákosi's counter-attack in the Politburo.

1955
8 January	Moscow disapproves of Nagy's course.
2–4 March	Central Committee condemns Nagy's reforms.
14 April	Nagy relieved of all party posts.
14 May	Signing of Warsaw Pact.
15 May	Austrian State Treaty.
26 May	Khrushchev in Belgrade.
18 October	Writers' Memorandum to the MDP Central Committee.

1956
14–25 February	Twentieth Party Congress, CPSU; Khrushchev's secret speech.
27 June	Petőfi Circle discussion on the press.
28 June	Uprising in Poznań.
17 July	Rákosi replaced by Ernő Gerő.
6 October	Interment of László Rajk and comrades.
16 October	Founding of the League of Hungarian Students MEFESZ in Szeged.

19 October	Gomułka elected first secretary in Warsaw.
22 October	Demands of students ('Sixteen Points') formulated at Technical University, Budapest.

23 October–4
November   Revolution and struggle for freedom.

23 October   Government delegation headed by Gerő returns home from Yugoslavia; the MDP Politburo meets to consider the planned student demonstration.

1:00 p.m.   prohibition of demonstration; 2:30 p.m. the prohibition is lifted and students from all universities begin to assemble.

3:00 p.m.   students march to Bem Square, then to the Parliament building where a large crowd gathers. In the evening the demonstrators demand that the Sixteen Points be broadcast, but at 8:00 p.m. the radio carries Gerő's speech against the demonstrators.

9:00 p.m.   Nagy makes a speech at the Parliament as armed clashes are breaking out at the radio building and spreading about the city.

9:37 p.m.   the Stalin statue is pulled down.

In the late evening, the MDP Central Committee begins a continuous session lasting until 28 October; Nagy is present but not his closest advisers.

During the night a military committee is formed in the party headquarters; around midnight Soviet troops reach Budapest and attack the demonstrators.

24 October   8:13 a.m.   announcement of Imre Nagy as prime minister.

8:30 a.m.   Nagy announces martial law, while strikes begin in most Budapest plants.

12:10 p.m.   Nagy calls for the ending of the fighting and promises amnesty for those who lay down weapons by 2:00 p.m. (this deadline is repeatedly extended).

Suslov and Mikoyan arrive in Budapest. Meanwhile, the first workers' councils are formed in the Egyesült Izzó Electrical Plant in Budapest and the DIMÁVAG Machine Factory in Diósgyőr.

25 October   In the morning, peaceable demonstrators, some fraternizing with the crews of Soviet tanks, are fired upon by security forces on Parliament Square in

Budapest, over 100 dead and wounded.

12:32 p.m.   radio announcement of Gerő's removal and replacement by János Kádár as first secretary of MDP. The first free newspaper, *Igazság*, appears as the organ of the revolutionary students.

26 October   Armed clashes throughout the country. Workers' and revolutionary and national committees form in most plants and localities.

Border police and security personnel fire on demonstrators in Mosonmagyaróvár and Miskolc, killing many; the massacres are followed by lynch-justice.

The party leadership refuses to recognize the uprising as a national democratic revolution against the proposal of Donáth and Losonczy.

4:45 p.m.   Central Committee appeal to end the fighting along with promises of 'changes' in general.

27 October   11:18 a.m.   Imre Nagy announces his new government consisting of communists less tainted by the Rákosi excesses or persecuted under Rákosi.

28 October   Negotiations between demonstrators and the leaders of the military. At MDP headquarters the military committee plans a massive attack on the insurrectionists in Corvin Passage, but Nagy averts its execution in favour of seeking a political resolution. The MDP Central Committee assigns direction to a six-member presidium.

1:20 p.m.   Nagy announces a truce.

5:25 p.m.   Nagy broadcasts on the radio, acknowledging the uprising as a national democratic revolution, announcing that Soviet troops would leave Budapest, and promising that the basic demands of the uprising, especially the abolition of the ÁVH, would be met.

Formation of the Revolutionary Committee of Hungarian Intellectuals.

UN Security Council places the Hungarian question on its agenda.

29 October   Tito's letter to the Central Committee welcoming developments in Hungary but also warning of pitfalls.

Israeli attack signals the beginning of the Suez crisis.

US Ambassador Bohlen informs the Soviet

government that it does not regard the new Hungary as its ally (as already stated by Secretary of State Dulles on 27 October).

30 October   Soviet government declaration of mutual respect for the independence of socialist states; announces willingness to negotiate on the removal of Soviet troops from Hungary.

Armed groups storm the Budapest headquarters of the MDP; twenty-four defenders of the building are killed in the attack and ensuing lynchings.

2:30 p.m.   Nagy announces the alteration of the government on the basis of the 1945 coalition, with the democratic parties represented in the cabinet. Old and new parties are forming and publishing their newspapers in last days of October and the first ones of November.

In the evening, a revolutionary defence committee is formed from army, police and insurrectionists.

Establishment of the West Hungarian revolutionary committee chaired by Attila Szigethy in Győr.

10:00 p.m.   Cardinal Mindszenty freed.

31 October   The Revolutionary Defence Committee names Béla Király as commander of the National Guard. In the afternoon, Imre Nagy announces the commencement of negotiations of Hungary's withdrawal from the Warsaw Pact.

In the evening, the Soviet leadership discusses with a Chinese party delegation the decision, already taken, to intervene in Hungary. Soviet troops in Romania and the Ukraine move towards Hungary.

1 November   In the morning, workers' councils and the government negotiate in the Parliament building (continuing in the afternoon at the building of the construction workers' union) and release an appeal for the resumption of work.

In the afternoon, Nagy summons Ambassador Andropov and informs him that Hungary is renouncing the Warsaw Pact in protest against the renewed Soviet troop movements. The government declares Hungary's neutrality. At 7:50 p.m. Nagy announces all this on the radio, hands a note to the legations accredited in Budapest and requests the UN to recognize the country's neutrality.

János Kádár and Ferenc Münnich enter the Soviet Embassy and are flown to Moscow to discuss the formation of a counter-government.

10:00 p.m.   Kádár's (earlier recorded) speech on the newly formed anti-Stalinist MSZMP is broadcast.

A Soviet party delegation meets Polish leaders in Brest to convince them of the need for intervention in Hungary.

2 November   Protests of the Nagy government against the renewed Soviet troop movements; Telegram from Nagy to Hammerskfold asks General Secretary of UN to mediate between Hungary and the Soviet Union and to call upon the Great Powers to recognize Hungary's neutrality.

Khrushchev and comrades negotiate in Bucharest with Romanian, Bulgarian and Czechoslovak leaders about intervention in Hungary. At night, Khrushchev's party convinces President Tito on Island Brioni to support the intervention and assist in 'eliminating' Imre Nagy from the political scene.

Kádár and Münnich in Moscow at the Presidium of the CPSU.

3 November   Third Nagy government formed with the participation of all post-war democratic coalition parties.

In the morning, negotiations with Soviet generals about withdrawal of troops, to be continued at 10:00 p.m. in Soviet HQ at Tököl.

Workers' councils of Csepel and Újpest decide to resume work on Monday 5 November.

8:00 p.m.   Radio speech of Cardinal Mindszenty supporting consolidation but equivocal about legitimacy of Nagy government.

Around midnight, General Maléter and negotiating team arrested in Soviet HQ.

4 November   4:00 a.m. Soviet troops attack Budapest.

5:05 a.m.   Broadcast (probably from Szolnok or Uzhgorod) about the formation of the Kádár government.

5:20 a.m.   Imre Nagy broadcasts the announcement of the Soviet attack. Armed groups in Budapest resume the fight without Nagy's call for resistance.

Later in the morning, Nagy and his associates take refuge in the Yugoslav Embassy and are granted asylum. Soviet and ÁVH units occupy the Parliament building. Minister of State István Bibó composes the official protest against the forcible removal of the legal government and the unconstitutional establishment of the Kádár cabinet.

Uniting for peace procedure in the Security Council in order to denounce Soviet aggression: the UN General Assembly holds special session.

7 *November*	The Kádár government is sworn in.
12 *November*	Founding of the Central Workers' Council of Greater Budapest (KMT).
22–23 *November*	Abduction of the Nagy group to Romania.
2–5 *December*	Resolution of the MSZMP Central Committee on 'the causes of the counter-revolution'.
11 *December*	Decree about martial law.
16 *December*	First death sentence against a participant of the Revolution for 'hiding weapons'.

1957

1–4 *January*	Summit meeting of east European communist leaders in Budapest.
19 *January*	József Dudás and János ('Uncle') Szabó, leaders of freedom fighters, executed.
26 *February*	Kádár reports to the MSZMP Central Committee on the initiation of proceedings against Imre Nagy.
21–27 *March*	Meetings in Moscow on the stationing of troops and the Nagy trial.
22–29 *June*	Failed coup by the Molotov-Kaganovich group against Khrushchev.
26 *June*	Execution of Ilona Tóth and co-defendants. The death sentence against the writers József Gáli and Gyula Obersovszky is commuted to prison terms in response to international protest.
13 *November*	Sentence in the 'writers' trial': Tibor Déry (nine years), Julius Hay (six years), Zoltán Zelk (three years) and Tibor Tardos (eighteen months in prison).
10 *December*	Execution of Antal Pálinkás-Pallavicini, commander of the escort of Cardinal Mindszenty.
30 *December*	Execution of László Iván-Kovács, one of the leaders of the Corvin Passage freedom fighters.

1958

17 March	Sentence in the trial of the leaders of the KMT.
16 June	Execution of Imre Nagy and co-defendants.
18 June	The historian, Domokos Kosáry, sentenced to four years in prison.
2 August	István Bibó and Árpád Göncz receive life sentences.
19 August-9 September	Army officers supporting the Revolution sentenced to long prison terms.
7 December	MSZMP Central Committee decides on a new mass collectivization of agriculture.

1959

25 September	Writers' Union, dissolved in 1957, reinstated.
28 September	Ten young freedom fighters from Budapest executed.

1960

April	Partial amnesty. Revolt at Vác penitentiary.

1961

26 August	László Nickelsburg and fellow fighters from Baross Square, the last 1956ers' sentenced to death, executed.

1962

14–16 August	Resolution of the MSZMP Central Committee on terminating the political trials.
20–24 November	Eighth Party Congress of MSZMP decides to lay the 'foundation of socialism'.
20 December	Following secret negotiations between the Kádár government and the USA, UN General Assembly removes the Hungarian question from its agenda.

1963

22 March	General amnesty for most of those sentenced in the 1957–58 trials.

1989

16 June	Reinterment of the martyrs of the Revolution.

1990

2 May	Freely elected Hungarian Parliament enacts the perpetual memorialization of the Revolution and the freedom struggle of 1956.

Glossary

INSTITUTIONS, PUBLICATIONS (AND THEIR ABBREVIATIONS)

ACC (Allied Control Commission)   four-power commission stationed in Hungary between armistice (1945) and peace treaty (Paris, 10 February 1947), chaired by Soviet Marshal Kliment Voroshilov.

ÁVH (*Államvédelmi Hatóság*, Office of State Security; formerly ÁVO, *Államvédelmi Osztály*, Department of State Security)   founded in 1946 it became the instrument of Stalinist terror. Its dissolution was a general demand during the uprising, one that Imre Nagy fulfilled on 28 October 1956.

Batthyány Memorial Light   a memorial with perpetual light in the centre of Budapest, erected in 1926 on the spot where, on 6 October 1849, Count Lajos Batthyány, Hungary's first parliamentary prime minister, was executed.

Beloiannis Electric Plant (formerly Standard Electric Plant)   an electric machinery enterprise named in 1952 for the Greek communist.

Central Workers' Council of Greater Budapest   see KMT.

Civic Democratic Party (*Polgári Demokrata Párt*, PDP)   founded in 1944, the small liberal party participated in the National Independence Front, but was dissolved in 1948.

Comecon (Council for Mutual Economic Assistance)   founded in 1949, the Council was primarily an instrument for the direction by Moscow of the economies of the states of the Soviet bloc; it was dissolved in 1991.

Committee for Historical Justice (*Történelmi Igazságtétel Bizottsága*, TIB)   a committee formed in 1988 to seek the rehabilitation of the victims of Stalinism (and especially of the reprisals after 1956); it was

189

responsible for the historic reinterment of Imre Nagy and his martyred comrades on 16 June 1989.

Csepel Iron and Metal Plant   the largest heavy industrial complex in Budapest, located on the Danube island Csepel (formerly Manfred-Weiss Plant, then renamed for Mátyás Rákosi in the 1950s) consisting of rolling mills and various machinery factories.

DIMÁVAG (*Diósgyôri Magyar Állami Vagon- és Gépgyár* – Hungarian State Rolling Stock and Machine Factory, Diósgyőr)   Hungary's largest industrial complex, including the neighbouring steel mills (in 1956 the Lenin Metallurgical Plant), located in Miskolc north-east of Budapest.

DISZ (*Dolgozó Ifjúság Szövegsége* – Union of Working Youth)   founded in 1950 according to the Soviet Komsomol model after all youth organizations had been brought under unified control.

DNP   see Popular Democratic Party.

Egyesült Izzólámpagyár (Tungsram – United Light Bulb Factory)   one of Hungary's best known industrial firms, located in Újpest in the north of Budapest.

Élünk (We Are Alive)   underground newspaper, successor of *Igazság* (Truth), edited by Gyula Obersovszky and József Gáli in early November 1956.

Free Kossuth Radio   the name adopted by Radio Budapest (Radio Kossuth) on 30 October 1956, after the broadcasts had embraced the ideas of the revolution. It remained on the air, from temporary studios in the Parliament building, until the early morning of 4 November.

FKGP (*Független Kisgazda Földmunkás és Polgári Párt* – Independent Farmers' Agrarian Workers' and Burghers' Party or Smallholders' Party)   founded in 1921 on the basis of earlier party organizations, it was the most influential moderate oppositional party of the inter-war period. Active in the anti-fascist resistance, it was the strongest party in free elections after 1945 but was ruined by the communists in 1947–48. On 30 October 1956 a provisional party executive was formed and the party paper *Kis Újság* (Small Newspaper) reappeared from 1 to 3 November.

Irodalmi Újság (Literary Gazette)   organ of the Writers' Union, became in 1953 the main vehicle for the writers' opposition. Its numbers during the revolution contained some of the most important manifestos. After the uprising was put down, the journal appeared until 1990 in exile.

KGB (*Komitet Gosudarstvennoi Bezopastnost'i* – Committee for State Security)   the Soviet security service since 1954, formerly known as GPU, NKVD, etc.

Kilián Barracks   formerly Maria Theresa Barracks, at the intersection of Boulevard and Üllői streets, counted as one of the headquarters of military resistance during the uprising.

Kis Újság   see FKGP.

KMT (*Nagybudapesti Központi Munkástanács* – Central Workers' Council of Greater Budapest)   founded on 12 November 1956, mainly at the initiative of the workers' council (revolutionary council) of Újpest, as a regional council in which most Budapest districts and large plants were represented. It was the principal alternative to the Kádár regime and Soviet occupation forces until its dissolution and the arrest of its leaders on 9 December.

MDFM (*Magyar Demokratikus Függetlenségi Mozgalom* – Hungarian Democratic Independence Movement)   underground group formed in November 1957 under the leadership of Miklós Gimes, editor of the newspaper *Október Huszonharmadika*.

MDP (*Magyar Dolgozók Pártja* – Hungarian Workers' Party)   the Stalinist state party formed in 1948 through the forced merger of the Social Democratic Party of Hungary (SZDP) with the Hungarian Communist Party (MKP); it fell during the revolutionary days of 1956 and was replaced by the MSZMP.

MEFESZ (*Magyar Egyetemista és Főiskolai Egyesületek Szövetsége* – Association of Hungarian University and College Unions)   originally (1944–5) a free association of anti-fascist student organizations, thereafter (1946–50) a student coalition (with slightly changed name, same abbreviation) increasingly subject to communist control. It was re-established in October 1956 at Szeged University in protest against DISZ (see above), as a League of Hungarian Students. After the suppression of the Revolution, the exiled MEFESZ continued to function for years in the west.

MKP (*Magyar Kommunista Párt* – Hungarian Communist Party)   founded in 1918 and frequently splintered, as well as being forced underground during 1920–44, the party was re-established in 1944 by communist resistance fighters and the returning emigrants from Moscow and became the instrument for the Bolshevization of Hungary.

MSZMP (*Magyar Szocialista Munkáspárt* – Hungarian Socialist Workers' Party)   founded on 31 October 1956 by those members of the Communist Party (MDP) who had joined the Revolution and, with Imre Nagy and János Kádár at its head, declared itself to be an anti-Stalinist party. After the Soviet intervention, the Kádár group appropriated the name, while a majority of the party's executive committee remained true to the Revolution and was charged along with Nagy. The MSZMP became a communist state party and remained so until 1989.

National Guard (*Nemzetőrség*)   an armed force constituted on 1 November 1956 and staffed by freedom fighters who, together with the police and reorganized elements of the army, were to preserve democratic order. National guards, recalling those of 1848–49, were formed in most cities and localities to defend revolutionary order.

National Independence Front (*Magyar Nemzeti Függetlenségi Front*)   see Patriotic People's Front.

National Revolutionary Committee (*Nemzeti Forradalmi Bizottmány*)   a political group led by József Dudás, at times in command of armed forces, that was critical of the policy of Imre Nagy and, until the last days of the Revolution, strove for more extensive changes.

NÉKOSZ (*Népi Kollégiumok Országos Szövetsége* – National Association of People's Colleges)   the central organization of the people's schools and colleges, an alternative form of education affording children of workers and farmers access to higher education and, at the same time, aiming at the development of a new elite. Though led by party members and communist sympathizers, NÉKOSZ and its constituent colleges were dissolved in 1949 in connection with the Rajk trial and many of its leaders were arrested.

Népszabadság (People's Freedom)   successor of *Szabad Nép* (see below); daily of the newly founded MSZMP, appeared first on 2 November 1956, became then the central organ of the state-party until 1990, when it changed to an independent daily.

NPP (*Nemzeti Parasztpárt* – National Peasant Party)   a radical peasant party formed in 1945 by populist writers and rural sociologists. It fell under the influence of the MDP, but was newly organized in October 1956 as the Petőfi Party, uniting a group of non-communist leftist intellectuals. Its party organ, *Új Magyarország* (New Hungary), appeared on 2 November 1956.

Október Huszonharmadika (23 October)   underground paper of the MDFM that appeared from 15 November until mid-December 1956.

Patriotic People's Front (*Hazafias Népfront*)   formed as an anti-fascist coalition in 1943–44, called National Independence Front, it became a hollow shell of the former parliamentary parties after 1948. In 1953, Imre Nagy planned to make the Front into a forum of public discussion and cooperation between communists and non-communists.

PDP   see Civic Democratic Party.

Peasant Union (*Parasztszövetség*)   organization of agriculturalists founded in 1941, that functioned after 1945 as a 'coalition' of the two peasant parties (FKGP and NPP).

Petőfi Circle (*Petőfi Kör*)   originating as a discussion group of young academics endorsed by DISZ, it became a focal point of younger and older anti-Stalinist intellectuals after the Twentieth Party Congress of the CPSU. After its debates of summer 1956 which mobilized thousands, it was suspended, but in the autumn it resumed its efforts. After 1957 the Circle was criminalized as a 'harbinger of the counter-revolution' and many of its members were arrested.

Popular Democratic Party (*Demokrata Néppárt*, DNP)   founded in 1944 as Christian Popular Democratic Party, its leaders were arrested or forced into exile by 1949; briefly reorganized in 1956.

Radio Free Europe (RFE)   a broadcasting station in Munich, sustained by public and private contributions from the USA, that from 1946 sent news and commentary into the lands of eastern Europe. The role of its Hungarian department in 1956 was strongly criticized from many sides.

Revolutionary Committee of Hungarian Intellectuals (*Magyar Értelmiség Forradalmi Bizottsága*)   formed on 24 October 1956 with the participation of professors, artists and writers to advance reform proposals and channel the professionals' ideas towards the Nagy government; also active in arranging humanitarian aid.

Revolutionary Council of Hungarian Intellectuals (*Magyar Értelmiség Forradalmi Tanácsa*)   successor to the Revolutionary Committee newly formed after 4 November with the best known artists and academics in its leadership; prohibited in January 1957.

Revolutionary Defence Committee (*Forradalmi Karhatalmi Bizottság*)   coordinating body formed on 29 October 1956 for the combining of all armed entities into a National Guard headed by General Béla Király.

Revolutionary Worker and Peasant Government (*Forradalmi Munkás-Paraszt Kormány*)   established by János Kádár and Ferenc Münnich on 4 November 1956 on Soviet soil as a legitimation of the Soviet intervention. It made its appearance as a counter-government in Szolnok, and the Kádár regime kept the hypocritical name until 1975.

Smallholders' Party   see FKGP.

Szabad Nép (Free People)   from 1944 until 1956 the central organ of the MKP, later the MDP. In the 1950s, *Szabad Nép* Hours were held in workplaces where attendance was obligatory and participants had to express their political views. Already in 1954 some of the staff rebelled against the dogmatic party leadership; in October 1956 the editors went over to the Revolution.

SZDP (*Szociáldemokrata Párt* – Social Democratic Party)   the party of the Hungarian workers since 1890, it had limited representation in

Parliament in the inter-war period. After 1945 the party was under constant pressure from the communists and in 1948 underwent a forced merger with the MKP, its leaders mostly arrested or sent into exile. Re-established on 30 October 1956, it was again prohibited early in 1957.

SZOT (*Szakszervezetek Országos Tanácsa* – National Council of Trade Unions) central organization of the trade unions as they were absorbed into the state under communist direction. Spurned by the workers, it was nevertheless revived in 1957 as the sole representation of employees and remained so until the fall of the Kádár regime.

The Tragedy of Man (*Az Ember Tragédiája*) a play by the Hungarian playwright Imre Madách (1823–64) portraying the history of human-kind from paradise to the future cooling of the earth; it is held to be the most important drama of nineteenth-century Hungarian theatre.

TIB see Committee for Historical Justice.

Új Magyarország see NPP.

UN Special Commission established at the meeting of the General Assembly on 10 January 1957, it issued a report on 7 June 1957 on the basis of hundreds of testimonials (taken abroad only since the Kádár regime admitted no UN observers to Hungary) and other documents in which the Soviet intervention and its results were labelled as aggression.

Warsaw Pact treaty between the Soviet Union and the people's republics concerning the stationing of Soviet troops in member countries and, more generally, coordinating military affairs in the Soviet orbit; signed in May 1955 and dissolved in 1991.

Writers' Union (*Magyar Írók Szövetsége*) founded in 1945 according to the Soviet pattern of a single representation of all writers, but already in 1953 and again until its practical dissolution in January 1957 arrayed on the side of reform and the Revolution. One of the most important centres of resistance in November and December 1945; restored in 1959.

INDIVIDUALS

Included here are such people, mostly Hungarians (and a few Soviet functionaries), who cannot be easily found in biographical reference works or whose activities in 1956 are less well known. They are identified by the roles they played in the period of the Revolution. No attempt has been made to provide detailed biographical data. Unknown dates are indicated by an asterisk.

Aczél, Tamás (1921–94)   Writer and journalist, an active member of the Communist Party and of the Hungarian Writers' Union since 1945. Laureate of the Stalin Prize for literature. Leading figure of the oppositional intelligentsia around Imre Nagy after 1953. 1966–94 professor at the University of Massachusetts.

Andropov, Yurii Vladimirovich (1914–84)   Soviet politician and party leader; ambassador in Budapest 1954–57.

Angyal, István (1928–58)   Construction technician and one of the best known commanders of fighting groups during the Revolution; leader of the armed group that fought in Tűzoltó Street. Tried and executed after the Revolution.

Aristov, Averky Borisewich (1903–73)   Member of the Soviet party presidium; secretary of the Central Committee (1955–60); Soviet ambassador in Warsaw after 1961.

B. Szabó, István (1893–1976)   Politician of the FKGP, active in reorganizing the Smallholders in 1956, minister of state in the last Nagy cabinet. Imprisoned 1957–59.

Bali, Sándor (1923–82)   Toolmaker and a leading member of the Central Workers' Council of Greater Budapest during the Revolution. Arrested in December 1956 and sentenced a year later to twelve years in prison.

Bang Jensen, Povl (1909–59)   Danish diplomat and deputy secretary of the UN Special Commission investigating the uprising in Hungary. The circumstances of his violent death in New York remain unclear.

Bárány, János (1930–59)   Toolmaker and leader during the Revolution of the freedom fighters of Tompa Street. Member of the Csepel Workers' Council he also organized a revolutionary federation of young workers. Sentenced to death in 1959 and executed.

Benjámin, László (1915–86)   Writer and poet; after 1945 a communist journalist and editor of literary periodicals. After 1953 a member of the oppositional intelligentsia around Imre Nagy; member of the executive of the Writers' Union in 1956. A librarian after 1956, he later became editor-in-chief of the weekly *Új Tükör*.

Bibó, István (1911–79)   Jurist, historian and political scientist. Professor at the university in Szeged 1946–50, department head in the Interior Ministry until 1949. Minister of state (for the Petőfi Party) in Nagy's last cabinet, he was sentenced to life imprisonment in 1958. After the 1963 amnesty, he worked as a librarian. Bibó's works and political stance experienced a renaissance after his death.

Biszku, Béla (b. 1921)   Pre-1945 communist who occupied various party and state offices. Party secretary of a Budapest district in 1955–56, he was interior minister 1957–61, deputy prime minister 1961–62 and secretary of MSZMP 1962–78; within the party a major figure in charge of the repression.

Brusznyai, Árpád (1924–58)   School principal; in 1956 vice-president, later president, of the Revolutionary National Committee of Veszprém. Sentenced to death and executed.

Csongovay, Per Olaf (b. 1930)   Film-maker who was one of the leaders of the armed group in Tűzoltó Street during the Revolution. Fled to Paris at the end of 1956.

Csoóri, Sándor (b. 1930)   Poet and writer; associated with the newspaper *Szabad Ifjúság* 1953–54, with the weekly *Irodalmi Újság* 1954–55, and with the monthly *Új Hang* 1955–56. One of the leaders of opposition during the 1980s, he was co-founder of the Hungarian Democratic Forum in 1987. President of the World Alliance of Hungarians since 1991.

Déry, Tibor (1897–1977)   Socialist, later communist writer; after 1955 a leading figure among oppositional writers around Imre Nagy. Expelled from the party after the press debate in the Petőfi Circle in June 1956, he was one of the spokesmen for the writers during and after the Revolution. In 1957 sentenced to nine years' imprisonment; amnestied in 1960.

Dobi, István (1898–1968)   Farmer and politician; member of the Smallholders' Party, later of the Communist Party. Prime minister 1948–52, head of state as chairman of the Presidential Council 1952–57. Member of the MSZMP Central Committee 1959–68.

Donáth, Ferenc (1913–86)   Jurist, politician and pre-1945 communist. After 1945 a state secretary in the Ministry of Agriculture and leading party functionary. Sentenced to fifteen years in a show trial in 1951, he was later rehabilitated. Active in the group around Nagy, he was interned with the Nagy group in Romania at the end of 1956. Sentenced to twelve years in prison in 1958, he was freed in 1960 and became a leading member of the democratic opposition in the 1980s.

Dudás, József (1914–57)   Engineer and active communist in Transylvania before 1945. In 1956 founded the Hungarian Revolutionary National Committee and challenged the Imre-Nagy government. One of the first to be executed because of his activity in the Revolution.

Eörsi, István (b. 1931)   Writer, poet, playwright and journalist. Sentenced to eight years in prison for his efforts in the Hungarian Writers' Union and the Central Workers' Council of Greater Budapest. Freed in 1960, he became active in the democratic opposition and as an author of samizdat literature.

Erdei, Ferenc (1910–71)   Sociologist and politician. Co-founder, vice-president, later general secretary of the NPP; held various ministerial posts 1948–56. Led the government negotiating team in Tököl where he was arrested by the KGB on 4 November 1956; freed again in a few weeks. Member of the Presidential Council 1965–71, general secretary of the Patriotic Popular Front 1964–70, and general secretary, later vice-president, of the Hungarian Academy of Sciences 1957–71.

Farkas, Ferenc (1903–66)   NPP politician; general secretary of the Petőfi Party in 1956; minister of state in Nagy's last cabinet.

Farkas, Mihály (1904–65)   Old communist active before 1945 in the Communist Youth International, after 1945 secretary of the MKP and MDP Central Committee; defence minister. Dismissed from the party because of his involvement in 'transgressions against legality' in summer 1956. Sentenced to sixteen years' imprisonment in 1957; freed in 1960.

Fazekas, György (1913–84)   Journalist and editor. Prisoner of war who joined the Soviet army. On the staff of the newspaper *Szabadság*; member of the inner-party opposition around Imre Nagy and in his secretariat during the Revolution. Sentenced to ten years in 1958; freed in 1963 and resumed work as editor.

Fekete, Sándor (b. 1927)   Literary historian; journalist on the staff of *Szabad Nép* 1952–56. Because of his anti-Kádárist activities and the pamphlet written under the pseudonym Hungaricus, sentenced to nine years in 1959. Amnestied in 1963.

Fischer, József (1901–95)   Architect and social democratic politician. Minister of state in Imre Nagy's last cabinet. After 1956 lived for thirty years in American exile.

Földes, Gábor (1923–58)   Theatre director; leader of the National Council of Győr. Because of the bloodbath in Monosmagyaróvár, despite his efforts to protect and rescue people, sentenced to death and executed.

Földes, László (b. 1914)   Politician; active in the resistance to the Nazis. Secretary of the MKP in Újpest 1945, later a leading party functionary. Played an important role as deputy interior minister in the reprisals after 1956. Later held various offices in economic affairs.

Földes, Péter (b. 1918)   Journalist; took part in the French Resistance movement. After 1953 he was part of Nagy's inner-party opposition and worked at Free Radio Kossuth in 1956. He passed his memorandum on political life in Hungary to the French ambassador in 1957, for which he was sentenced to thirteen years in 1960. Freed in 1969, he worked as a translator.

Földvári, Rudolf (b. 1921)   Locksmith and party functionary. First secretary of the Budapest party committee in 1953–54, of the committee of Borsod-Abaúj-Zemplén County 1954–56. Member and later chairman of the revolutionary council of the county in 1956. Sentenced in 1958 to life imprisonment; freed in 1961 and worked as translator and technical editor.

Fónay, Jenő (b. 1926)   Engineer; member of the armed group at Széna Square during the Revolution. Sentenced to death but pardoned. President of the Federation of Hungarian Political Prisoners (POFOSZ) since 1989.

Fry, Leslie A. Charles (1918–76)   British diplomat; envoy in Budapest 1955–57.

Gáli, József (1930–81)   Writer and playwright. Editor of *Igazság* and *Élünk* in 1956. Sentenced to death in 1957 but international protest brought a reduction of sentence to fifteen years. Freed in 1961, he resumed his writing despite the illness he had contracted in Auschwitz.

Gerő Ernő (1898–1980)   Communist politician, representative of the Comintern in France and in the Spanish Civil War in the 1930s. Architect of economic policy in Hungary after 1945, deputy prime minister. After Rákosi's fall, he was first secretary of the MDP from 17 July to 25 October 1956. During 1956–60 he lived again in the Soviet Union.

Gimes, Miklós (1917–58)   Journalist; foreign correspondent of *Szabad Nép* in 1954, later a principal associate of the paper *Magyar Nemzet*. One of Nagy's most active colleagues in the 1955–56 opposition. On 30 October 1956 he published the first issue of *Magyar Szabadság*. A leading figure in the resistance after 4 November, he edited the newspaper *Október Huszonharmadika*. He was tried and executed in the Imre Nagy trial.

Göncz, Árpád (b. 1922)   Jurist, agronomist and writer; active in anti-Nazi resistance and member of the FKGP 1945–47. Because of revolutionary activity in 1956, sentenced to life imprisonment in the István Bibó trial. After the 1963 amnesty, writer and translator of literary works. Participant in the democratic opposition, founding member of the Committee for Historical Justice (TIB) and the Alliance of Free Democrats. In 1989 president of the Hungarian Writers' Union; in 1990 became president of the Republic of Hungary.

Grebennik, K.★   Major-General and Serov's deputy in the KGB. Soviet commandant of Budapest after 4 November 1956.

Gulyás, Lajos (1918–57)   Protestant pastor in Levél (Co. Győr–Sopron). Member of the Regional National Committee in 1956. Despite his efforts to mediate and to save people, he was sentenced to death and executed for the bloodbath in Mosonmagyaróvár.

Haraszti, Sándor (1897–1982)   Editor, journalist and communist politician. Sentenced to death in a show trial in 1951, he was released in 1954. One of Nagy's associates in the opposition, he edited the newspaper *Népszabadság*. Interned with Nagy in Romania, he was sentenced to six years in prison in 1958.

Háy, Éva (b. 1915)   Writer; joined her husband in appealing to the free world against the Soviet aggression on 4 November 1956. Emigrated to Switzerland in 1964.

Háy, Julius [Gyula] (1900–75)   Writer and dramatist; an émigré in Vienna, Berlin and Moscow from 1920 to 1945. Active in inner-party opposition, sentenced to six years because of his revolutionary activity. After his release emigrated in 1964 to Switzerland.

Hegedüs, András (b. 1922)   Sociologist and communist politician. Before 1956 a leading figure in Stalinist policies; deputy prime minister 1953; prime minister 1955–56. Emigrated to Moscow 1956–58. At the onset of the 1960s, organized and led the sociological research group of the Hungarian Academy of Sciences. Dismissed in 1968 for opposing the intervention in Czechoslovakia.

Hegedüs, B. András (b. 1930)   Economist and sociologist; secretary of the Petőfi Circle in 1956. Active in inner-party opposition, he was sentenced to two years in prison in 1959. Founding member and officer of TIB; co-director of the Institute for the History of the 1956 Hungarian Revolution since 1989.

Heltai, György (1914–94)   Political scientist condemned in a show trial in the Rákosi period. Deputy foreign minister during the Revolution. Emigrated to Belgium where he founded the Imre Nagy Institute, later a university professor in the United States.

Illyés, Gyula (1902–83)   Poet, essayist of poor peasant origin, the leading writer of mid-twentieth-century Hungary. His 'One Sentence of Tyranny' was published in *Irodalmi Újság* on 2 November 1956.

Iván-Kovács, László (1930–57)   Miner and soccer player. At times commander of the armed rebels in Corvin Passage during the Revolution. Condemned to death and executed.

Jánosi, Ferenc (1916–68)   Protestant pastor and chaplain; Imre Nagy's son-in-law. After 1945, major-general, general secretary of the Patriotic Popular Front in 1954–55. Member of the inner-party opposition, he was interned with Nagy in Romania and later sentenced to eight years in prison.

Jónás, Pál (b. 1922)   Economist active in the resistance movement during the Second World War. Chairman of MEFESZ after 1945; spent 1948–54 in the forced labour camp at Recsk. Elected as chairman of the reorganized Petőfi Circle on 3 November 1956. Since 1956 in the United States as a university professor.

Kádár, János (1912–89)   Communist politician; in jail 1951–54, regional party secretary 1954–55, member of the Politburo from July 1956, elected first secretary of MDP on 25 October; co-founder of MSZMP, minister of state in the last Nagy cabinet. Leader of the Soviet-imposed government and the ruling party of Hungary in differently styled position from 4 November 1956 to May 1988.

Kállai, Gyula (b. 1910)   Journalist and communist politician; active in wartime resistance. Foreign minister 1949–51, condemned in 1951 in a show trial but rehabilitated in 1954. Deputy minister for education 1955–56, then member of the Central Committee and the MSZMP Politburo; prime minister 1965–67.

Kardos, László (1918–80)   Ethnographer and director of Györffy College; general secretary of NÉKOSZ. A leader of the Revolutionary Committee of Hungarian Intellectuals, he was sentenced to life imprisonment in 1958. Released in 1963, he resumed his scholarly activity.

Kelemen, Gyula (1897–1973)   Mechanic and social democratic politician; state secretary for industry 1945–48. Condemned in a show trial under Rákosi. General secretary of the reorganized SZDP 1956; minister of state in last Nagy cabinet.

Kende, Peter [Pierre] (b. 1927)   Journalist and political scientist. Associated with *Szabad Nép* from 1947 but fired in 1955 as oppositionist. Worked in 1956 on *Magyar Szabadság* and *Október Huszonharmadika*. Living in Paris since 1957, he was editor and publisher of *Magyar Füzetek* (Hungarian Notebooks), since 1989 co-chairman of the Board of the Institute for the History of the 1956 Hungarian Revolution, Budapest.

Kéthly, Anna (1889–1976)   Clerk; social democratic and trade union activist, member of Parliament since the 1920s. Under Rákosi condemned and incarcerated. In 1956 chair of SZDP, minister of state in Nagy government. Chair of the Hungarian Revolutionary Council in Strassbourg in 1957.

Király, Béla (b. 1912)   Professional military officer and historian. Victim of a show trial in 1951, condemned to death, sentence reduced to life imprisonment; released in 1956. During the Revolution, commander of the National Guard and of military forces in Budapest. Emigrated to the United States in 1957, where he became professor of history, editor and author of books on Hungarian history and 1956. Member of the Hungarian Parliament 1990–94.

Kodály, Zoltán (1882–1967)   Composer. In November 1956, president of the Revolutionary Committee of Hungarian Intellectuals.

Kopácsi, Sándor (b. 1922)   Worker; police officer after 1945; police colonel, chief of Budapest police in 1956. A follower of Imre Nagy, he fashioned the cooperation with the armed groups. One of the organizers of the National Guard and member of the Revolutionary Defence Committee, he was sentenced to life imprisonment in the Nagy trial. Released in 1963, emigrated to Canada in 1975, but he returned to Hungary in 1989.

Kósa, Pál (1921–59)   Cabinet-maker. Chairman of the Revolutionary Committee of Újpest during the Revolution. Sentenced to death and executed.

Kosáry, Domokos (b. 1913)   Historian; director of the Institute for Historical Research until 1949, thereafter librarian. Sentenced to five years in prison in 1958; freed in 1960 and became archivist, later fellow of the Institute for Historical Research. Member of the Academy of Sciences; its president since 1990.

Kovács, Béla (1908–59)   FKGP politician, general secretary of the Hungarian Peasant League; minister of agriculture 1945–46. Arrested and sentenced by Soviet military in 1947; a prisoner in various Soviet camps until 1956, then chairman of the newly organized FKGP, minister of state in Nagy government.

Kovács, István (b. 1911)   Communist functionary since the party's underground activity; was first secretary of the Budapest Party Committee 1954 to October 1956.

Kovács, István (b. 1917)   Major-general and chief of the general staff during the Revolution in 1956; member of the Revolutionary

Defence Committee. Arrested during negotiations in Tököl on 3 November 1956; sentenced to six years' imprisonment in 1958.

Kővágó, József (b. 1913)   Engineer and FKGP politician; mayor of Budapest 1945–47. Show trial victim under Rákosi. Again during the Revolution mayor of Budapest. Vice-president of the Hungarian Revolutionary Council in Strasbourg; later emigrated to the United States.

Krassó, György (1932–91)   Economist; participated in the fighting during the Revolution. Sentenced in 1957 to ten years in prison, but was freed in 1963. Founded the samizdat publishing house Magyar Október (Hungarian October). He led the Hungarian October Party that he had founded from 1989 until his death.

Litván, György (b. 1929)   Historian; active member of the inner-party opposition around Imre Nagy. Because of his activities in 1956–57, sentenced to six years' imprisonment. After his release, librarian, later fellow of the Institute for Historical Research. Founding member of the TIB; director of the Institute for the History of the Hungarian Revolution 1956 since 1990.

Lőcsei, Pál (b. 1922)   Journalist and sociologist. Fired in 1954 from the newspaper *Szabad Nép*, he was a founder of *Magyar Szabadság*. Received an eight years' sentence in 1958; amnestied 1963. Founding member of TIB, fellow of the Institute of Sociology.

Losonczy, Géza (1917–57)   Journalist, politician and pre-1945 communist. Condemned in a show trial under Rákosi. After release, editor of the journal *Magyar Nemzet*, a leader of the inner-party opposition and one of the closest associates of Imre Nagy. Minister of state in the Nagy government. Interned with Nagy in Romania, he died in detention in Budapest while on hunger strike.

Lukács, Georg [György] (1885–1971)   Philosopher; people's commissar for education in the Hungarian Soviet republic of 1919; lived as émigré until 1945 in Vienna, Berlin and Moscow. A leading ideologue of the MKP, he was excluded from public affairs in 1949. Minister for education in Nagy's second government in 1956. Interned with Nagy in Romania, he devoted himself to scholarly activity after his return.

Maléter, Pál (1917–58) Professional military officer. Captured by the Soviets during the Second World War, he later fought as a partisan against Nazi Germany. In the Defence Ministry after 1945, in 1956 he became one of the military leaders of the Revolution. Promoted to major-general, he was defence minister under Nagy. Tried, sentenced and executed.

Malinin, Sergey Nikolaevich★ Soviet general; one of the leaders of the Soviet military commission in Hungary in 1956.

Mansfeld, Péter (1941–59) High school student who joined the battles at Széna Square in 1956. Arrested in 1958, he was executed as soon as he reached 18 years of age.

Marián, István (b. 1924) Leading young communist and professional military officer. As lieutenant-colonel in 1956, he was in command of the military department at the Technical University in Budapest and became a leader of MEFESZ. His revolutionary activity led to a sentence of life imprisonment in 1958. After the 1963 amnesty, he became a translator.

Markos, György (1902–76) Journalist and economist; participated in armed resistance to fascism. Professor of economics at the university in Budapest, he was general secretary of the Revolutionary Council of the Hungarian Intellectuals.

Marosán, György (1908–92) Baker and social democratic, later communist, politician. Despite his active role in terminating the SZDP under Rákosi, he was victim of a show trial. Rehabilitated, he became a member of the Politburo of the MDP, later of the MSZMP, secretary of the Central Committee, and a minister in the Kádár government of 4 November. One of the most prominent advocates of reprisal, he was removed from all his offices in 1962.

Márton, András (b. 1924) Professional officer and commander of a military academy in 1956. He was named on 31 October to command the defence of Budapest. Given ten years in prison in 1958; freed in 1963 and became a translator.

Mécs, Imre (b. 1934) Electrical engineer and politician. Participant in the student movement at the Technical University in 1956; sentenced first to death, then to lifelong imprisonment; amnestied in 1963.

Leading member of the democratic opposition, founding member of TIB; member of Parliament since 1990.

Mecséri, János (1920–58)   Officer and lieutenant-colonel in 1956. In command of a division from Esztergom, later on the staff of Maléter. Condemned to death in 1958, along with six comrades, and executed.

Menon, Kumara Pladmanabha Siwansakawa★   Indian ambassador in Moscow and Budapest. He was special envoy of President Nehru in Budapest 2–7 December 1956 and conveyed the MDFM's proposed compromise to the Soviet government. (Not related to Krishna [Wengalli Krishnan] Menon, 1896–1974, jurist and statesman; India's chief delegate to the UN in 1956.)

Méray, Tibor (b. 1924)   Writer and editor. Worked for *Szabad Nép* after 1945. Party secretary of the Writers' Union in 1953. Joined the opposition around Imre Nagy in 1954. Emigrated to France in 1956. Editor, later chief editor, of *Irodalmi Újság*, author of several books on 1956 and Imre Nagy.

Mérei, Ferenc (1909–86)   Psychologist and pioneer of modern child psychology and pedagogy in Hungary. As professor at the university in Budapest in 1956, he was one of the leaders of the revolutionary student committee. Condemned to ten years in prison in 1959. After release in 1963, became head of a psychodiagnostic laboratory.

Mező, Imre (1905–56)   Tailor and communist politician; active in the Spanish Civil War and the French Resistance. Union and party functionary 1945; second secretary of the Budapest party committee 1954; a sympathizer of Imre Nagy. Fatally wounded in the attack on party headquarters in 1956.

Miklós, Béla, Dálnoki (1890–1948)   Professional soldier. In October 1944, as commanding general of the I Hungarian Army, went over to the Soviets and became prime minister of the provisional government from December 1944 until November 1945.

Mindszenty, József (1892–1975)   Archbishop of Esztergom, Cardinal and Primate of Hungary. On trumped-up charges, sentenced in 1949 to life imprisonment in a show trial. Freed in 1956, he fled on 4 November to the US embassy and left Hungary in 1971.

Molnár, Miklós (b. 1918)   Journalist and historian; editor of *Irodalmi Újság* until dismissal in 1955. Active member of the Nagy opposition; one of the founders of the paper *Magyar Szabadság* in October 1956. After 4 November involved in the Hungarian Democratic Independence movement. Emigrated in 1957; university professor in Geneva, author of several books on 1956.

Münnich, Ferenc (1886–1967)   Jurist and communist politician; émigré in the Soviet Union and participant in the Spanish Civil War. Police chief in Budapest after 1945, later diplomat. Interior minister in Nagy's second cabinet in 1956. As of 4 November, deputy prime minister in Kádár's counter-government. Member of the MSZMP Politburo 1957–65; chair of the Council of Ministers 1958–61; minister of state 1961–65.

Nagy, Balázs (b. 1927)   Social scientist and politician; secretary of the Petőfi Circle in 1956. In exile, he was founding member of the Imre Nagy Institute in Brussels, but left it to become active in the Trotskyist movement. Lives in France.

Nagy, Elek (1926–94)   Officer; removed from the army in the 1950s and worked as a turner in Csepel. Chairman of the Workers' Council of Csepel in 1956. Condemned for his revolutionary activity, he was a worker and a translator after his release.

Nagy, Ferenc (1903–79)   Co-founder of the FKGP in 1930; prime minister 1946–47; forced into exile by the MKP. One of the leading figures of the Hungarian emigration in the United States.

Nagy, Gáspár (b. 1949)   Poet and educator. Secretary of the Writers' Union 1981–85 but forced to resign because of a poem dedicated to Imre Nagy. Editor since 1988, and member of the Writers' Union executive.

Nagy, Imre (1896–1958)   Agrarian economist and communist politician. Prime minister 1953–55 and October-November 1956. Condemned in a secret trial and executed on 16 June 1958.

Németh, László (1901–75)   Writer, physician and teacher. Leading ideologue of the populist movement of the interwar period. In two important articles of 2 November 1956 in Új Magyarország and

Irodalmi Újság, he spoke out for the Revolution and against all restorationist tendencies.

Nickelsburg, László (1924–61)   Head of a crafts cooperative. Leader of an armed group fighting at Baross Square during the Revolution. After being legally sentenced to imprisonment, he was recalled before the court and executed.

Obersovszky, Gyula (b. 1927)   Journalist, poet and film-maker; a founding editor of the papers *Igazság* and *Élünk* in 1956. Condemned to death, his sentence was commuted to life in prison. He revived briefly the two newspapers after 1989.

Örkény, István (1912–79)   Writer and playwright, in 1954–56 member of the literary opposition. After the Revolution for years silenced.

Pákh, Tibor (b. 1924)   Jurist and translator. Sentenced to fifteen years for high treason because of his revelations about Soviet-Hungarian relations. Actively involved in opposition after his release.

Pálinkás-Pallavicini, Antal (1922–57)   Professional soldier of aristocratic origin, in 1956 major of the Hungarian People's Army, who escorted Cardinal Mindszenty from his place of captivity to Budapest and remained the commander of his guard. Arrested in 1957, sentenced to death and executed.

Perbíró, József (1908–93)   Jurist and professor at the university in Szeged; chairman of the Revolutionary Council in Szeged in 1956. Sentenced to life in prison; economic adviser after his release.

Péter, Gábor (1906–93)   Communist politician; head of the political police of the ÁVO (later ÁVH) 1945–54. Arrested in 1953 for 'trespasses against socialist legality' and sentenced to life imprisonment, the term later reduced to fourteen years. Freed in 1960.

Piros, László (b. 1917)   Butcher, communist politician and trade union leader. Commander of border police 1950; interior minister 1954–56. During the Revolution, fled to Moscow, returned on 4 November as part of the Soviet invasion. Became director of a salami factory in Szeged.

Pongrátz, Gergely (b. 1932)   Agronomist and clerk. Commanded the armed group fighting in Corvin Passage during the Revolution. Emigrated to the United States and became a farmer. Returned to Hungary in 1990 and has been elected chairman of various '1956er' organizations.

Rácz, Sándor (b. 1933)   Toolmaker. In 1956 a member of the Workers' Council of the Beloiannis plant in Budapest; chairman of KMT. Sentenced to life in prison in 1958, he was released in 1963 and worked as a toolmaker.

Rajk, Júlia (née Földi) (1914–81)   Pre-1945 member of the Communist Party and librarian. Arrested with her husband László Rajk in 1949 and sentenced to five years' imprisonment. Rehabilitated in 1954, she became an active member of the inner-party opposition and was interned with Imre Nagy in Romania. Became an archivist upon returning home, researching the atrocities of the Stalinist regime.

Rajk, László (1909–49)   Leading functionary of the underground communist party before 1944, one of the leaders of the MKP, later MDP. Interior minister 1946–48, later foreign minister. Sentenced to death in a show trial in 1949 and executed. Rehabilitated in 1956 and ceremoniously reinterred on 6 October.

Rákosi, Mátyás (1892–1971)   Communist politician. Imprisoned 1924–40, then an émigré in the Soviet Union. General secretary of the MKP and MDP; prime minister 1952–53. Central figure in Hungary's Stalinist dictatorship. Forced from office in summer 1956, he lived in the Soviet Union until his death.

Révai, József (1898–1959)   Communist politician and party functionary. After 1945 in charge of ideological work of the MKP and MDP; member of the Politburo. Editor-in-chief of *Szabad Nép*; minister of education 1949–53.

Rónai, Sándor (1892–1965)   Stonemason and leading social democratic politician. After 1948, member of the MDP Politburo, minister, finally head of state.

Serov, Ivan Aleksandrovich (1905–91)   Army general who headed the KGB until 1959; playing a leading role in the reprisals of 1956 in Hungary.

Sulyok, Dezső (1897–1965)   Lawyer, FKGP politician. One of the most determined opponents of communist takeover. In 1947 forced to emigrate to the USA where he was a leader of Hungarian émigrés.

Szabó, János ('Uncle Szabó') (1897–1957)   Truck driver. During the Revolution he led the armed group fighting at Széna Square. Condemned to death and executed.

Szabó, Zoltán (1912–81)   Writer and social scientist; representative of the village research movement. Chairman of MADISZ in 1945, lived in England after 1949, later in France. Associated with Radio Free Europe; general secretary of the Union of Hungarian Writers Abroad.

Szakasits, Árpád (1888–1965)   Social Democratic journalist and politician. Advocated the union with the MKP. Became president of state but then spent six years in a Stalinist prison. Inactive in the Revolution, he later supported Kádár.

Szántó, Zoltán (1893–1977)   Communist politician, a leader of the underground party before 1945, thereafter party functionary and ambassador. In 1956 a member of the executive of the newly formed MSZMP. Interned along with Nagy in Romania; returned home in 1958 and distanced himself from his colleagues.

Szász, Béla (b. 1910)   Writer and journalist. Press secretary of the Ministry of Agriculture in 1949. Sentenced in a trial connected to the show trial of Rajk to ten years in prison. Emigrated to England in 1957. Commentator on the BBC, editor from 1959 to 1963 of the journal *Szemle* of the Imre Nagy Institute in Brussels.

Széll, Jenő (1912–94)   Pre-1945 communist, politician and author; envoy to Bucharest; founder of the Institute of Folk Art. Active in the inner-party opposition; head of Hungarian Radio in 1956. Sentenced to five years; released in 1962 and served as translator and editor.

Szigethy, Attila (1911–58)   Politician of the Peasant Party; member of Parliament. Deputy council president in Győr-Sopron in 1950–54. Chairman of the National Council of Győr, later of West Hungary, in 1956. Arrested in 1957, he took his own life under unclear circumstances.

Szilágyi, József (1917–58)   Politician; regional police commissioner in 1945. Active member of inner-party opposition led by Nagy. Head of Nagy's secretariat during the Revolution. Condemned to death in a secret trial in 1958 and executed.

Szirmai, Ottó (1917–58)   Theatre director; party secretary at Hungarian Radio. Participated in the fighting at Tűzoltó Street. Condemned to death and executed.

Sztáray, Zoltán (b. 1918)   Writer and social scientist; active in the anti-fascist resistance, he was in a forced labour camp 1948–53. Left Hungary in 1956, was founding member of the Imre Nagy Institute, later emigrated to the United States. Lives and works in California.

Tamási, Áron (1897–1966)   Novelist; one of the leaders of the Petőfi Party formed in 1956. In September 1956 elected to the executive of the Hungarian Writers' Union.

Tánczos, Gábor (1928–79)   Philosopher, teacher, youth leader and leader of the Petőfi Circle. Interned with Nagy in Romania and sentenced in 1958 to fifteen years. After the 1963 amnesty, sociologist.

Tardos, Tibor (b. 1918)   Writer; active in the French Resistance. Associated with *Szabad Nép* and *Szabad Ifjúság* 1947–54. For his speech at the 'press debate' of the Petőfi Circle excluded from the MDP. In the writers' trial of 1957, sentenced to eighteen months in prison. Emigrated to France in 1963.

Tihanyi, Árpád (1916–57)   School principal. After the bloodbath in Mosonmagyaróvár, despite his efforts to mediate and to save people, he was condemned to death and executed.

Tildy, Zoltán (1892–1961)   Protestant pastor and FKGP politician. Prime minister 1945–46; president of the Republic 1946–48. Kept under house arrest for years during the Rákosi regime. Minister of state in the second Nagy government. Sentenced to six years in the Nagy trial, but freed 1959.

Tóth, Ilona (1933–57)   Clinician; member of the insurrectionist group organized in the hospital in Péterffy Sándor Street. Condemned to death and executed.

Újhelyi, Szilárd (b. 1915)   Jurist, politician and pre-1945 communist. After 1945, state secretary in the Welfare Ministry. Condemned in a show trial in 1951, released in 1954. Active in inner-party opposition and interned with the Nagy group in Romania. Director of the film industry after his return.

Váradi, Gyula (b. 1921)   Metal worker; professional military officer; major-general in command of tank troops. Chairman in 1956 of the Revolutionary Defence Committee. Sentenced to seven years in 1958, released in 1960; works as head of a technical department.

Vásárhelyi, Miklós (b. 1917)   Journalist, politician and pre-1945 communist. After 1945, foreign affairs editor of *Szabad Nép*; later associated with various newspapers. A member of the inner-party opposition, he was among those closest to Imre Nagy. Press chief for the Nagy government in 1956, he was interned in Romania and sentenced to five years in prison in the Nagy trial. Founding president of TIB, member of Parliament 1990–94.

Veres, Péter (1897–1970)   Writer and politician. Member of Parliament from 1945 until his death, minister in several cabinets, chairman of the National Peasant Party. Chairman of the Writers' Union 1954–56.

Zelk, Zoltán (1906–81)   Socialist, later communist, poet. After 1953, a member of the oppositional movement of communist writers. Member of the executive of the Writers' Union in September 1956. Sentenced to three years in prison in 1957, released in 1958.

Selected Bibliography of English-Language Reference

(Compiled in cooperation with Bill Lomax)

ON THE HISTORICAL BACKGROUND (1945–1956)

Bibó I 1991 *Democracy, Revolution, Self-Determination* (ed.) Nagy K. Translation by Boros-Kazai Social Science Monographs, Atlantic Research and Publications, Boulder, Highland Lakes New Jersey

Garai G 1982 'Rákosi and the anti-Zionist campaign in Hungary' *Soviet Jewish Affairs* **12** (2): 19–36

Gati C 1984 'The democratic interlude in post-war Hungary' *Survey* **28** (2): 99–134

Gati C 1986 *Hungary and the Soviet Bloc* Durham, Duke UP

Király B 1982 'The aborted Soviet military plans against Yugoslavia' in Wucinich W S (ed.) *At the Brink of War and Peace: The Tito-Stalin Split in a Historic Perspective* New York, Columbia U P: 253–72

Kovrig B 1979 *Communism in Hungary: From Kun to Kádár* Stanford, Hoover Institution Press

Mindszenty J 1974 *Memoirs* Weidenfeld

Nagy F 1948 *The Struggle Behind the Iron Curtain* New York, Macmillan

Schöpflin G 1981 'Hungarian People's Republic' in Szajkowski B (ed.) *Marxist Governments: A World Survey* Macmillan

Schöpflin G 1979, 'Hungary' in MacCauley M (ed.) *Communist Power in Europe 1944–1949* Macmillan

Szász B 1971 *Volunteers for the Gallows* Chatto

ON 1956

I. Books

Aczél T (ed.) 1966 *Ten Years After* MacGibbon & Kee

Aczél T and Méray T 1960 *The Revolt of the Mind* Thames & Hudson

American Friends of the Captive Nations 1957 *Hungary Under Soviet Rule*. Survey of developments, published annually

Anderson A 1964 *Hungary 1956* Solidarity

Aptheker H 1957 *The Truth About Hungary* New York, Mainstream

Arendt H 1958 *The Origins of Totalitarianism* 2nd edn New York, Meridian

Bain L 1960 *The Reluctant Satellites* New York, Macmillan

Barber N 1960 *A Handful of Ashes* Allan Wingate

Barber N 1974 *Seven Days of Freedom* New York, Stein & Day

Beke L (pseudonym) 1957 *A Student's Diary: Budapest Oct 16–Nov 1, 1956* Hutchinson

Belokov A and Tolstikov V 1957 *The Truth About Hungary: Facts and Eyewitness Accounts* Moscow, Foreign Languages Publishing House

Berecz J 1986 *1956 Counter-Revolution in Hungary: Words and Weapons* Budapest, Akadémiai Kiadó. Translated by István Butykay. Translation revised by Charles Coutts

Bone E 1957 *Seven Years Solitary* Hamish Hamilton

Bursten M A 1958 *Escape From Fear* Siracuse, Siracuse University Press

Calhoun D F 1991 *Hungary and Suez, 1956. An Exploration of Who Makes History* Lanham, University Press of America

Cavendish A 1988 *Inside Intelligence* Granta/Penguin

Coutts C 1957 *Eye-witness in Hungary* Daily Worker

Davidson B 1957 *What Really Happened in Hungary* Union of Democratic Control

Delaney R F (ed.) 1958 *This is Communist Hungary* Chicago, Regnery

Dewar H and Norman D 1957 *Revolution and Counter-Revolution in Hungary* Socialist Union of Central-Eastern Europe

Dornbach A (ed.) 1994 *The Secret Trial of Imre Nagy* Westport Connecticut, Prager

Faludy G 1962 *My Happy Days in Hell* Andrew Deutsch

Fehér F and Heller A 1983 *Hungary 1956 Revisited, the Message of a Revolution* Allen & Unwin

Fejtő F 1957 *Behind the Rape of Hungary* New York, McKay

Fejtő F 1971 *A History of the Peoples' Democracies* Pall Mall Press

Free Europe Committee 1956 *The Revolt in Hungary* New York, Free Europe Committee

Fryer P 1956 *Hungarian Tragedy* Dobson

Gadney R 1986 *Cry Hungary! Uprising 1956* Weidenfeld & Nicolson

Géza Dr (pseudonym) (As told to Geoffrey Dias) 1958 *Doctor in Revolt* Muller

Gleitman H 1957 *Youth in Revolt: the Failure of Communist Indoctrination* New York, Free Europe Press

Gorka P 1986 *Budapest Betrayed* Oak-Tree

Halász de B I L 1963 *A Bibliography of the Hungarian Revolution 1956* Toronto, University of Toronto Press

Haraszti-Taylor E (ed.) 1995 *The Hungarian Revolution of 1956 A Collection of Documents from the British Foreign Office* Astra Press

Hay J 1974 *Born 1900* Hutchinson

Heller A 1957 *No More Comrades* Chicago, Regnery

Helmreich E C (ed.) 1957 *Hungary* New York, Praeger

Horváth J 1960 *Revolution for the Privilege to Tell the Truth* New York, Kossuth Foundation

Hungarian People's Republic 1956–1957 *The Counter-Revolutionary Forces in the October Events in Hungary* (4 volumes) Budapest, Information Bureau of the Council of Ministers

Hungarian People's Republic 1958 *The Counter-Revolutionary Conspiracy of Imre Nagy and his Accomplices* Budapest, Information Bureau of the Council of Ministers

Hungaricus (pseudonym of Fekete S) 1959 *On a Few Lessons of the Hungarian National-Democratic Revolution* Brussels, Imre Nagy Institute for Political Research

Ignotus P 1964 *Political Prisoner* New York, Collier

International Commission of Jurists 1957 *The Hungarian Situation and the Rule of Law* The Hague

International Confederation of Free Trade Unions 1957 *Four Days of Freedom: the Uprising in Hungary and the Free Unions of the World* Brussels, ICFTU

International Research Associates 1957 *Hungary and the 1956 Uprising: Personal Interviews 1000 Hungarian Refugees in Austria* New York, IRA

International Union of Socialist Youth 1957 *Why? The History of a Mass Revolt in Search of Freedom* Vienna, IUSY

Irving D 1981 *Uprising!* Hodder & Stoughton

Juhász W (ed.) 1965 *Hungarian Social Science Reader: 1945–1963* New York, Aurora

Juhász W 1957 *The Hungarian Revolution: The People's Demands* New York, Free Europe Press

Kádár J 1962 *Socialist Construction in Hungary: Selected Speeches and Articles: 1957–1961* Budapest, Corvina

Kállai Gy 1957 *The Counter-Revolution in Hungary in the Light of Marxism-Leninism* Budapest, Zrínyi

Kecskemeti P 1961 *The Unexpected Revolution: Social Forces in the Hungarian Uprising* Stanford, Stanford University Press

Király B K and Jónás P (eds) 1977 *The Hungarian Revolution of 1956 in Retrospect* Boulder, Colorado, East European monographs

Kissinger H 1944 *Diplomacy* New York, Random House

Kopácsi S 1989 *In the Name of the Working Class* Fontana/Collins

Kovács I (ed.) 1959 *Facts about Hungary* New York, Hungarian Committee

Kővágó J 1959 *You are All Alone* New York, Praeger

Kovrig B 1958 *National Communism in Hungary* Wisconsin, Marquette University Press

Laping F and Knight H 1975 *Remember Hungary 1956* New York, Alpha

Lasky M J (ed.) 1957 *The Hungarian Revolution: A White Book* Secker & Warburg

Leonov V 1957 *The Events in Hungary* Moscow, Foreign Languages Publishing House

Lettis R and Morris W E (eds) 1961 *The Hungarian Revolt: October 23–November 4, 1956* New York, Scribner

Lomax B (ed.) 1980 *Eye-Witness in Hungary: the Soviet Invasion of 1956* Spokesman

Lomax B (ed.) 1990 *Hungarian Workers' Councils in 1956* Social Science Monographs, Atlantic Research and Publications, Boulder, Highland Lakes New Jersey

Lomax B 1976 *Hungary 1956* Allison & Busby

Lukács Gy 1983 *Record of a Life* Verso

Márton E 1971 *The Forbidden Sky* Boston/Toronto, Little Brown

Méray T 1959 *Thirteen Days that Shook the Kremlin* Thames & Hudson

Mikes G 1957 *The Hungarian Revolution* Andre Deutsch

Molnár M 1971 *Budapest 1956* Allen & Unwin

Nagy I 1957 *On Communism: In Defence of the New Course* Thames & Hudson

Nemes D (ed.) 1971 *Chapters from the Revolutionary Workers' Movement in Hungary: 1956–1962* Budapest, Pannonia

Pálóczi-Horváth Gy (ed.) 1957 *One Sentence on Tyranny: Hungarian Literary Gazette Anthology* Waverley Press

Pálóczi-Horváth Gy 1959 *The Undefeated* Secker & Warburg

Pfeiffer E 1958 *Child of Communism* Weidenfeld & Nicolson

Pryce-Jones D 1969 *The Hungarian Revolution* Benn

Radványi J 1979 *Hungary and the Superpowers: the 1956 Revolution and Realpolitik* Stanford, Hoover Institution Press

Sanderson J D 1958 *Boy with a Gun* New York, Henry Holt

Sartre J P 1969 *The Spectre of Stalin* Hamish Hamilton

Scarlett D 1959 *Window Onto Hungary* Broadacre

Schramm W L (ed.) 1959 *One Day in the World's Press* Stanford, Stanford University Press

Shawcross W 1974 *Crime and Compromise: János Kádár and the Politics of Hungary Since Revolution* Weidenfeld & Nicolson

Stillman E (ed.) 1958 *Bitter Harvest: the Intellectual Revolt Behind the Iron Curtain* Thames & Hudson

Stillman E 1957 *The Ideology of Revolution: the People's Demands in Hungary, October–November 1956* New York, Free Europe Press

Szabó T 1958 *Boy on the Rooftop* Toronto, Little Brown

Sztáray Z 1960 *Books on the Hungarian Revolution: A Bibliography* Brussels, Imre Nagy Institute for Political Research

The Truth About the Nagy Affair, Facts. Documents. Comments. 1959 (preface by Albert Camus) Secker & Warburg

Time-Life 1956 *Hungary's Fight for Freedom – A Special Report in Pictures* New York, Time-Life Magazine

Trory E 1981 *Hungary 1919 and 1956: the Anatomy of Counter-Revolution* Crabtree

United Nations 1957 *Report of the Special Committee on the Problem of Hungary* New York, General Assembly Official Records

Unwin P 1991 *Voice in the Wilderness: Imre Nagy and the Hungarian Revolution* Macdonald

Urbán G 1957 *The Nineteen Days* Heinemann

Urquhart M 1957 *Hungary Fights* Brown Watson

Váli F 1961 *Rift and Revolt in Hungary* Oxford University Press

Varga L 1967 *Human Rights in Hungary* Gainesville Florida, Danubian Research & Information Center

Wagner F S (ed.) 1967 *The Hungarian Revolution in Perspective* Washington, DC, Freedom Fighters Memorial Foundation

Woroszylski W 1957 *Diary of a Revolt: Budapest Through Polish Eyes* Segal & Jenkins

Zinner P E (ed.) 1956 *National Communism and Popular Revolt in Eastern Europe* New York, Columbia University Press

Zinner P E 1962 *Revolution in Hungary* New York, Columbia University Press

II. Articles

1959–1963 *The Review* Quarterly Journal of the Imre Nagy Institute for Political Research, Brussels

Arendt H 1958 'Totalitarian imperialism: reflections on the Hungarian Revolution' *The Journal of Politics* **20**: 5–43

Békés Cs 1992 'New findings on the 1956 Hungarian Revolution'

Bulletin Cold War International History Project, Woodrow Wilson International Center for Scholars, Washington DC Fall: 1–3

Békés Cs 1995 'The 1956 Hungarian revolution and world politics' *The Hungarian Quarterly* **36** (138): 109–21

Cable J 1988 'Britain and the Hungarian Revolution of 1956' *International Relations* (9): 317–33

Campbell J C 1989 'The Soviet Union the United States and the twin crisis of Hungary and Suez. In *Suez 1956. The Crisis and its Consequences* Louis W M and Owen R (eds) Clarendon Press

Gati C 1986 'Imre Nagy and Moscow 1953–1956' *Problems of Communism* **33**: 32–49

Granvile Johanna 1995 'Imre Nagy, hesitant revolutionary' *Bulletin*, Issue 5, Cold War International History Project

Griffith W E 1960 'The revolt reconsidered' *East Europe* **9**(1): 12–20

Hedli D J 1974 'United States involvement or non-involvement in the Hungarian Revolution of 1956' *International Review of History and Political Science* **11**: 72–8

Hegedüs A 1985 'Additional remarks by a major participant in the Hungarian Revolution of 1956' *Studies in Comparative Communism* **18**: 115–23

Khrushchev 1995 'CPSU CC Presidium meeting on East European crises, 24 October 1956' (Introduction, Translation and Annotation by Mark Kramer) *Bulletin* Issue 5, Cold War International History Project

Király B K 1966 'From death to revolution' *Dissent* New York: 709–24

Király B 1958 'Hungary's army under the Soviet' *East Europe* **7**(3): 3–14

Király B 1958 'Hungary's army: Its part in the revolt' *East Europe* **7**(6): 3–15

Litván Gy 1994 'The political background of the Imre Nagy trial. In *The Secret Trial of Imre Nagy* Dornbach A (ed.) 161–82

Lomax B 1985 The Hungarian Revolution of 1956 and the origins of the Kádár regime' *Studies in Comparative Communism* **18**(2–3): 87–113

Lomax B 1980–81 'The working class in the Hungarian revolution of 1956' *Critique* **(13)**: 27–54

Madariaga S de 1957 'Suez and Hungary' *Swiss Review of World Affairs* **6**: 10

McCauley B 1981 'Hungary and Suez 1956: the limits of Soviet and American power' *Journal of Contemporary History* **16**: 777–800

Nagy B 1964 'The formation of the Central Workers Council of Greater Budapest in 1956' *International Socialism* **18**: 24–30

Rácz S 1984 'Hungary 56: the workers' case' *Labour Focus on Eastern Europe* **7**(2): 2–17

Rainer M J 1993 '1956 – The other side of the story. Five documents from the Yeltsin file' *The Hungarian Quarterly* **34**(129): 100–14

Rainer M J 1992 'The 1956 Revolution in the provinces' *Budapest Review of Books* **2**(2): 64–8

Rainer M J 1992 'The reprisals' *The New Hungarian Quarterly* **33**(127): 118–27

Rainer M J 1995 'The Yeltsin dossier: Soviet documents on Hungary, 1956' *Bulletin* Issue 5, Cold War International History Project

Soviet Documents 1995 'On the Hungarian Revolution 24 October – 4 November' *Bulletin*, Issue 5, Cold War International History Project

Taylor E 1956 'The lessons of Hungary' *The Reporter* **27**: 17–21

Index

Italicised page numbers refer to biographical entries in the Glossary.

Index